AP

STRESS, CROWDING, and BLOOD PRESSURE in PRISON

ENVIRONMENT AND HEALTH
Andrew Baum and Jerome E. Singer,
Series Editors

STRESS, CROWDING, and BLOOD PRESSURE in PRISON

Adrian M. Ostfeld
Stanislav V. Kasl
David A. D'Atri
Edward F. Fitzgerald
Yale University School of Medicine

LEA LAWRENCE ERLBAUM ASSOCIATES, PUBLISHERS
1987   Hillsdale, New Jersey   Hove and London

Lawrence Erlbaum Associates, Inc., Publishers
365 Broadway
Hillsdale, New Jersey 07642

Library of Congress Cataloging-in-Publication Data

Stress, crowding, and blood pressure in prison.

   (Environment and health)
   Bibliography: p.
   Includes index.
   1. Prisoners—Mental health. 2. Crowding stress—
Physiological aspects. 3. Blood pressure. 4. Prisons—
Overcrowding—Psychological aspects. 5. Hypertension—
Etiology. I. Ostfeld, Adrian M. II. Series. [DNLM:
1. Crowding. 2. Hypertension—etiology. 3. Hypertension
—psychology. 4. Prisons. 5. Stress, Psychological.
WG 340 S9152]
RC451.4.P68S74   1987   616.85′2   87-5295
ISBN 0-89859-574-6

Printed in the United States of America
10 9 8 7 6 5 4 3 2 1

Contents

Introduction and Overview

The purpose of the book is to present, in a single location, the rationale, background, methods, principal results, analyses, interpretations, and conclusions of our studies at Massachusetts correctional institutions. In the major study (Middlesex County House of Correction), 568 inmates participated in a longitudinal effort that followed them through imprisonment, changes in prison housing and activities, release and, often, back into prison. Less extensive cross-sectional studies of other inmate groups, guards and correctional treatment, service and clerical personnel were carried out in four other institutions.

In fulfilling the purpose of the book it is necessary to convey something of the atmosphere of the site of the major study. Our staff, who worked there daily, came to feel comfortable in the institution but the authors who went there three or four times a year never reached the point of feeling secure in the prison. There were regular reminders that they were in a qualitatively different setting from any other research location they had worked in.

One reminder was the outside exercise yard surrounded by a barbed-wire fence topped with a razor ribbon. Sometimes a massive steel door or a sudden fusilade of curses reminded us where we were. But the most frequent reminder came when each inmate in the study was asked to prepare for having an electrocardiogram. Part of the instructions call for removing all metal objects from the pockets. About one man in three removed metal spoons, stolen from the cafeteria and honed to a sharp edge on the prison floor.

The starting point for the work was our interest in the effects of the social environment on human blood pressure. We were particularly intrigued by reports indicating that enforced aggregation of rats and mice resulted in large blood pressure increases in these mammals for long periods of time. That work is mentioned in chapter 1. We began to wonder if involuntary human aggregation would have similar effects on blood pressure and whether the prison or jail was the best place to find out. These speculations led to the hypothesis that inmates' blood pressures would be higher in dormitories where inmates are aggregated rather than in cells; that hypothesis was confirmed in cross-sectional studies of 251 inmates in three institutions (chapter 4). Aware that cross-sectional data may be an inadequate basis for causal inference, we began to plan a longitudinal study (chapter 6) that would tell us more about the process of aggregation in dormitories and the time ordering of blood pressure increases and might reveal, in addition, whether moving from a dormitory back to a cell resulted in lower pressures.

As our conceptualizations continued to evolve, we began to consider using blood pressure as a non-self-report measure of the stressful effect of the prison environment on inmates and employees (chapter 3). That orientation is the focus of this book. The longitudinal study of 568 inmates and the cross-sectional studies of 355 prison employees were designed with that orientation in mind.

In addition to blood pressure as a measure of prison stress, we have collected a variety of data from inmates and employees. These include sociodemographic and background characteristics and serial measures of: (a) affective reactions, (b) perceptions of guards and the prison environment, and (c) a variety of symptoms of psychophysiological distress as the men experienced changes in prison housing, work and leisure, release from prison, status in the community and (sometimes) return to prison (chapters 8, 9, 10). Data from the institution that was the site of the longitudinal study included reasons for imprisonment, prison disciplinary actions, and major disruptions of routine as well as records of medical histories and examinations of inmates, their infirmary visits, medical diagnoses made, and treatments prescribed (chapter 11). The records of inmate health enables us to enlarge the scope of the study by including analyses of the prevalence of health problems, symptoms, and infirmary visits and to compare the health status of these inmates with those in other studies. The data on prison events and disciplinary action provided an opportunity to explore the effects of these occurrences on blood pressure (chapter 8).

Because we are quite aware of the limitations of our data and because we realize that the institutions and people we studied may be different from many other prisons, we have avoided the preparation of lengthy lists of recommendations for how to run prisons, handle inmates, and administer staff. But we have not altogether shrunk from this task. At the end of the book, we present certain recommendations for prison policy, for inmates, for inmate's family and friends, for prison medical care, and for further studies (chapter 13).

Now, some words on what this book is not about. Although blood pressure is a most important measure for us, none of our data bear directly on the problem of high blood pressure or hypertension; the blood pressure changes we observed were usually small. Furthermore, although crowded prisons are a focus of contemporary attention and we repeatedly consider the issue of "crowding," it is not the intention of this volume to develop an elaborate theory of crowding that could then be tested in the prison setting. Rather, the focus is on the prison environment and the psychosocial characteristics, health, perceptions, and blood pressure responses of inmates and staff.

ACKNOWLEDGMENTS

The research project culminating in this book required help from many. Some worked with us from start to finish; others helped for months or years.

We gratefully acknowledge Eleanor Eliopoulos, Field Director of the project, whose wisdom, personal courage, hard work, and sense of humor kept the project going all that time; and Helen O'Brien and Ruth Surprenant, nurses, who carefully maintained the quality of the data.

We also thank Janett Nabors, who skillfully took the raw data from the field and transformed it into an orderly body available for analysis. Her talent with research budgets is also gratefully acknowledged.

Linda Morrissey typed a seemingly endless array of drafts, tracked down obscure references, and maintained communication between all concerned.

Our thanks also go to Paula Bryant, Barbara Carless, Peter Charpentier, Ann Clark, William Hamilton, Ph.D., Joan Hendricks, Kathleen Reynolds Maturo, and Marcia Richardson. Some helped with coding and data entry, others with programming, preliminary literature reviews, analysis of parts of the data or typing and filing. All helped to get the job done.

Three correctional officials provided entry and goodwill as we went about our work at the Middlesex County House of Correction. Our special gratitude to them. They are Sheriff John Buckley, Master John Benz, and Ray Johnson, R.N.

1 The Study of Human Crowding

It is the intent of this chapter to introduce the reader to the literature on crowding and examine the evidence on the link between crowding and health and well-being. The review is selective, but not intentionally idiosyncratic, and emphasizes conceptual issues, major research themes, and some controversies over the evidence. This chapter, as well as chapter 2 dealing specifically with the prison setting, provides the reader with a broad background for the rationale and methods of our study and should also be a suitable framework for interpreting the results of our study.

In this chapter we do not cover the substantial animal literature on crowding. Although there is no question that such work, especially the early classics (e.g., Calhoun, 1962; Christian, 1961), has provided a major impetus to the studies of human crowding, it is at the same time very difficult to decide which animal findings (if any) are generalizable to the human situation. As this text indicates, in spite of the many disagreements regarding the best conceptualization of the phenomenon of crowding and of its consequences, there is wide consensus that we are dealing with an environmental condition (susceptible to objective definition and assessment) which is richly embedded in a matrix of socio-cultural and psychological influences. These modifying influences are deemed to be sufficiently powerful so that considering only the objective environmental condition would be seen as a seriously underdeveloped study design. Generalizing from animal studies to humans would imply that the objective environmental condition of crowding is the same for animals and humans and animal and human perception of and reaction to the environmental condition are also the same. These assumptions are not supported by data currently available.

This chapter is organized around three topics that appear quite naturally when one is trying to provide an overview of the major scholarly and research themes on human crowding: (a) conceptual and methodological issues; (b) studies of the urban residential environment; and (c) studies of college students, which include both their residential setting and the acute experimental laboratory setting. Chapter 2 deals specifically with the prison setting.

CONCEPTUALIZING AND INVESTIGATING THE PROBLEM OF CROWDING

The authors' concern with the literature on stress and health (e.g., Kasl, 1984a, 1984b) has helped us realize that there is a high similarity between the theoretical and methodological problems which characterize the stress field, and the domain of human crowding. The reader familiar with the stress literature will become easily oriented to the issues that plague the human crowding literature. They include: (a) no agreed-upon terminology; (b) no agreement on conceptualization; (c) uncertainty about appropriate dimensions (subcategories, finer classification); and (d) disagreement over relative emphasis on subjective versus objective formulations of the stimulus (environmental) condition.

Disagreement over terminology, by itself, is more a nuisance (especially to reviewers) than a fundamental obstacle to progress in the field; one simply needs to be more careful in one's reading and in communicating ideas and results. However, such disagreement is also likely to be a symptom of more basic uncertainties that plague the field. For example, Schmitt (1966) has defined *density* as population per acre and crowding as persons per room. Stokols (1972), however, uses *density* to refer to a "physical condition defined purely in terms of spatial parameters," (p. 275) while crowding to him indicates "a motivational state aroused through the interaction of spatial, social and personal factors and directed toward the elimination of perceived space restriction" (p. 275). Freedman (1975) would seem to be opposed to the terminological distinction between objective condition of density and the experience of crowding. To Schmidt and Keating (1979), crowding is "an attributional label applied to a setting when situational density results in a loss or lack of personal control" (p. 680). One could go on. Over time, even the same author may betray some inconsistencies. A few years later, Stokols (1976) has coordinated the term *crowding* more closely to formulations in the stress field, by stating that crowding is "a form of psychological stress in which one's demand for space exceeds the available supply" (p. 63). Stokols (1976) finds it also necessary to talk of "perceived crowding," (p. 69) as if now crowding means to him an objective condition in need of qualification ("perceived") when it is the subjective counterpart.

Disagreement over terminology represents inconsistent use of words as labels. Disagreement over conceptualization refers to a different issue, although in fact, the two may go hand in hand; it denotes disagreement over how crowding should be characterized in terms of theoretical constructs, not just the vernacular or words in the dictionary. With respect to the subjective experience of crowding, numerous authors have offered conceptual definitions or have attempted to zero in on the criterial aspects of the experience or the process (Altman, 1975a; Baldassare, 1978; Booth & Cowell, 1976; Cohen & Sherrod, 1978; Cox, Paulus, & McCain, 1984; Cox, Paulus, McCain, & Karlovac, 1982; Epstein, 1981; Gove, Hughes, & Galle, 1979; Kirmeyer, 1978; Schmidt & Keating, 1979; Stokols, 1972, 1976; Taylor, 1980). It is possible to discern several common themes in the various conceptualizations: (a) behavioral constraints, loss of environmental control, thwarted goal attainment; (b) stimulus overload, cognitive overload; (c) unwanted or negative social interaction, need to accommodate to others, lack of privacy; and (d) uncertainty, unpredictability.

It is not quite clear from the theoretical literature whether the aforementioned elements in their *totality* are meant to represent the experience of crowding, or whether different writers are zeroing in on *specific* individual elements as their own notion of what the essence of the experience is, and would not agree that the other elements should also be subsumed under the terminology of crowding. Another ambiguity in the theoretical literature comes from the fact that many authors do not explicitly pay attention to the time dimension (process aspects) in their conceptualization. Thus, it is not clear if the previous elements are meant to characterize the initial experiential consequence of exposure to the environmental stimulus (i.e., the "objectively" defined crowding) or some later stage in the process. If the latter is so, do these later stages always have to be experienced before one can invoke the term *crowding*? Stokols' (1976) emphasis on crowding and "demand for space [that] exceeds the available supply" (p. 63) and perception of crowding as "desire to augment space" (p. 66) would seem to relegate the other elements (such as behavioral constraints, cognitive overload, and unwanted interaction) to later stages of the process. Cox, Paulus, and McCain (1984) talk of crowding as "levels of density that are aversive" (p. 1148) and quite explicitly suggest that the other elements be examined as aspects of the process that may lead to negative effects of crowding.

It needs to be recognized that the psychological-experimental approach to conceptualizing crowding leads to significant problems that go beyond lack of consensus. Because the elements that have been proposed as criterial for the experience of crowding (such as behavioral constraint, cognitive overload, and unwanted interaction) are in fact not unique to crowding, but have their antecedents in many other social experiences, one finds that with further elaboration of theory the concept actually becomes more amorphous

and increasingly overlaps with quite different constructs. Thus, Stokols
(1976) introduces two refinements in his theory: distinctions between primary and secondary environments, and between neutral crowding and personal crowding (which he calls "thwarting"). Clearly, the most adverse effects would be expected for the combination of personal crowding in primary
environment. But then Stokols falls over the brink by suggesting that fighting
in marriage is an example par excellence of this pathogenic combination. The
inexorable psychologizing of the concept of crowding has led to an example
that has all the right elements of the experience of crowding, yet makes no in-
tuitive sense whatever, because every last vestige of a link to some specific environmental condition that includes spatial parameters has been severed. A
second illustration may reinforce the argument. A "good" (i.e., reflecting input of several theorists) composite definition of crowding would be: excess of
social stimuli (demands), plus inability to control *when* one receives the demands and *how* one should respond. However, this could also be a good description of a controlling-demanding boss, or of the job demand-control
model, which is assuming some importance in the stress-at-work literature
(Baker, 1985).

The drift of the concept away from spatial parameters will, not surprisingly, show up in empirical research as well. One illustration will suffice. In
their study of overcrowding in the home, Gove, Hughes, and Galle (1979) report a correlation of .40 between their "felt demands" scale (one of two measures of subjective crowding) and their "children are a hassle" scale. The
former includes such items as: people making demands, constantly doing
something for others, and being frequently interrupted. The latter has such
items as: children get in the way, and children make too many demands. It is
difficult to understand how an investigator would see an association between
the two scales as specifically implicating crowding (or even establishing anything beyond a tautology) unless he or she had first put on blinders provided
by a specific psychological conceptualization of crowding.

Definitions and conceptualizations of crowding that are tied to some *objective* characteristic of the environmental (stimulus) condition do not encounter the same set of problems that have been just noted for the approach
that focuses on the experiential (subjective) aspects. However, certain issues
still have to be confronted; primarily, they seem to concern the choice of the
specific criterial characteristics (dimensions) for the definition of crowding
and the need to subdivide; that is, to create subcategories or more refined dimensions. Thus, studies of residential crowding primarily reflect the notion
that "crowding is usually a matter of too many people" (Reddy, Baum, Fleming, & Aiello, 1981, p. 529) and seek to operationalize some relationship between number of people and amount of space. Kirmeyer (1978) breaks down
the notion of population per unit of land into several levels: net residential
acreage, structures per residential acre, dwellings per structure, rooms per

dwelling, and people per room. Galle, Gove, and McPherson (1972) utilize a similar classification in their study of urban ecology. At the minimum, it appears accepted that one needs to separate within-structure density (e.g., people per floor, people per building) and within-unit density (e.g., people per room; Baum, Shapiro, Murray, & Wideman, 1979). Studies of small group ecology (Sommer, 1967) and investigations of "personal space" (e.g., Fischer & Byrne, 1975) are more concerned with actual distance between persons (bodies) and the functional setting in which they find themselves.

The most difficult task for the approach that utilizes objective environmental characteristics to define crowding, is how to go beyond the notion of space per person and to also incorporate what might be called *architectural features* of the space. This would reflect the ways in which the space is divided and arranged because that bears on issues of privacy, oral communication, visual contact, transmission of noise, and so on. The distinction between within-structure and within-unit density addresses this issue, but only in a very limited way. In fact, it really begs the issue because the whole point is to find out how to operationalize appropriately "structures" and "units" in the particular setting that is being examined. For example, in research on the prison setting (Cox, Paulus, & McCain, 1984; Paulus, McCain, & Cox, 1985) it is not clear whether the prison dormitory should be viewed as a structure or as a unit, and what architectural features (if any) might make one term or the other more appropriate. Similarly, research on college dormitories (e.g., Aiello, Baum, & Gormley, 1981; Baum, Shapiro, Murray, & Wideman, 1979) does not make it clear that the unit should be a single dormitory room, as opposed to, for example, a cluster of several rooms that open up to a shared living room area. Specific features, such as which doors can be locked, could be decisive in characterizing the boundaries of a unit. The generic notion of what a unit actually is has not been discussed in the literature, and the concept is worth additional attention.

Perhaps the best classification schema of properties of the built environment, relevant to social behavior and health, has been developed by Geddes and Gutman (1977) in a true interdisciplinary collaboration of social science and architecture. This classification schema consists of 48 categories of environments, based on the conjunction of six levels of environmental scale and eight "properties" of environments. The six levels are: building, site plan, neighborhood layout, local community, region, and macro-region. The eight environmental properties are: spatial organization, circulation and movement systems, communication systems, ambient properties, visual properties, amenities, symbolic properties, and architectonic properties. The authors also offer a very useful discussion of the desiderata or requirements of an environmental classification, given from the perspective of the planner or builder concerned with the impact of the built environment on health and behavior.

A Perspective on Crowding

Although we have just delineated some of the conceptual problems that plague the human crowding literature, we are not eager to offer our "solutions." We are aware that within the stress field, passionate pleas for uniformity of language or for the superiority of a particular conceptualization are invariably ignored, and we suspect that the same would hold for the crowding research area. Consequently, we only offer a few general ideas that characterize our thinking about crowding and about ways of studying its impact. The following points are interrelated.

First, we prefer to view the term *crowding* as merely designating an area of research, a research topic (with somewhat imprecise boundaries). Its ordinary dictionary meaning is satisfactory for us and we do not feel that attempts to transform it into a precise higher order scientific construct are really necessary in order to accumulate scientifically valid or useful information. What is important is that our research designs permit a clearcut identification of what the independent variable is (the stimulus, the environmental exposure) and that the designs also reveal at least part of the causal sequence that links the independent variable to some indicator of impact.

Second, we believe that is is very important that the presumed independent variable in crowding studies be defined in terms of (anchored to) environmental conditions susceptible to *objective* description. Conversely, when the independent variable in our study is defined in *subjective* terms (not anchored in objective reality) and is, furthermore, a response variable rather than a stimulus condition (such as, "felt demands"), then we run into many difficulties in attempting to impose a cause–effect interpretation on our data. The details of the argument in favor of this position have been developed elsewhere (Kasl, 1985). Other authors (e.g., Archea, 1977; Taylor, 1980) have also emphasized the need to anchor one's subjective variables to objective situational dimensions.

Third, we are fully in agreement with the general notion that crowding as an objective environmental condition is richly embedded in a matrix of sociocultural and psychological influences and that the dynamics of impact, and the variation in impact, cannot be apprehended without a consideration of these influences. However, we quickly part company with those who translate this insight into the need to measure complex, broad constructs (which would encompass these complex, broad processes), or into the strategy of dealing with crowding purely at the psycho-social level. Rather, we believe that the usual research strategy applies, whether the dynamics are simple or complex: measure separately as many of the applicable dimensions or elements as possible, and let the data analysis reveal how they relate to each other (additive and independent, interactive, or moderating).

Moos (1979) provides a useful framework for the generic study of the health impact of environmental exposures. He offers several categories of variables that are suggestively linked in an idealized schema of a causal sequence: (a) environmental system, to (b) cognitive appraisal, to (c) arousal or activation, to (d) coping and adaptation efforts, to (e) health status changes or health-related behaviors. (Moos' model also includes: (a) a category called *personal system*, which appears to be a set of characteristics capable of moderating any and all of the other variables; and (b) the usual set of feedback loops to reflect the likely complexity of the processes involved.) The major point we are making in these arguments is that the study of crowding should be firmly anchored in the objective description of the "environmental system," and not in some complex package of reactions that are farther down in the causal sequence.

An Overview of the Evidence

A reading of the various reviews of the crowding literature (e.g., Aiello & Thompson, 1980; Cox, Paulus, McCain, & Karlovac, 1982; Epstein, 1981; Freedman, 1975, 1979; Kirmeyer, 1978; Moos, 1979; Taylor, 1980, 1981) leaves one with several impressions: (a) The documentation of adverse effects of crowding is in considerable disarray, and summarizing statements of evidence are difficult to formulate. "Small and inconsistent effects" would seem to characterize the conclusion of a number of reviewers. However, the reader should be warned that the question of "how small is small" has been passionately debated (Booth, Johnson, & Edwards, 1980a, 1980b; Gove & Hughes, 1980a, 1980b). (b) It is likely that indicators of adverse impact are not interchangeable and that a different picture will emerge for different outcomes. (c) There can be little doubt that the effects of crowding are mediated by — and moderated by — a potentially large set of other variables. However, at present this is more a matter of inference than documentation. When these other influences are systematically investigated, the conclusion of "inconsistent effects" may be rendered unduly pessimistic. (d) Current conceptualizations, such as those utilizing the person–environment fit notion (Stokols, 1979) or emphasizing the full range of transactions and manipulations in which individuals engage in their "spatial behavior" (Baldassare, 1978, p. 29), are considerably richer than present research design methodology can implement. (e) In addition to adequate operationalization of central variables (discussed previously), adequacy of research designs (or rather, their "sufficiency" or "power" for detecting cause–effect relationships) remains a fundamental issue in human crowding research outside of the laboratory. Two basic problems are: (a) How to control for the effects of extraneous or confounding variables, given that crowding is usually part of a larger package of poverty and disadvantage, and (b) how to set up a longitudinal and prospective design that permits the identification of the distal health and behavioral *outcomes*, while it also enables one to study the details of the *process* (of responding, coping, and adapting) that may be the crucial mechanisms in determining the outcome.

STUDIES OF THE URBAN
RESIDENTIAL ENVIRONMENT

The relevant research evidence comes primarily from two rather distinct types of studies: those using aggregate data ("ecological" studies) and those using data on individuals, coming mostly from epidemiologic surveys.

The first approach has not yielded particularly consistent results (e.g., Freedman, 1975; Kirmeyer, 1978). It also remains under attack by methodologists (e.g., Choldin, 1978) who continue to elaborate on the pioneering criticism of Robinson (1950) and his discussion of ecological fallacy. However, this approach has not been abandoned completely. A recent example of it (Centerwall, 1984) illustrates the methodology at its simplest. The procedure correlates one aggregated measure, such as percent of crowded households, with another aggregated measure, such as rates of domestic homicide, over the units of aggregation, most often census tracts. The earlier reports showed that acres of the city characterized by overcrowded living conditions (generally indexed by persons per room) yielded higher rates of tuberculosis (Stein, 1950), venereal disease and infant mortality (Schmitt, 1955), juvenile delinquency (Gordon, 1967), and hospitalizations with the diagnosis of schizophrenia (Hare, 1956). The more recent reports (e.g., Galle, Gove, & McPherson, 1972; Levy & Herzog, 1974; Manton & Myers, 1977) have resorted to multivariate data analysis strategies in order to attempt to control for the influence of other social structural variables (notably socio-demographic and those related to class-ethnicity). However, the list of potential confounding variables is large, and different investigators add different new variables to the model (e.g., Sengel, 1978). Generally, it may be expected that as additional or more refined measures of social structural variables are introduced, the contribution of crowding or population density to social pathology will be reduced (Ward, 1975). We must also remember that these studies do not attempt to adjust for many other possible indicators of quality of residential environment in which crowding is firmly embedded, such as the indicators used by Wilner (Wilner, Walkley, Pinkerton, & Tayback, 1962) or in the Annual Housing Survey (U.S. Department of Commerce, 1975).

Even though the three multivariate ecological analyses (Galle, Gove, & McPherson, 1972; Levy & Herzog, 1974; Manton & Myers, 1977) use different sets of indicators for crowding/density and adjust for different sets of confounders, all three seem to suggest the existence of a residual association between crowding/density and all-cause or cause-specific mortality (the one outcome variable they have in common). This thus appears to be a replicable finding. However, there are two fundamental questions that must be raised about this kind of an ecological association. One gets right back to Robinson (1950): Does the correlation of aggregated data accurately reflect the correlation that would be obtained at the individual level? The best answer seems to be that there is commonly a serious inflation of the value of the individual-level coefficient when computed on aggregated data; reversals of the direction of association are also possible but presumably quite a bit less likely. In any case, without independent information, estimating the magnitude and direction of the individual level of association is impossible. The second question is a more technical one and concerns our ability to estimate multiple-partial associations in the face of extremely high multicollinearity. For example, Galle, Gove, and McPherson (1972) try to partial out the effect of social class and ethnicity on mortality, the magnitude of which is represented by a multiple correlation of somewhere between .83 and .94 (see Ward, 1975, for reanalysis). At best, extreme caution must be used when working with such very high correlations. It might also be noted that if individual level zero-order correlations are inflated by the aggregation to differing extent, then the multivariate analysis at the aggregate level may over-correct, or under-correct, the effects of the confounding variables, as compared to carrying out the analysis solely at the individual level.

It would thus seem to be a fair conclusion that "ecological" studies of this kind can safely tell us only where the high rates of a particular pathology are, and that they are unsuitable vehicles for studying etiologic questions. It might be noted in passing that the practice of aggregating individual characteristics (such as being divorced) in order to create an areal characteristic, an ecological descriptor (percent divorced in a census tract) is an ambiguous way of creating dimensions of the urban residential environment. Only by combining areal analysis with individual level analysis will one be able to disentangle the effects of living in areas where there are many or few divorced people from the effects of one's own marital status.

In the second approach, *individual level* studies of urban crowding have focused, more often than not, on one specific independent variable: persons per room. A second theme running through this literature is an interest in the effects of living in a high-rise structure. There is also some interest in assessing the impact of crowding at the level of the neighborhood.

Persons per room represents far from satisfactory operationalization of the concept of crowding. First, it tends to be substantially associated with number of children in the family; for example, the correlation was 0.83 in the Chicago study (Gove, Hughes, & Galle, 1979). Second, it may not be adequately sensitive to the unique situation of persons living alone; for example, an old study of tuberculosis and crowding was able to show an association with social isolation instead, because the variable "living alone" was not submerged in the persons-per-room dimension (Brett & Benjamin, 1957). Booth, Johnson, and Edwards (1980b) discuss other problems with the measure, such as (a) how to make it sensitive to the special case of unrelated adults living in the dwelling unit, and (b) how to adjust for the fact that a linear increase in family size doesn't necessarily create a linear increase in the need for additional rooms. We should also note that most studies do not attempt to collect additional information about the rooms, such as their specific configuration and how they are used. That this may be an unfortunate omission is illustrated by a study (Michelson, 1970) that found that physical crowding and lack of privacy per se were not an important influence on school achievement of children; rather, it was how the space at home was used — that is, setting aside time when a particular room was devoted only to quiet pursuits.

Two studies of residential crowding have come to dominate the picture: the Toronto study (e.g., Booth & Cowell, 1976; Booth, Johnson, & Edwards, 1979; Duvall & Booth, 1978) and the Chicago study (Gove, Hughes, & Galle, 1979). The differences between these two studies — in methods, in results, and in interpretations — have been more than adequately aired (Booth, Johnson, & Edwards, 1980a, 1980b; Gove & Hughes, 1980a, 1980b).

The Toronto study includes approximately 560 families living in high density census tracts; 522 wives and 334 husbands were interviewed, while physical examinations were done on approximately 58% of the wives and 64% of the husbands. Initial analyses with two independent variables — people per room and households per block — revealed no significant associations with numerous biological health and mental health variables. The authors then went on to develop several new indices of crowding. The items for these indices came from a pool from which items not even minimally relating to any one of five selected dependent variables were first discarded. Two indices of neighborhood crowding, one objective (e.g., number of households in block, street width) and one subjective (e.g., stores too crowded, playgrounds too crowded), still failed to relate to a variety of dependent variables, including blood pressure, cholesterol, urinary catecholamine, "stress diseases," psychiatric impairment, days sick in bed, and doctor visits. Two indices of household crowding, one objective (e.g., kitchen set in wall of another room, number of hours respondent is at home and awake in a room with 2 or more people) and the other subjective (e.g., troubled by lack of space, too many people around) fared somewhat better, but the significant associations were still few and weak. The fact that the highest (unadjusted, zero-order) correlations were between the subjective index and the Langner (1962) scale of psychiatric impairment (0.26 for men, 0.20 for women) is less than impressive, because here the direction of causation is most ambiguous. Additional analyses of all measures of crowding in relation to other outcomes, such as spousal relations, reproductive behavior, and children's school performance (Booth, Johnson, & Edwards, 1979) also revealed very few sporadic associations. Overall then, it is not surprising that Booth (1976) views the general study results as demonstrating minimal detrimental effects of residential crowding.

The authors of the Chicago study, on the other hand, have taken the view that their results reveal a strong association between crowding and poor mental health and poor social relationships in the home (Gove, Hughes, & Galle, 1979). Their study design involved approximately 25 interviews from each of 80 census tracts in Chicago, which were selected so as to provide an adequate range in crowding, as well as to reduce the normal collinearity between crowding and socio-economic status. Persons living alone were excluded from the study. The project utilized one measure of objective crowding, persons per room, and two measures of the subjective experience of crowding: (a) a 4-item felt demands scale (e.g., others always make demands, never any peace and quiet), and (b) a 3-item lack of privacy scale (e.g., enough privacy, can never be by oneself). The two subjective scales are well correlated with each other ($r = .49$) but less so with persons per room (r's .30 and .33, respectively). The outcome variables included several indicators of mental health: psychiatric symptoms, positive affect, marital health balance, nervous breakdown, happiness, self-esteem, alienation, and manifest irritation. Indices of social relations in the home included: positive and negative mental relations, marital relations balance, closeness to spouse, getting along with children, and involvement in arguments and physical violence. An overall self-rating of physical health was also obtained. The data analysis routinely included statistical adjustments for socio-demographics: age, sex, income, education, race, and marital status. The combined influence on the three crowding measures accounted for most unique variance in the "children are a hassle" scale (15.8%). Crowding accounted for moderate amounts of variance (5% to 8%) in several other scales: psychiatric symptoms, manifest irritation, marital relations balance, and getting along with others. The overall rating of physical health was not related to crowding, although another variable, which the authors consider a physical health indicator, "cannot get good rest," was reasonably well correlated (6.7% of variance). It is also worth noting that if one tries to compare the relative contribution of the objective index of crowding versus the two subjective indices, to the above mentioned associations, then the following observation holds: Invariably, the subjective indices make a stronger contribution to the unique variance in the various outcomes than does the objective index.

Comparisons of the Toronto and Chicago results seem to suggest the following lines of "reconciliation": (a) There is a real difference in results: The Chicago study obtained significant associations (albeit quite weak) for the objective index, persons per room, and a variety of psychosocial outcomes, while the Toronto study did not. (b) There is an apparent difference in results. The Chicago study seemed to account for somewhat more variance with its crowding indices than the Toronto study. However, it is a fair guess that the two subjective indices in the Chicago study are "independent" variables with a greater conceptual (content) overlap with several of the dependent variables to which they are related, than is the case in the Toronto study. (c) There is a false difference in results. The authors of the Chicago study are eager to use certain subjective labels ("strong," "important") in connection with their results, while the authors of the Toronto study are not so inclined.

There are several other studies of crowding that should be briefly noted. One is the well-known work of Mitchell (1971), who examined fairly extreme levels (by Western standards) of urban density and residential crowding in relation to indices of mental health. The overall finding was somewhat of a surprise. Only a very weak impact of crowding on mental health could be detected. It seemed that crowding (sheer limitation of space) was not as significant an influence on mental health as were forced interaction (with members of another household sharing the same unit) and the difficulty of escaping temporarily from the dwelling (living on upper floors, poor income). Another study of mental health examined crowding (persons in household per number of rooms) in relation to depression and psychophysiological symptoms (Schwab, Nadeau, & Warheit, 1979). This Florida survey revealed poorer mental health in the more crowded residential conditions, after adjustments for age and income; it also appeared that the impact was stronger on female respondents and those in a broad middle-age category (23–59). In a study of State College, Pennsylvania (Rohe, 1982), residential crowding was found unrelated to several indices of poor health, such as visits to doctor, headaches, and reports of nervous tension. Crowding, however, was observed to have an impact on residential satisfaction. Another study, a cross-sectional survey of female heads of household (Gruchow, 1977), examined persons per room in relation to a biochemical indicator of stress: vanillyl-mandelic acid (VMA), a urinary catecholamine metabolite and an indicator of sympathetic-adrenal medullary activity. No overall association between crowding and VMA was observed ($r = -0.04$). However, the expected positive association was obtained in a subset of respondents, defined by their own childhood characteristics: those who had been the youngest and/or who had had no more than one sibling. Analysis of blood pressure data on 1,000 Detroit residents (Kasl & Harburg, 1975) revealed generally weak negative correlations (i.e., against expectation) between crowding (ratio of persons in household to rooms in dwelling, adjusted for number of children) and systolic and diastolic blood pressure, computed separately for eight groups, defined by sex, race, and area of residence.

There are also some surveys of residential crowding that are not concerned with distal outcomes, such as mental health, but only proximate outcomes, such as perceptions. Such studies are also useful to the extent that these perceptions may mediate or modify the more distal outcomes. One study, for example, has suggested a non-linear relationship between persons per room and sense of crowding (amount of time the person feels crowded in the dwelling unit). Only in the upper ranges of the objective measure was an increase in objective crowding accompanied by an increase in sense of crowding (Gillis, 1979). This might suggest the need for more complex analyses when working with this variable, persons per room. Another study (Schmidt, Goldman, & Feimer, 1979) examined physical and psychological correlates of perceptions of crowding at three levels: residence, neighborhood, and the city. The objective (physical) predictors for residential crowding were people per room and people per lot size ($R = .47$). For neighborhood crowding, the objective predictors were quite weak: distance from commercial or industrial areas and distance from nearest park ($R = .18$). For city crowding, no significant physical predictors were found. Psychological predictors for residential crowding consisted of ability to attain desired level of privacy and freedom to get away ($R = .45$). For neighborhood crowding, the subjective predictors were preference for number of people in city and perception of traffic problems ($R = .45$). The same variables also predicted perception of city crowding ($R = .58$).

There is also a somewhat small literature on the impact of living in *high-rise* dwelling units (e.g., Cappon, 1971; Gillis, 1977; McCarthy & Saegert, 1978; Power, 1970; Stevenson, Martin, & O'Neill, 1967; Williamson, 1981). It is best to view these studies as dealing with a topic possibly related to crowding, rather than with crowding per se. This is because it is difficult to know what specific dimensions might be involved, and what is the best way of formulating the dynamics that might underlie the observed association. For example, a Canadian study of residents of public housing (Gillis, 1977) showed that living in the upper floor levels was associated with more psychological strain among the women and less psychological strain among the men. Controlling for household composition, child supervision, confinement, and social isolation did not alter this finding. However, it is difficult to know what is the best way to conceptualize this variable, floor level, particularly in view of the statistical controls. Another study looked at residents of low income housing projects and compared those living in a 14-story apartment building with those living in 3-story walk-ups (McCarthy & Saegert, 1978). The adverse impact of the high-rise seemed rather broad. The residents there experienced: higher social overload; greater tenant anonymity; lower sense of control, safety, and privacy; lower residential satisfaction and attachment; and greater residential powerlessness. They were also lower on mutual aid and less socially active outside of the building. One may speculate about the relevant dynamics here. For example, it is possible that the building itself defines the boundaries for social interaction and friendship formation. In the high-rise, these boundaries are too large and include too many people; the proximity to a few people in the 3-story walk-ups may favor friendship formation but the proximity to too many people may foster withdrawal. On the other hand, there is good evidence that poorly planned high-rise public housing becomes a management nightmare with rapid deterioration of housing quality and increase in safety problems (e.g., Kriesberg, 1968; Rainwater, 1970; Yancey, 1971). This latter possibility has little to do with crowding per se, but would still be an adequate explanation of the differences that were obtained. Overall then, the literature on high-rise living cannot as yet support many firm conclusions regarding physical or mental health effects and it is not yet clear what aspects of high-rise living — including those broadly related to the notions of crowding — may prove to be the crucial operating factors.

The study of crowding in other settings, such as at work, appears to be a neglected area with only a few studies available. For example, in a Navy study of men on 18 ships (Dean, Pugh, & Gunderson, 1978), total illness rates were found unrelated to either an objective index (amount of volume per man) or a subjective measure of crowding. In another study (O'Brien & Pemroke, 1982), clerical workers performing routine duties were compared across three different sections of varying densities (floor space per person). A subjective index of perceived crowding was found unrelated to satisfaction with pay, supervision, coworkers, and work itself. The objective measure, however, did show higher satisfaction with work itself in the low density section. A third study (Szilagyi & Holland, 1980) involved a longitudinal design in which data on professional employees in a large petroleum company were collected 4 months before and 4 months after a move to a new building. Employees who experienced an increase in social density (defined as number of employees within a 50 ft. walking distance) reported greater work satisfaction, better friendship opportunities, more job feedback, lower role stress, and less job autonomy. These are predominantly beneficial effects, and, in fact, the density increase represented greater closeness to the most needed colleague and greater task facilitation. This last study is a useful reminder that in the work setting — and possibly the residential setting as well — there may be an optimal level of separation–closeness to co-workers, for performance and for needed social interaction. Increases in density which represent a move toward the optimal therefore, cannot be expected to have adverse effects. It must also be presumed that different work setting will have different optimal levels. Commuting to work on the train may be a setting where the optimum level is quite low; a Swedish study (Lundberg, 1976) found that as the train became more crowded, the rate of adrenaline excretion was higher, as were the feelings of discomfort. The role of adaptation was suggested by the finding that persons commuting longer distances had lower levels of adrenaline and noradrenaline excretion than did those commuting lesser distances.

Overall, these mostly residential studies of crowding suggest several conclusions: (a) Impact on physical health is probably rarely going to be observed, and may require a combination of very high levels of crowding and suitable specific disease etiologic dynamics (e.g., Aaby, Bukh, Lisse, & Smits, 1984). (b) Adverse effects on mental health and well-being are somewhat more likely to be observed, but the findings are much too tenuous to promise more than a weak relationship. Associations with subjective measures are stronger and more replicable, but at the same time involve a stronger likelihood of conceptual and methodological confounding. (c) Objective crowding is most easily linked to perceptions and, probably, to indices of satisfaction. Their linkages to health outcomes are unclear. (d) Most field research in this area is subject to many practical limitations and, consequently, the study designs fall short of being able to encompass the full range of process and outcome dynamics that appear to be involved in this complex topic.

We need to remind the reader that even though the above conclusions are rather pessimistic, our reading of the general empirical literature on the relationship of health and well-being to the residential environment (Kasl, 1976; Kasl & Rosenfield, 1980) would suggest that the crowding evidence makes it in no way an unusual parameter within the total spectrum of housing dimensions.

STUDIES OF STUDENT HOUSING

From a purely architectural perspective, it makes a lot of sense to discuss the research on the dormitory setting with other studies of the residential environment, particularly those concerned with living in high-rise apartments. However, as we have noted earlier, the psycho-social matrix of the residential setting strongly modifies, if not dominates, the nature of the impact. Thus, from diverse psychosocial perspectives, the situation of the student in the dormitory is special and unique: The student is in a particular stage of the life cycle, there is a characteristic time course to the tenure in that setting, the role demands on the student are of a particular kind, the significant others are almost always non-family members, and, overall, the cultural norms and expectations that apply there are unlikely to be found anywhere else.

Some of the studies of crowding in college dormitories are cross-sectional analyses of the impact of number of roommates (most often one vs. two), especially when the number of roommates exceeds the number for which the unit was originally designed. Thus, Hughey (1983) has reported lower self-perceptions among those living in the more crowded conditions, and Karlin, Epstein, and Aiello (1978) have reported lower grades as another consequence. Baron, Mandel, Adams, and Griffen (1976) observed that residents in overcrowded triplets expressed greater feelings of crowding, perceived less control over room activities, expressed more negative interpersonal feelings, and reported a more negative room ambience, than those in double rooms housing only two students. However, Ronchi, and Sparacino (1982) were unable to detect significant effects on blood pressure, heart rate, or psychosomatic symptoms. Some studies have also been concerned with describing sex differences in adaptation. Both groups Karlin, Epstein, and Aiello (1978) and Walden, Nelson, and Smith (1981) have noted that male students tend to withdraw or escape to alternate locations, while female students tend to spend more time in dense rooms and attempt to make them more home-like.

Some investigators of crowding in the dormitory setting have opened up a second research theme concerned with interpersonal relationships (e.g., Aiello, Baum, & Gormley, 1981; Baum, Shapiro, Murray, & Wideman, 1979; Gormley & Aiello, 1982; Reddy Baum, Fleming, & Aiello, 1981). The general issue is the creation of coalitions and isolates in units that contain three or more students. The authors are, in effect, testing the hypothesis that the symptoms of interpersonal stress associated with crowding are mediated by group formation. The results that have been obtained are rather strange, and, in our opinion, lead to quite different conclusion altogether. First of all, being an isolate (i.e., students saying they felt "left out" by their roommates) was more common in tripled rooms, and less common *both* in doubles and quadrupled rooms. Thus, being an isolate appears unrelated to crowding, but may be related to the dynamics of odd numbers versus even numbers of students living together. In any case, being an isolate does not seem to be mediating effects of crowding. Second, isolates stand out as being clearly different: They have more problems of any kind, including self-confidence, interpersonal, and somatic. However, this appears to be a mere measurement tautology; asking about feeling "left out" simply taps into a large reservoir of "neurotic" problems. (However, in doubles, coalition formation is not possible and feeling "left out" cannot be easily used as a proxy for neurotic complaints.) Third, in the study comparing doubled with tripled students (Aiello, Baum, & Gormley, 1981), no main effects of crowding were observed for most variables; thus the effects of being "left out" are self-selection effects and could be presumably observed if other screening questions had been used (e.g., "do you hate your parents") to divide the subjects into two groups. In the Reddy, Baum, Fleming, and Aiello (1981) study, there did seem to be a true interaction between being an isolate and the number of roommates; however, the negative effects (such as reporting crowding as a problem) were the strongest in the triples, not the four-student rooms. Thus, this result (deemed "counterintuitive" by the authors) hardly implicates objective crowding.

These findings, once again, illustrate the complexities one can get into when the psychological approach dominates our thinking about crowding. In this instance, students self-designated as rejected or left out will have many problems: interpersonal difficulties can be expressed in terms that constitute psychological definition of crowding (e.g., perception of lack of control over different aspects of dormitory life), but in fact are not related to any environmentally defined antecedents. Thus, findings, such as a strong association between perceived crowding and visits to student health center (Stokols, Ohlig, & Resnick, 1978) remain ambiguous, if not suspect.

The social psychological approach of Aiello, Baum, and their colleagues, with its emphasis on both the objective and the psychological measurement of crowding, is thus quite necessary to encompass the phenomenon of crowding.

Some of the work of Baum and his colleagues on crowding in the dormitory setting (e.g., Baum, Aiello, & Calesnick, 1978; Baum, Calesnick, Davis, & Gatchel, 1982; Baum & Valins, 1977) has dealt with a specific contrast in the architectural design of the dormitories: long versus short corridors or suite style accommodations. Although the square footage in this contrast is comparable, in the long corridor design many more students are forced to share the lounge, the bathrooms, and the hallway space. The results suggest that during the early phases of adaptation (7–9 weeks) the students in the long corridor design are more competitive and try to re-establish control. Thereafter, they become less involved and show indications of helplessness; they perceive more crowding and they have a lower sense of control over their environment. Students who use "screening" (structuring social events and ranking them by priority) as a coping style in their daily lives are more successful in adapting to the long corridor environment. These observational data have been followed up with an intervention study (Baum & Davis, 1980) in which some of the long corridors were divided into two by changing three bedrooms into a common lounge space. After the initial adaptation period, the previously observed negative effects were apparent only in the unmodified long corridors, whereas students in the modified long corridors were like the students in the short corridors. The authors also noted that the number of doors remaining open in the evening declined after the initial period, but only in the unmodified long corridors.

These are interesting results that clearly point to the environmental condition that is responsible for the observed effects. The similarity of the results with the findings of the McCarthy and Saegert (1978) study of the 14-story apartment building versus 3-story walk-ups, is striking. Although the appropriate interpretation of the underlying dynamics may not be quite clear, it is likely that the concept of an "architecturally determined residential group size" (Baum & Davis, 1980, p. 71) that is too large for friendship formation, will play an important role. Such an impaired friendship formation process then leads to the other consequences which, fundamentally, may reflect the phenomenon of exposure to fairly intimate contacts with relative strangers rather than with friends.

EXPERIMENTAL LABORATORY STUDIES

We do not intend to provide a detailed overview of this class of studies because we believe that the generalizability of the results beyond the specific setting in which the data were obtained is often a serious problem. The issue is, in part, the potential artificiality of the laboratory setting (and its own unique norms of behavior) and the difficulty of translating the laboratory manipulation into the most appropriate analogue in the "real-life" setting. Even a more important issue, however, in our opinion, is the difficulty of extrapolating acute, short-term effects into long range, enduring consequences, which are really the ones on which we must focus if we are trying to link crowding to health and well-being. The recent review of endocrine responses to stressful experience (Rose, 1980) is a striking demonstration of the many instances in which the endocrine response (particularly cortisol), although exquisitely sensitive to acute stressors, underwent extinction when the individuals were re-exposed to those stressors, or exposed to chronic stressors.

However, the experimental control that can be achieved in the laboratory setting is an obvious advantage and the focused testing of hypotheses represents a great economy of effort. The laboratory findings can provide useful information, provided we are cautious about accepting their applicability to other situations. One particularly important question is the extent to which many of the laboratory manipulations, creating crowded conditions, involve invasion of "person space" or violation of the "body buffer zone," a concept that refers to the notion of an invisible boundary surrounding each person and defining a territory that others must not enter (e.g., Sommer, 1967, 1969; Worchel & Teddlie, 1976). Because it doesn't appear that the field studies of crowding in the residential environment involve such extremes as to represent invasion of personal space, we may have great difficulty linking the laboratory studies with the field studies.

The primary manipulation in the laboratory studies is some form of violation of the normative expectations about the appropriate interaction distance between strangers (Epstein, 1981). Such an increase in crowding appears to have adverse effects on task performance (Epstein, 1981; Paulus, Annis, Seta, Schkode, & Mathews, 1976; Seta, Paulus, & Schkode, 1976), but this is far from a universal finding. Not all manipulations are equally powerful and not all tasks are equally sensitive to such a manipulation. Other dimensions, such as availability of resources and importance of task behavior may condition the effects of the manipulation (McCallum, Rusbult, Hong, Walden, & Schopler, 1979). Perceptions of control may ameliorate the adverse effects (Epstein, 1981), as may other types of manipulation which provide an attribution source for the experienced arousal (Worchel & Yohai, 1979). Individual differences may also be important. For example, people who prefer large amounts of space between themselves and others may be more susceptible to the effects of the manipulation than those who get along with less space (Aiello & Thompson, 1980). Similarly, those who have a stronger desire for control may be more susceptible than those whose desire is weaker (Burger, Oakman, & Bullard, 1983). Also, tasks that require cooperation may be influenced by gender differences: Under crowded conditions, male groups may function better in an achievement setting, whereas female groups perform better if the situation demands socio-emotional group maintenance (Epstein, 1981).

In fact, the study of gender differences in crowding appears to have generated a fairly replicable body of evidence with respect to a variety of outcomes. Although the perception of being crowded may be the same for males and females, the subjective meaning of the experience may differ by gender (Ross, Layton, Erickson, & Schopler, 1973). Females appear to respond more positively to high crowding and display fewer manifestations of stress than do males in the same situation (Burch & Walker, 1978; Freedman, Levy, Buchanan, & Price, 1972; Marshall & Heston, 1975).

Laboratory studies of crowding have examined a number of other outcomes, such as negative mood and various physiological indicators of arousal (stress?), such as cardiac functioning and skin conductance. The evidence favors the general conclusion of an adverse impact (e.g., Epstein, 1981; Nicosia, Hyman, Karlin, Epstein, & Aiello, 1979), but much variability of results exists, as was the case for task performance as the outcome variable. For example, in a study of subjects working on a series of tasks and being seated either very close together or far apart (Walden & Forsyth, 1981), the effects of close proximity on self-reported stress and systolic blood pressure were observed only when a second manipulation was also present (anticipating side effects of "medication"), which led to a negative appraisal of the situation. In another study, the main effects of the crowding manipulation, room size, were minimal compared to the effects of low expected compatibility of group members or the effects of a "high gaze" manipulation (Schaeffer & Patterson, 1980). And in a study of aggression after being crowded, as measured by an opportunity to administer electric shock to another student, the impact of the manipulation was seen only under a competitive set, but not a cooperative set, and not when there was a 30-minute delay in the opportunity to administer the shock (Mathews, Paulus, & Baron, 1979). Incidentally, the effect of crowding was to reduce aggression, which led the authors to speculate that crowding may promote social withdrawal rather than aggression; only male students were studied.

SUMMARY

In this chapter we examined some of the literature on human crowding, focusing particularly on the evidence regarding the effects of crowding on health and well-being. The concept of crowding remains imprecise and there exists as yet no convergence of opinion regarding the best way of conceptualizing and measuring the essential aspect(s) of this concept. As with the concept of "stress," crowding has been used as a stimulus condition, as a response variable, and as some complex process that encompasses both the stimulus and the response. Among those preferring to think of crowding as a stimulus condition, opinion is divided on the relative need for objective versus subjective definitions of the stimulus. In this chapter, we argued for the need to approach crowding as an objectively defined environmental condition and we illustrated some of the conceptual and methodological problems one encounters when the subjective (purely psychological) approach to the stimulus condition is emphasized.

Given these uncertainties and disagreements in the field of crowding, we feel that the most reasonable approach for the moment is to leave the term crowding alone (i.e., utilize an ordinary dictionary definition) but to take pains in our studies to identify clearly the environmental exposure, the outcomes which can be linked to that exposure, and some of the processes which underlie the linkages. That is, we need to shift from a conceptual–theoretical preoccupation to an emphasis on strong research designs that illuminate cause–effect relationships and in which both the exposures and the outcomes are of some public health significance.

The empirical evidence (examined in this chapter) for adverse effects of crowding on health and well-being comes basically from studies of the residential environment. The research is clearly not very extensive and, possibly, a critical mass of studies has not yet been accumulated. On balance, the evidence is weak and, for various methodological considerations, unconvincing; on the other hand, the evidence that does exist cannot be easily dismissed. The best guess is that an impact exists which — in *descending* order of magnitude — includes: perceptions, housing satisfaction, social–leisure interaction, quality of life, mental health, role performance, physiological indicators, and disease states. The near lack of impact on physical health in the modern industrial society setting may reflect a historical change: The extremes of residential crowding are no longer common, nor are the infectious diseases that were potentiated by crowding.

Two major research challenges persist. One is how to isolate the effects of crowding from a host of interrelated variables reflecting poverty-disadvantage, social class, stage in life cycle, and other dimensions of the residential environment. The other is how to study in the field setting the complex and rich processes and mechanisms that have been suggested by theory and laboratory experiments. The overall research task is exceedingly difficult because these two challenges are, in some sense, incompatible: to isolate, yet also to study in its full complexity. Innovative research designs should reveal better the specific conditions of human vulnerability to crowding.

2 Studies of Crowding and of Health in the Prison Setting

This chapter has a dual purpose: to review relatively limited research literature that is specifically concerned with crowding in prison, and then to sketch out the more general picture of health and health care of prisoners. The first topic provides continuity with the previous chapter, whereas the second topic provides a broad introduction to the prison setting from a public health perspective. Together, these topics are intended as background to our cross-sectional and longitudinal studies of inmates at three Massachusetts correctional institutions.

EFFECTS OF CROWDING IN PRISON

Chapter 1 considered the evidence on the impact of crowding on health and well-being that came primarily from the study of the non-institutional residential setting. The evidence was characterized as rather weak and inconsistent. In the present chapter, the evidence from the study of the prison setting, although more limited in quantity, implicates more convincingly the dimension of crowding in affecting health and well-being. There are several possible explanations for being able to detect more clearly an impact of crowding in this particular setting: (a) The degree of crowding experienced by the inmates is likely to be considerably higher than the crowding typically experienced in the residential studies. (b) The prison setting, with its atmosphere of uncertainty and threat of violence may make the issues of space and privacy more salient, thus enhancing the effects of crowding. (c) The involuntary nature of the confinement and the environmental constraints of the setting may

[handwritten margin note: MND P 22-3 Data & Conclusion accurate]

reduce the inmates' capacity to cope with the consequences of crowding. (d) The social environment of crowding is not the family setting typically seen in the residential studies, but the setting of strangers who typically represent a disadvantaged segment of our society (young, unmarried males, from the lower social classes, with unstable family histories).

The bulk of the prison research has been done by Paulus, Cox, McCain, and their colleagues (e.g., Cox, Paulus, McCain, & Schkade, 1979; McCain, Cox, & Paulus, 1976; Paulus, Cox, McCain, & Chandler, 1975; Paulus & McCain, 1983; Paulus, McCain, & Cox, 1978). Two papers (Cox, Paulus, & McCain, 1984; Paulus, McCain, & Cox, 1985) provide good overviews of this program of research. These investigators have studied a variety of jails and prisons, and have utilized archival data (institutional records) as well as their own de novo data collection. Three primary aspects of crowding have been examined: (a) number of inmates housed, in relation to the original capacity of that institution (institutional crowding); (b) amount of floor space available per inmate (spatial density); and (c) number of individuals in an inmate's housing unit (social density). Institutional crowding was primarily examined in the archival data analyses. Spatial density was mostly examined by comparing single cells of different sizes. Social density is involved in comparisons of single cells with double cells and with dormitories.

The archival analyses suggest that institutional overcrowding leads to higher rates of: (a) disciplinary infractions and inmate-on-inmate assaults; (b) suicides, violent deaths, and total deaths; (c) psychiatric commitments; and (d) reconviction rates. These analyses are "ecological" (aggregate data) analyses, that is, cross-sectional comparisons of different institutions and change over time comparisons in single institutions that experienced considerable fluctuations in census. In many reports, statistical controls for potential confounders were carried out. These were: age, race, ethnicity, type of housing, security level, and inmate/guard ratio. In spite of the limitations of the aggregate data methodology, the evidence appears impressive, particularly the consistency of findings from different times, and with different outcomes.

With respect to spatial density, the investigators have come to the broad conclusion that only minimal effects can be observed, such as on ratings of favorableness, but not on various health outcomes. This appears to be true of comparisons of individual cells (of double cells) that vary in amount of space. It is less clear that the conclusion also holds for variations in space for the dormitory setting, and the investigators acknowledge the possibility that amount of space may have some importance in the context of multiple occupant housing.

Paulus and his colleagues see the impact of social density as being rather broad and well documented in their studies. Inmates prefer singles over doubles and doubles over dormitories. Units of high social density, such as dormitories, are described in more negative terms: noisy, crowded, poorly arranged, too many people. Inmates in high social density conditions give evidence of negative mood and have higher illness complaint rates; some studies also show somewhat higher blood pressure levels. These investigators have also demonstrated the benefits of cubicles (partitions) in the prison dormitory setting: such segmentation seems to ameliorate the adverse impact of the dormitory setting. With respect to time course of impact, this team of investigators has made two observations: (a) There appears to be an initial period of adaptation (approximately 6 weeks), and it is primarily after this period that the effects of social density become apparent. (b) As exposure to high social density conditions lengthens, there appear to be more negative consequences, suggesting that this is a situation to which it is difficult to adapt. In some of the settings investigated, assignment to housing conditions appeared without bias (i.e., arbitrary, although not strictly random), which permitted a check on the role of background characteristics. On the whole, the investigators could not identify specific characteristics that would point to differential vulnerability.

The findings from this program of research by Paulus and his colleagues suggests several comments. One observation is that it appears that the most powerful effects are due to institutional overcrowding. However, we cannot be sure that this is the case because the de novo studies of social density did not include the same outcome variables, such as suicide or general mortality, as did the archival analysis. (This is, undoubtedly, due to the need for large numbers and longer periods of observation in order to detect impact on such outcomes.) Also, when one compares different levels of social density within a single institution, the overall impact of level of institutional crowding may wash out because it contributes separately at all levels of social density. It is also interesting to speculate to what extent the impact of institutional overcrowding may reflect social rather than spatial dynamics: That is, the original design of the prison sets up norms and expectations for the inmates, and overcrowding beyond intended capacity is then seen as violation of inmates' rights. A comparison of two institutions that differ in designed capacity but not in actual space per inmate (thus making one overcrowded in the design sense, but both comparable on spatial density) might reveal the extent to which our speculation is plausible.

It might also be noted that the results with the two variables of greatest interest to our own study, blood pressure and illness complaints, are somewhat unclear. With respect to blood pressure, the authors state that "in most of our studies, blood pressure has not varied with the degree of crowding in prison housing" (Paulus, McCain, & Cox, 1985, p. 122). However, they note three studies where it did, and in all three the contrast was a confounded one, including both spatial and social density differences. This suggests that one needs a "double dose" of both forms of crowding before blood pressure ef-

[Margin annotations:]

mm3p24 Crwdng = poor hlth

mm3p24 cubicles >> hlth

mm3p24 6 weeks TF [linear hlth ↓]

mm3p24 overcrwdng lrgst factr

mm3p24 overcrwdng © unsure

mm3p24 overcrwdng ↓ rights

mm3p24 bld P ∅ affctd (BP)

fects may be observed. There is also some suggestion that only some inmates may be vulnerable to the blood pressure effects. For example, violent inmates may be least vulnerable, while those inmates who are non-workers (i.e., spend most of their time in the cell or dorm) may be most vulnerable (Paulus & McCain, 1983). The results with respect to illness complaints appear to suggest a more consistent effect of crowding, although negative findings also exist (e.g., Paulus & McCain, 1983). Here the issue is more the inherent ambiguity of this measure when it is obtained without additional data. We do not know to what extent it reflects differences in actual illness experiences versus differential tendencies to react to some symptom or illness experience. In fact, in many prison settings it could simply reflect a temporary escape from the crowded setting, in no way triggered by the presence of symptoms.

Beyond the program of research by Paulus and his colleagues, there are a few scattered other studies providing additional information on the impact of prison crowding. Three of these are archival analyses. One has confirmed the association between institutional overcrowding and elevated reconviction rates (Farrington & Nuttall, 1980), while another suggested that rates of assault and total disciplinary rates may not be related to overcrowding once one adjusts for age (Ekland-Olson, Barrich, & Cohen, 1983). A third study (Ruback & Carr, 1984) is of interest because it deals with a woman's prison. In the archival part of the study, infraction rates were observed to rise as prison census rose, and this finding held even after adjustment for covariates (age, race, previous arrests, history of violence). In the individual part of the study, dealing with self-reports of inmates, higher symptoms of distress were observed among those who perceived little control over their living situation and those who had lived alone before imprisonment. In another study, Megargee (1977) examined the relationship between prison population size, amount of personal space, and the incidence of disruptive behaviors in correctional institutions. Decreased personal space and greater population density were associated with higher rates of misconduct.

HEALTH STUDIES OF PRISONERS

Toch (1975, 1977) has portrayed imprisonment as a drastic life change, often characterized by sensory deprivation, threats of violence, restricted activity, and loss of social supports. Imprisonment has been ranked the sixth most stressful event on the schedule of 42 life events developed by Holmes and Rahe (1976). It is thus fair to speculate that imprisonment would have a significant effect on health and well-being of prison inmates, and that numerous studies would have addressed this broad hypothesis. In fact, surprisingly little research has been conducted in this area (Goldsmith, 1975).

It must be understood that the literature is not devoid of studies of the health of prisoners. However, the vast majority of such studies are descriptive epidemiologic designs giving the prevalence of health problems and medical conditions of prison inmates. At best, such studies may indicate the need for medical care among prisoners, particularly the currently unmet needs. However, for detecting the impact of the experience of imprisonment, one needs longitudinal designs in which early and later health status assessments permit a better estimate of the change in health status that might be specifically attributed to the imprisonment. A cross-sectional look at the health status of prisoners, even when compared to good age- and sex-specific national norms, cannot securely indicate the impact of imprisonment because prisoners are such a self-selected group whose health status prior to imprisonment could already be markedly different. This would be particularly likely for offenses that are associated with substance abuse.

In the review that follows, we have omitted the research literature on prisoners of war (e.g., Beebe, 1975; Nefzger, 1970). We view it as only peripherally relevant because the prisoner-of-war experience differs significantly from criminal incarceration. The former may commonly include severe malnutrition, beating, and torture — events that seriously confound physical with psychological stressors. The potential for these same events may exist in some American correctional institutions, but their occurrence is much less frequent and the primary source of stress is psychological (e.g., Toch, 1975, 1977). Of course, the reasons for incarceration in the two institutions are also quite different, as would be the self-selection characteristics of the two groups. Overall therefore, the prisoner-of-war literature cannot really contribute to our understanding of civilian criminal incarceration.

As indicated already, the studies that we do review are primarily descriptive studies of prevalence of health problems and of medical-care needs. They are useful in summarizing the current state of knowledge regarding prison health and in indicating areas that need additional attention. They cannot directly illuminate the general issue of health impact of imprisonment or the specific issue of health impact of crowding in correctional institutions. However, they can give us some additional insight into the characteristics of the subjects and of the setting that we study when we undertake to examine the topic of health and crowding in prison.

GENERAL HEALTH SURVEYS

Several investigators have conducted general surveys of the health problems and medical conditions of prison inmates. One of the earliest was Rector's

(1929) survey of selected state and federal prisons across the country. He observed that practically all of the institutions were overcrowded (50% to 100% above normal capacity) and medically understaffed. The most prevalent physical illness, determined by examination, was syphilis (16%). He also reported high rates of psychologic disturbances including mental retardation (40%), psychopathic personality disorders (33%), neurosis (10%), and psychosis (5%). His recommendations for standards of medical care in prisons were physical examinations by qualified physicians at intake and discharge, complete dental and optical care, and daily sick call conducted by a physician, including the dispensing of prescription drugs.

More recent investigations have been conducted by the American Medical Association (AMA) as part of their program to improve services for the nation's medically underserved. In conjunction with the American Bar Association, the AMA first developed and submitted to 2,900 sheriffs throughout the country, a questionnaire on medical services in their jails (AMA, 1973). Forty percent responded, and they reported grossly inadequate conditions. For instance 66% provided only first aid treatment, and 17% had no medical facilities at all. The results prompted a second and more detailed study (Modlin, 1979). In that study, health histories, physical examinations, and laboratory tests were performed on 641 inmates from 28 jails in six states. The findings indicated that 30% had abnormal liver function suggestive of hepatitis, 13% had a positive tuberculin test, and 6% has positive tests for syphilis. Eighteen percent had been daily users of heroin, and 50% reported daily intake of alcohol before imprisonment. Ninety percent of the inmates voiced at least one medical complaint, and the physical examination revealed approximately three abnormalities per person.

These AMA studies have been important in the development of minimal standards, the implementation of a national certification program for jail medical services, and have influenced legal decisions regarding the constitutionality of denying necessary medical treatment to prisoners. Their epidemiologic significance, however, is limited by the lack of specific information concerning the demographic characteristics of the inmates, the selection of the inmates for study, and the assessment and diagnostic procedures employed.

Several studies of the health status of prisoners have been conducted in New York City, which has one of the largest correctional systems in the nation. Litt and Cohen (1974) have investigated 31,323 juveniles who were detained in youth facilities by order of family courts until disposition plans were completed by probation officers. Their study extended over a 60-month period. Through health histories, physical examinations, and laboratory tests performed at intake, these researchers found that 46% of the children had medical problems. These conditions included abnormal liver function (9%), venereal disease (3%), and positive tuberculin tests (2%). One-third were identified as drug abusers. Over 2,000 youths were admitted to the prison infirmary or Montefiore Hospital during the study period. Among the most frequent diagnoses in them were drug and alcohol withdrawal (12%), trauma (8%), and skin infection (5%). The study is noteworthy because of its large sample size and emphasis on juvenile offenders, but, like the AMA studies, it is epidemiologically limited by its lack of detailed information concerning methodology and patient characteristics.

Novick, Della Penna, Schwartz, Remmlinger, and Loewenstein (1977) have conducted a similar investigation of adult and juvenile prisoners. The study population consisted of all 1,420 persons admitted to any New York City correctional institution for a 2-week period in 1975. Sixty-two physicians were utilized to determine the prevalence of specific current and past health conditions from physical examinations and health histories. More than one quarter of the inmates reported a current illness or medical complaint, and three-fifths received at least one diagnosis by the examining physician. The most frequent specific diagnoses were drug abuse (16%), psychiatric disorder (13%), physical trauma (6%), and alcohol abuse (5%). An additional 18% were noted as having abnormalities of the teeth and mouth. A history of hepatitis was reported by 8%, attempted suicide by 5%, and epilepsy by 4%. Forty-one percent stated that they currently or previously used illicit drugs. Seventeen percent gave histories of repetitive alcohol abuse. Sociodemographic variables were examined, and the results were often presented by age, sex, race, or education. Potential methodologic problems include the use of a large number of physicians to collect the data, thus introducing variability in diagnosis, and the need to conduct the examinations and histories rapidly and under less than ideal conditions, thus affecting the accuracy of their notations.

Several states have studied the health of their inmate populations. In Michigan, for example, 458 inmates randomly selected from the state's inmate population were assessed through physical examinations, health histories, and laboratory tests (Michigan State Office of Health and Medical Affairs, 1975). The most common conditions identified by a collation of data from all sources were genitourinary problems, hypertension, visual disorders, hearing difficulties, and liver dysfunction. The referral rates for these five classes of conditions ranged from 13% to 82%. Ninety-seven percent also required dental treatment other than cleaning. Only 15% had MMPI profiles in the normal range, with sociopathic as the most frequent diagnostic classification (51%). Because the clinical assessments, were carefully performed, the study presumably portrayed accurately the health status of a state prison population. However, data analyses were limited, and little information was presented regarding variation among inmates in the frequency of conditions beyond associations with basic demographic variables.

The health status of inmates in a Minnesota jail has been investigated by Derro (1978a, 1978b). Health histories, physical examinations, and laboratory tests were performed on 491 men at admission who were serving sentences of at least 30 days. Common abnormalities were dental or gingival conditions (66%), skin disorders (12%), and psychiatric problems (7%). Within a 2-year period after intake, 312 members of the original cohort (64%) made a total of 1,257 clinic visits, yielding a rate of 2.0 visits per inmate per year. Injuries were the most frequent problem (15%). The generalizability of the study, however, may be limited by the fact that the population was predominately White and housed in a county workhouse.

One hundred and fifty-eight female inmates were questioned about their health status in a Massachusetts correctional institution (Climent, Rollins, Ervin, & Plutchik, 1973). Seventy-six percent had a history of head injuries, 39% had frequent headaches, and 14% had seizure disorders. Also of note were surgery other than gynecologic (82%), major infectious disease (42%), and allergies (20%). The study is important because it involves the largest sample of female prisoners investigated to date. The results, however, are of limited epidemiologic significance, because the main thrust of the study was to relate medical and psychiatric variables to violent behavior, and not to document the health status of inmates or the medical consequences of imprisonment.

A different approach has been followed by Jones (1976). He has estimated the health effects of imprisonment by comparing morbidity rates for inmates with rates for probationers and parolees. The primary source of data was personal interview, supplemented by prison medical records. A 20% random sample of Tennessee's adult male felon population was followed for 6 months.

The results indicated that inmates reported morbid episodes at higher rates than did non-incarcerated probationers and parolees. Their annual incidence rate for acute physical conditions, for example, was 432.4/100 persons, compared with 55.7/100 persons for parolees and 51.0/100 persons for probationers. The most common chronic diseases were gastrointestinal disorders like gastric or duodenal ulcers and gastritis or duodenitis. The prevalence rates of these conditions for inmates were 102.9/1,000 persons and 93.1/1,000 persons, respectively, versus 46.1/1,000 persons and 21.4/1,000 persons for probationers and parolees combined. More than 16% of the inmates had received one or more psychiatric diagnoses. Similar data were not gathered for probationers or parolees. These latter two groups nevertheless reported lower psychologic distress and less desire to commit suicide than did the prisoners. Inmates visited a physician more frequently (4.3 visits per person per year in contrast to 2.5 for probationers and 0.9 for parolees). Prisoners also had higher rates of restricted activity, bed disability, and hospitalizations for acute and chronic conditions.]

[Jones' study is broad and comprehensive, but it lacks a sound theoretical framework. Many of the analyses were conducted without a guidance of a priori hypotheses, and the results were interpreted with little reference to pertinent public health or social science literature. He has failed to distinguish, for example, between illness and illness behavior, a problem resulting from his use of patient self-report and medical records. His attempt to introduce non-incarcerated offenders such as parolees or probationers as control groups is useful, but it results in non-comparable sources of data. Differences in the utilization of health services, for instance, may reflect differences in cost or access, and not measure the health effects of imprisonment]

DISEASE-SPECIFIC SURVEYS

Hepatitis

The Center for Disease Control investigated an outbreak of hepatitis B that was associated with a plasmapheresis unit and parenteral drug abuse in a Kansas state prison (Koplan, Walker, Bryan, & Berquist, 1978). A representative survey of prisoners for hepatitis B surface antigen (HBsAg) and antibody to HBsAg (anti-HBs) was conducted. Eight percent of 286 inmates had HBsAg whereas 34% had anti-HBs. This estimate is much greater than general population values, and it also exceeds the 1% to 2% rate of HBsAg found in other inmates studies (Kliman, 1971; Krotoski, 1972; Muniz, Malyska, & Levin, 1971). It suggests that the prevalence of HBsAg carriage in prisoners may be greater than previously believed. The significance of this finding is underlined by the fact that prison populations are frequently used in plasmapheresis programs and occasionally as blood donors.

Tuberculosis

In a study of approximately 15,000 adult male prisoners in New York City, the number of inmates with active pulmonary tuberculosis was 2/1,000 persons, as determined by chest examination and radiography (Abeles, Feibes, Mandel, & Girard, 1970). More than 17% of adolescents 16 to 21 years old had a positive tuberculin skin test. Similar results have been reported for inmates in New Orleans (Thompson, Trachtman, & Greenberg, 1978), and prisoners in Arkansas had rates of active tuberculosis equal to 6.7/1,000 persons and positive tuberculin skin tests of 32% (Stead, 1978). The ease of contagion in penal institutions has been demonstrated by King and Geis (1977), who have shown that the placement of a single inmate with undiagnosed tuberculosis in a crowded dwelling unit led to a positive tuberculin skin test of 71% among inmates who had previous negative results.

Seizure Disorders

The prescription rates for anti-convulsant medications in 10 Illinois correctional institutions housing 12,030 persons have been surveyed to estimate the point prevalence of seizure disorders among inmates (King & Young, 1978). The results indicated a rate of 1.9%. The study may be criticized for using prescription rates as indicators of epilepsy, because this procedure does not allow for the inclusion of unaware or untreated cases or for the confirmation of diagnosis for treated individuals. The observed prevalence of 1.9% nevertheless agrees closely with the 1.6% and 1.8% figures found respectively in the previously described Minnesota (Derro, 1978a, 1978b) and New York City (Novick, Della Penna, Schwartz, Remmlinger, & Loewenstein, 1977) studies, which used health histories and physical examinations to determine prevalence. Gunn, however, has used more detailed diagnostic procedures, including in-depth interviews and neurologic examinations, and has reported lower prevalances of 0.7% to 0.9% in British prison populations (Gunn, 1974, 1977; Gunn & Fenton, 1969).

Psychiatric Disorders

Swank and Winer (1976) examined 445 inmates through referral of self-request for psychiatric evaluation. Forty-two percent reported previous psychiatric hospitalizations. The leading diagnoses were functional psychosis (23%), anti-social personality (15%), and alcoholism (12%). The extent of selection bias was evident by comparing these figures with data collected on a more nearly random sample of 100 inmates upon admission. For the latter population the following estimates were made: previous psychiatric hospitalization, 14%; functional psychosis, 3%; anti-social personality, 13%; and alcoholism, 18%. The more seriously ill and disruptive inmates were more likely to be referred or to receive psychiatric evaluation. By extrapolating from referrals, Petrich (1976) has estimated that 4.6% of approximately 2,625 inmates of a county jail were mentally ill. This may be an underestimate because 39% of those referred were not examined and therefore were not included. The most common diagnoses were alcoholism or drug addiction, anti-social personality, and schizophrenia. Through a review of records, Roth and Ervin (1971) determined among 1,154 federal prisoners, a history of psychiatric hospitalization for 18%, a diagnosis of personality disorder for 31%, and a life-time prevalence of 8% for psychosis.

In a series of studies, Guze and his colleagues (Guze, 1976; Guze, Goodwin, & Crane, 1969; Guze, Woodruff, & Clayton, 1974) have confirmed high rates of alcoholism, drug addiction, and anti-social personality in prison populations. An intriguing study by Bauer and Clark (1976) has shown that long-term offenders had more pathologic profiles on several MMPI subscales than short-term offenders, controlling for age, race, and education. Their cross-sectional design limits causal inferences, but they nevertheless concluded that incarceration has harmful effect on personality.

Suicide

Novick and Remmlinger (1978) have examined mortality of prisoners in New York City over a 5½-year period from 1971 to 1976. Suicide was the leading cause, accounting for 52 (41%) of 128 deaths. The rate was highest among males 35 to 44 years old, (i.e., 194.4/100,000 persons compared with 13.1/100,000 persons for New York City males of the same age). Seventy-one percent were detainees awaiting trial, and over three-quarters had been previously identified by the mental health staff of the prison as having psychiatric problems. Of special note is the fact that no female inmate committed suicide during the study period. In another study of male prisoners, a much lower suicide rate (10.5/100,000) was reported by Rieger (1971). This discrepancy may be explained by differences between the two studies both in setting (federal prison for Rieger versus city facilities for Novick & Remmlinger) and in legal disposition (100% convicted and sentenced inmates for Rieger vs. 71% detainees awaiting trial for Novick & Remmlinger).

A prison-based case-control study of 30 suicide attempters and 30 randomly selected inmates of Arizona jails in 1970 has indicated that suicide attempters were younger, more likely to have been separated or divorced, to have been arrested for a non-violent crime, and more often a recidivist than other prisoners (Beigel & Russell, 1972). In that study no suicide attempt occurred after 6 weeks of imprisonment. Unlike the previously discussed studies of suicide, however, it did not involve the systematic investigation of all relevant correctional and medical records. The data were collected through a mailed questionnaire circulated to all sheriffs in the state, a procedure sensitive to biases of non-response and recall.

STUDIES OF MEDICAL UTILIZATION

Other studies have focused upon the utilization of medical services by prison populations. Engebretsen and Olson (1975), for instance, have investigated the health problems of 333 men who presented at sick call in a Florida county jail. These inmates were part of a prison population of approximately 600 men, and made a total of 407 physician visits over a 6-month period of

1973. Five hundred and twenty-eight conditions were identified. They were most commonly: psychosocial problems (37%), including drug and alcohol abuse, anxiety–depression, and phenothiazine responsive emotional disorders.

In contrast, the most frequent reason for visiting a physician in the previously described study by Derro (1978b) was injury. Mental disorders ranked seventh in the Derro research, whereas accidents were ninth in the work by Engebretsen and Olson. This difference may be due to the fact that the latter investigators only studied physician visits that had occurred after screening by guards and nurses. Inmates with minor injuries or other routine medical problems were treated by the nurses or prevented from gaining access to the physicians by the guards. A distorted picture of primary care resulted when compared to the Derro study, in which all medical encounters were recorded and examined.

The magnitude of the bias may be estimated by reviewing the results of an experiment by Howe, Froom, Culpepper, and Mangone (1977). They introduced two new options (a non-prescription drug pharmacy and a nurse screening station) to New York state prisons, which previously only maintained physician-attended sick calls. The total number of medical encounters remained the same in the 20 institutions over a 1 year period, but the number of visits specifically to physicians was reduced from 100% to 21%. The utilization data of Jones (1976) discussed previously are subject to the same criticism as the work of Engebretsen and Olson because his population was also required to submit requests for medical care to paraprofessionals before referral to a physician was possible.

The studies of Derro and of Engebretsen and Olson are medically oriented in that they focus on diagnosis, course and care, and are similar to other research conducted in the Canadian provinces of Ontario and Saskatchewan (Botterell, 1972; Young & Carr, 1976). In contrast, Twaddle (1976) has emphasized the social science perspective to the utilization of health services in prison. Conceiving of a visit to a prison medical facility as a measure of illness behavior in the context of a specific organizational setting, he has examined the medical records of almost 1,600 incarcerated men in a large midwestern prison over a period of 5 months in 1972. By investigating in detail 293 inmates randomly selected from this population, Twaddle has shown that 35% accounted for all of the visits made by the 293 men in 1 month. Infirmary visits were more likely among younger men, black inmates, those in prison for 1 year or less, and those who resided in the higher security areas of the prison. A history of previous medical problems, particularly chronic diseases, was also positively correlated with utilization, as was a history of previous hospitalization. Marital status, criminal history, length of sentence, work assignment, and number of disciplinary reports were unrelated to or only weakly associated with sick calls.

Twaddle has proposed several explanations for his findings, including the stress of imprisonment. His design, however, did not provide for a direct test of attribution of "cause." His analysis of the data was rudimentary, and consisted entirely of one- and two-way frequency distributions. He failed to test for statistical significance, and thereby omitted an assessment of the extent to which his findings may be the consequence of sampling variation. Another limitation concerns the fact that data regarding the reasons for visiting the infirmary were not available. Consequently, his investigation is limited to a simple count of visits with no further examination of specific types or classes of visits.

ADAPTATION TO PRISON

⌈Miller (1973) wrote that "no matter what the degree of inmate psychopathology, the stress of punitive confinement is great and the adaptive patterns are limited and, generally, non-utilitarian once confinement has ended" (p. 26)⌋ He undertook a description of the sequence of adaptive processes used by young men during their imprisonment. His observations were based on contact with inmates as a prison psychiatrist in a medium security prison housing 525 youthful inmates. This was supplemented by a series of interviews with inmates, many just prior to release, and by conversations with other prison psychiatrists. He divided the sequence of stress and problems into phases, and identified various modes of coping.

The "Initial" phase, occurring during the first 4 to 6 weeks of confinement in prison, can be characterized by feelings of denial, often followed by depression, anxiety, and even panic. The inmate must deal with the issue of forcible restraint, separation, feelings of abandonment, and interpersonal disruption. He then begins an initiation process, turning his attention to the prison community. He is tested, harassed and closely observed, and, in coping with this process, begins to establish a role for himself.

The next, or "Middle" phase is one in which the inmate focuses most of his interest and energy on the prison community itself. He is intent on securing self-esteem, and the goods and services he requires. He assumes certain kinds of role behavior in order to protect himself and secure a degree of individual power, while building alliances and friendships with other inmates or groups of inmates. A good deal of sexual behavior takes place within the prison, often resulting from the evolution of an initially platonic friendship.

The final, or "Terminal" phase varies in duration depending on when the inmate is released. If an inmate serves all of his sentence, this phase begins about 6 weeks before his release. This tension–anxiety syndrome is known as the "short-time syndrome." The inmate experiences a return to consciousness of memories, thoughts and feelings associated with his home community, in addition to contemplating the aspects of the prison community that have had an important impact on him. He is severing ties developed in the prison while anticipating reunion with family and friends on the outside. Concern with sexual problems may complicate this phase. Doubts about adequacy arise, compounded by the shame felt by many inmates who have engaged in homosexual behavior during confinement.

EVALUATION OF HEALTH STUDIES OF PRISONERS

Most of the studies reviewed provide descriptive accounts of illness and illness behavior among incarcerated populations. The majority are prevalence surveys, usually conducted at intake. They are subject to a variety of methodologic criticisms, but generally indicate that inmates suffer from poor health in disproportionate numbers and utilize prison medical services more frequently than the general population uses community facilities. The quality of the care prisoners receive is a separate issue, and most research indicates that it is grossly inadequate (e.g., Novick & Al-Ibrahim, 1977). Standards have been established to insure at least minimal levels of competency (AMA, 1979; The Jails and Prisons Task Force of the Program Development Board of the American Public Health Association, 1976; Commission on Accreditation for Corrections, 1977), but the national implementation of changes in prison health care has been difficult (Goldfarb, 1975; King & Whitman, 1981; Mitford, 1973).

Relatively few investigations have been analytic. Exceptions include the studies of Jones (1976) and Twaddle (1976). They go beyond a simple statement of the distribution of disease in prison populations to examine respectively the health status of prisoners compared to non-incarcerated populations (Jones, 1976), and the factors associated with the utilization of medical services in prison (Twaddle, 1976). Jones' work, however, lacks theoretical guidance and does not possess a rigorous, quantitative methodology. Twaddle's study has stronger theoretical underpinnings, but is also quantitatively weak. Both studies suffer from the fact that their designs were cross-sectional. Correlations were noted, but temporal sequences could not be demonstrated, so causal inferences remain tenuous. This limitation is shared by all of the studies reviewed, because none are longitudinal. A great need exists for research that follows inmates from admission to discharge and links health status and change in health status over time to antecedent events.

Most of the prison health studies conducted to date adhere to the medical perspective, and focus on the nature of the disease with little emphasis on underlying causal mechanisms like stress (AMA, 1973; Engebretsen & Olson, 1975). The social science studies, on the other hand, employ stress and other theoretical constructs, but do not examine characteristics of the illness episode (Twaddle, 1976). Investigations are required that combine the best features of both approaches. In other words, studies should be designed to provide for in-depth examinations of health conditions at intake and of changes in health conditions subsequently, as well as reasons for visiting the prison infirmary after admission, while simultaneously testing hypotheses derived from a strong theoretical base. Research that uses these methods and pursues these goals would contribute significantly to our understanding of the prison environment, and, as King and Whitman (1981) have noted in their review of morbidity and mortality among inmates, "directly affect the lives and health of prisoners, public and judicial policies, and the health of the general population" (p. 26).

3 Blood Pressure as a Measure of Psychosocial Stress

Blood pressure was used in the studies described in this book as a non-self-report measure of the stressful effects of the prison environment. We did not intend our studies to be a search for etiological clues to hypertension. In order to understand how blood pressure change may be a measure of response to the psychosocial stress of prisons, it is useful to consider any analogy (Fig. 3.1). We consider together factors influencing the level of blood pressure from moment to moment and factors influencing the level of water in Long Island Sound at any instant.

Three types of factors may be seen as determining the level or depth of water in Long Island Sound at a single place and time. The first is the basic depth of the water, a level beneath which the water never or rarely goes. Then there are factors influencing the depth or level of water whose effects are discernable over hours, days, and months. The tide is an example of such factors. Finally, the depth of the water at any instant and at a given point is determined by the presence and height of the waves. The effect of a wave on the depth of water at a single location and time comes and goes in seconds.

Now consider the analogy with blood pressure. There is in each individual a basal blood pressure below which, in the waking state, the blood pressure never goes. This basal pressure is influenced by genetic factors and by gender, and is equivalent to the basic depth of the water in Long Island Sound. Then there are factors that influence the level of blood pressure over days, months, and years. The effects of these factors, like the tides, last longer, sometimes very much longer, than an instant and are often reversible. Such factors are obesity, education, and occupation, possibly salt, potassium, calcium and alcohol intake, age, race, and season of the year. Finally, there are factors influencing blood pressure almost instantaneously and lasting for a few sec-

37

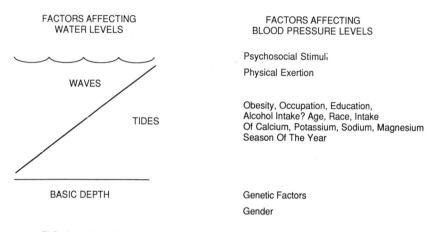

FIG. 3.1.   Parallels in factors affecting levels of blood pressure and depth of water.

onds, minutes, hours, or days. These factors, often psychosocial stimuli or physical exertion, may be compared to the depth of waves in their rapid and reversible effect on blood pressure. For a fuller discussion of these issues, the reader is referred to Guyton (1977) and Pickering (1974).

Thus, a single blood pressure reading reflects the combined influence of the basal blood pressure, of relatively enduring influences whose effects are summated over months or years (such as age, race, education, obesity), of psychosocial influences that may last for days or weeks (such as increase in workload on the job), and of momentary changes in the psychosocial environment (such as a sudden change in the topic of a conversation or the appearance of a threatening figure). A second reading minutes later would be expected to be different only because of the momentary changes, whereas another reading a week or two later would presumably reflect the momentary changes and the longer lasting environmental changes, but not the relatively enduring influences that take months or years to develop.

There is measurement error in taking blood pressures and there may be error in assessing the depth of a body of water. For the sake of simplicity, we have excluded these issues from our discussion.

In the prisons we studied, the effects of all factors other than psychosocial stress on blood pressure changes were probably negligible and some could be adjusted for statistically. Genetic factors, gender and race are constant. During a sentence of a few months, occupation and education do not change. Age change is small. Inmate's weight has been carefully monitored with weight recorded every time blood pressure was measured (chapter 7). We know that weight change has been quite small and probably without effect on blood pressure. the content of prison meals available to inmates was identical with a single exception, that of pizza on Friday nights as a privilege earned by a small minority of inmates. We have no reason to believe that inmates' intake of sodium, potassium, and calcium fluctuated very much from day to day or week to week. None of the inmates were drunk or showed drug effects during the occasions of data collection. All pressures were measured after inmates had been seated quietly for at least 5 minutes and had had no cigarettes for at least 40 minutes, so it is unlikely that physical exertion or tobacco were a factor in blood pressure changes. The chronological relationship of blood pressure change to change in housing mode (see chapter 6) was the same in all seasons of the year. None of the factors just listed could have been responsible for the blood pressure changes we observed except for psychosocial stress.

PSYCHOSOCIAL STRESS AND BLOOD PRESSURE

It has been noted frequently that when blood pressures are taken serially under the same social and physical conditions, each successive reading tends to be lower than the previous one, for the first few readings. The drop in blood pressure is usually largest between the first and second readings. In longitudinal studies where the interval between measurements is a year or more (Kagan, Gordon, Kannel, & Dawber, 1958; Paul, Lepper, Phelan, Dupertuis, McKean, & Park, 1963) and in surveys in which the pressures are taken minutes apart (Veale, Hamilton, Irvine, & Smirk, 1962) the same phenomenon occurs. It is important to realize that self-reports of anxiety in a novel but subsequently unchanging situation may also decline with each successive report. Perhaps the reduction of anxiety to its usual levels and the lowering of blood pressure to characteristic readings represent parallel responses to declining mental vigilance and arousal. In short, blood pressure usually declines because of the greater familiarity of the subject with the process of blood pressure measurement, familiarity with the social circumstances under which the pressure is taken and reduced concern about the results and meaning of the reading.

Blood pressure has been shown to increase promptly after the appearance of some threat in the environment. Knowing that blood will be drawn increases pressure as the needle and syringe draw near (Tolubeeva & Flegontova, 1940). The appearance of an unfamiliar physician has been shown to produce major blood pressure increases in hospitalized patients (Richardson, Honour, Scott, & Pickering, 1964). Blood pressure readings made in the home are consistently lower than those recorded in the office by a physician (Ayman & Goldshine, 1940). Brod, Fencl, Hejl, and Jirka (1959) and Hejl (1957) monitored blood pressure, cardiac output and resistance to blood flow before, during, and after the approach of an unfamiliar laboratory technician. They engaged their participants with arithmetic tasks while monitoring the variables just listed. Both stimuli, the new technician and the mental arithmetic induced increases in systolic and diastolic pressures that were far from trivial. However, the changes in blood pressure outlasted the stimuli by only a few minutes.

Several investigators have noted, both in hypertensive and normal participants, that the introduction of disturbing personal topics into the conversation between physician and patient is associated with an increase in heart rate and systolic and diastolic pressures. The blood pressure returned to pre-stress levels within minutes after the conversation was redirected to more neutral topics (Hickam, Cargill, & Golden, 1948; Wolf, 1958; Wolf, Pfeiffer, Ripley, Winter, & Wolff, 1948). It was also noted that in some hypertensive patients, the blood pressure dropped considerably after such aggressive acts as hitting a despised brother-in-law and shouting at a coworker.

Fraser and Cowell (1919) noted that among soldiers engaged in combat in World War I, the blood pressure was substantially higher than among men of the same regiment who were kept in reserve away from the fighting. Ehrstrom (1945) noted higher pressures in Finnish soldiers in the front lines than during peace. Ruskin, Beard and Schaffer (1948) observed diastolic pressures of 95 and over in 103 of 180 casualties (57%) from a vast explosion in Texas City. As a comparison group they employed surgical patients seen in the 2 months before the explosion and noted similarly high diastolic pressures in only 34%. Graham (1945) measured blood pressure in 695 men aged 20 to 38 who had spent a year or more in a British Armoured Brigade in North Africa in World War II. All had participated in a decisive battle 4 to 8 weeks before their pressures were measured and had spent those weeks in a safe and relatively comfortable training area. The average systolic pressure was 154, the average diastolic 90. One hundred eighty seven of the men had diastolic pressures exceeding 100. These are extraordinarily high levels for a group of healthy young men.

Much of this early work on psychosocial stimuli and blood pressure change was concerned with trying to establish that an enduring adverse social environment and certain stable characteristics of personality (traits, perceptions, and attitudes) caused high blood pressure. Except for the studies already cited, all of which examined powerful and unusual life circumstances, the attempts to find social-environmental causes of high blood pressure ended in disappointment. The possible link to stable characteristics of personality was occasionally seen, but only in highly select subjects, known hypertensives receiving some medical care, and very often, psychiatric treatment as well. However, the evidence for acute psychosocial stimuli producing acute blood pressure changes became overwhelming, but not particularly in need of further documentation. The overall effect was a much reduced level of such blood pressure studies after 1960 or so.

More recent work has attempted to note the characteristics of life events that raise blood pressure acutely and for brief time periods, and the longer term effects on pressure of psychosocial stress persisting over months and years. Among the latter stressors, occupation, race, sociodemographic characteristics, and job loss have been examined most thoroughly.

Ostfeld and Shekelle (1967) characterized those acute and brief life experiences causing prompt increases in blood pressure in the following way. From the point of view of the person or persons involved, these experiences: (a) have an uncertain outcome; (b) may cause bodily or psychological harm; (c) cannot be handled appropriately by either running or fighting; and (d) call for increased vigilance until the experience ends or is clarified.

As a preliminary test of this hypothesis, Ostfeld carried out some observations on medical students. Each of 20 freshmen medical students was randomly selected from the class roster and matched with another first year student so that the blood pressure of each pair, taken during their prematriculation examination, differed by no more than 10mm systolic and 5mm diastolic. Eighteen of the 20 could be matched. All students were male and between 21 and 27 years of age.

One member of each group (decided by coin flips) received a curt note instructing him to report to the laboratory. The other member of each pair received a longer, more courteously worded note extending an invitation to come to the laboratory. All 36 students participated. All 18 men receiving curt notes (uninformed group) had their blood pressure taken promptly by a technician who said as little as possible and they were then dismissed. With the other men (informed group), Ostfeld spent 15 to 35 minutes showing them the laboratory and reassuring them that all that was wanted was a blood pressure measurement, that they were not at risk for hypertension and were in no academic difficulty. Then the same technician recorded the blood pressures. The technician did not know the hypothesis to be tested and he measured all pressures in the same room, with the same mercury sphygnomanometer, at approximately the same time of day, and after the subjects had been seated for 5 minutes. The group receiving curt notes was informed about the experiment and its purposes within an hour of leaving the laboratory.

The means and standard errors of the students' blood pressures in their pre-matriculation examination and in the laboratory are shown in Table 3.1.

Two points deserve comment. The informed group, the group with the longer letter and the laboratory tour, had lower pressures in the laboratory than in the earlier examination. However, the uninformed group had appreciably higher readings in the laboratory than at the prematriculation exam. The data do confirm the hypothesis that familiarity with and knowledge

TABLE 3.1
Means and Standard Errors in Prematriculation and
Laboratory Examinations

		Pre-matriculation Examination Mean and S.E.	Laboratory Examination Mean and S.E.
Informed Group N = 18	Systolic	119 + 1.7	112 + 1.3
	Diastolic	71 + 1.1	67 + 0.8
Uninformed Group N = 18	Systolic	117 + 1.9	129 + 2.3
	Diastolic	70 + 1.2	78 + 1.4

about a situation are associated with lower pressures than are noted in unfamiliar situations in which expectations are uncertain.

Obrist et al. (1979), who have worked principally with animals, also carried out an interesting series of experiments with healthy male college students. They observed that blood pressure increased more when a difficult but manageable task was presented to the subjects than when either a very easy or impossibly difficult task was presented. Tasks that arouse and challenge because they are not too easy or too difficult induce blood pressure increases. Easy tasks do not arouse and challenge nor do impossibly difficult ones. In the latter case recognition of the impossibility of performing the task leads to giving up rather than to arousal. Obrist et al. (1979) noted that simply telling subjects to get ready for the experiment caused an increase in blood pressure. It was also apparent that subjects whose pressures responded briskly to one task would not necessarily show a major increase when faced with another task.

Other valuable studies have examined the effect on blood pressure of job loss, stressful occupations and residents of high stress residential areas. Kasl and Cobb (1970, 1980) have reported results of a followup study of unemployed automobile workers. After an initial increase, those men unable to find jobs exhibited a drop in blood pressure that led to convergence of the pressures of the employed and unemployed group. The authors suggested that, after prolonged unemployment, the men stopped trying to cope and, as Obrist's work would suggest, had a decrease in pressure.

Some recent work has tried to note the factors leading to blood pressure elevation in certain occupations and segments of American society. One of the more striking associations was noted in a study of 4,325 air traffic controllers and 8,435 second class airmen. The air traffic controllers had a 4-fold greater point prevalence of hypertension and a 5.6-fold greater annual incidence of hypertension than the airmen. Those air traffic controllers who worked in the busiest airports had 1.6 times more hypertension than air controllers at less busy airports (Cobb & Rose, 1973). Harburg, Erfurt, Hauenstein, Chape,

Schull, and Schork (1973) in Detroit, Michigan, have shown that hypertension prevalence rates were higher among residents of census tracts characterized by economic deprivation, residential and family instability, crime, and crowded living circumstances. These relationships held for black men and white women.

In the United States, it is generally true that persons in lower socioeconomic positions, especially blacks in lower socioeconomic positions have a higher prevalence of hypertension than those in higher positions (Stamler & Stamler, 1976). Syme et al. (1974) observed that hypertension had a high prevalence in the lowest but not the highest of socioeconomic groups among both blacks and whites in a population numbering over 22,000 in California. In that population, social class had more to do than race with prevalence of high blood pressure.

Dohrenwend and Dohrenwend (1970) have reviewed a good deal of the literature on the psychosocial circumstances of people in various social and racial groupings. They concluded that those living in the lowest social class groups are more often faced with uncertain and demanding environmental challenges when aspirations cannot be achieved and life is very chancy. Faced with such challenges, some may choose to try to cope and, perhaps, raise their blood pressure, whereas others may choose to withdraw.

AGGRESSION, HOSTILITY, AND BLOOD PRESSURE

Other studies of psychosocial variables in blood pressure have developed evidence that repression or suppression of hostile feelings and aggressive impulses accompanied by guilt over expression of aggression are partly responsible for higher blood pressures in certain individuals and groups. Some of the relevant studies are psychiatric (Ayman, 1933) or psychoanalytic (Alexander, 1939). Others are based on uniform psychological and social assessments of defined populations (Harburg, Erfurt, Chape, Hauenstein, Schull & Schork, 1973). One study of prisoners is particularly relevant. The study (Meyer, 1968) was carried out at a state prison in southern Michigan. The participants included 23- to 35-year-olds who had served at least 2 years and whose recent imprisonment involved direct physical aggression. The inmates were classified as low or high aggressors based on their behavior during imprisonment. The two groups were matched by age, weight, race, and prior medical history. There were 34 members in each group. All were given the Masters Incomplete Sentences Test, a measure of guilt over expression of aggression, and the Cattell 16 PF test. Three blood pressure measurements were taken, two were taken 10 minutes after the first. The last two blood pressure measures were averaged to obtain the dependent variable. Meyer found that subjects whose behavior in the previous 18 months exhibited little aggression had significantly higher diastolic pressures than those who reported little guilt.

WHAT RELEVANCE DOES THIS KNOWLEDGE OF FACTORS AFFECTING BLOOD PRESSURE HAVE TO OUR PRISON STUDY?

What does prison housing have to do with psychosocial stress and with blood pressure? In a cell housing one person, that single individual is not forced to interact closely and almost continually with other inmates. Fewer situations arise in which coping behavior is required. There are fewer uncertain, potentially harmful interactions with other inmates requiring great vigilance and arousal. In a cell, there are no other inmates 5 feet away threatening assault, or rape, or demanding subservience. Even communication with guards and other prison staff is principally outside the boundaries of the cell. In the dormitory, housing shared by dozens of men, the situation is quite different. Other inmates are all around. A hierarchy of leaders and followers emerges. There are threats of physical attack, of sexual assault, of struggle for social dominance, and for space. Nothing but open space separates inmates from inmates and guards from inmates. The guards have their informers. There is ill will between the informers and the other inmates. There are many ambiguous, potentially and actually threatening events. Coping behavior is required more often than in the cell. There is another way in which dormitory housing may raise blood pressure. Because this mechanism did not occur to us until some data analysis had been completed, we cannot call it an a priori hypothesis. It is to some extent an explanation after the fact. In the dormitory, there is not only a hierarchy of leadership but a tendency toward polarization into a majority that accepts the hierarchy and fits in with it and a minority who do not but cannot openly oppose or criticize the majority. The minority, to save their own skins, must repress any manifestation of anger, hostile intent, or aggressive action. Consequently, they may be the ones whose blood pressures rise in the dormitory.

As suggested by our earlier work (chapter 4) and the literature reviewed in this chapter, we expected to find more instances of increase in blood pressure among the men housed in dormitories than occurred among men in cells. Some of these blood pressure increases may last only 10 or 15 minutes to an hour. Some rise in blood pressure may endure for hours, days, weeks, or months. The duration of the blood pressure increases may be dependent on the duration of the psychological stress, its intensity, the psychological characteristics of the inmate, the presence or absence of a family history of hypertension and thus of increased susceptibility to factors affecting blood pressure, and on other events in the prison such as the emergence of friends and defenders of the distressed inmate.]

The constraints of prison security and organization and the limited personnel of our research team meant that periods of data gathering had to be precisely and regularly scheduled and involved only one inmate at a time, regardless of what was happening to that inmate or to other inmates. For these methodological details, see chapter 6. Briefly, data were gathered on admission to prison, 2 and 4 weeks later, and at monthly intervals thereafter. We were required to collect all data in a single large room next to the infirmary. We could not measure pressures or collect other data in cells or dormitories. We could not measure pressures just before, during, or just after fights, threats, assaults, visits, receipt of good or bad news by phone, or solitary confinement in "lower report."[All the blood pressure values described are the means of two consecutive determinations. These procedures had the effect of obscuring or reducing the amount of blood pressure change we could measure occurring after prison events evoking fear, rage, or arousal.]

Our scheduling meant that we missed many of the sudden and quickly reversible blood pressure changes in the inmates. Therefore, the requirements of the prison and the limits of our protocol made it much more difficult to confirm our hypotheses about blood pressure and the prison environment than if we had been able to measure pressures in the cells and dormitories and at much shorter intervals. As is seen, statistically significant changes in blood pressure did occur after housing change and in parallel with other prison events.

4 The Initial Cross-Sectional Study

In pilot cross-sectional studies already published (D'Atri & Ostfeld, 1975), our interest initially centered on the relationship between housing mode and blood pressure in prisons. As outlined in Chapter 3, the use of levels and changes in blood pressure as a means of gauging a person's response to environmental change and psychosocial stress has been our central concern. Blood pressure level and blood pressure change as indicators of response to psychosocial stress have these advantages for our purposes:

1. They are not dependent on self-report.
2. They are quantitative.
3. The meanings of levels of blood pressure and amounts of change are relatively standard.
4. They take very little time to measure and can be taken repeatedly.
5. They can be measured in a wide variety of settings.
6. With proper methodology, the potentially confounding effects on blood pressure of physical exertion, smoking, drugs and alcohol usually can be identified and avoided or accounted for.
7. They are viewed as medical rather than investigational by inmates and are therefore acceptable to them.

The initial cross-sectional study began as an attempt to replicate in man the findings of Henry, Meehan, and Stephens (1967) and Henry, Stephens, Axelrod, and Mueller (1971) in other mammals. We tested one major hypothesis: that there will be an association between blood pressure level and housing mode in the jails and prison setting; specifically that men living in dormitories will have higher pressures than men confined to cells.

THE STUDY SITE

Data were collected in three male correctional institutions in Massachusetts. Each of these institutions had two or more modes of housing for its inmates. There are several very important differences in the three institutions. The first is that Institution A housed both sentenced and unsentenced (those awaiting trial) inmates, whereas Institutions B and C housed only sentenced inmates. The second is that the inmates of Institution A were allowed out of their cells or dormitories for only approximately 2 hours per day. This 2-hour period included meal times and a period of exercise. In Institution B, the average length of time per day that an inmate was out of his cell or dormitory was approximately 8 to 10 hours, and in Institution C, this average length of time was approximately 9 hours.

The greatest degree of restriction of inmate activities occurred in Institution A. Institution B, in which inmates were allowed out of their cells or dormitories for certain job details and recreation periods, adhered to a fixed time schedule for its inmates. Institution C was, by comparison, the most relaxed of all institutions. Its inmates were allowed to go to and from their cells or dormitories when not involved with a job detail. Because of these differences, data from each institution were examined separately.

HOUSING MODE ASSIGNMENT

The assignment of an inmate to a particular mode of housing was determined by multiple factors in these institutions, some subtle and some obvious. The space available when an inmate was admitted, efforts to avoid the appearance of preferential assignment to dormitories considered by staff and inmates as less punitive and more comfortable housing, the race of the inmate, and other factors probably had some influence on housing assigned.

Institution A and 3 housing modes; single-occupancy cell, double-occupancy cell, and small dormitories with three or more inmates. Institution B contained single occupancy cells and two larger dormitories capable of housing 40 or more men at that time. Institution C had single occupancy cells and a single larger dormitory.

ENUMERATION OF STUDY POPULATIONS

Once the populations were identified, collection of data was attempted from the entire enumerated population of each institution in this way:

1. The enumerated population of Institution A was the entire population housed at that facility.

2. The enumerated population at Institution B included the entire populations in each of the two dormitories and one entire wing of single cells.
3. The enumerated population at Institution C included the entire population of the large dormitory and the entire enumerated population of the
   prison cells.

Only those inmates in the institutions on the day in which data collection
commenced constituted the study population.

INTERVIEW DATA

The format of data collection varied slightly between institutions in that inappropriate or uninformative items were deleted and some additional measures were added in the latter stages of the study. Detailed training was given
to all persons who collected either interviews or data on blood pressure. Each
interview schedule was pretested before its administration. Institution A was
completed first, and then B and C, in that order. Data were collected in the
cells and dormitories.

The items that were collected in all three institutions included the usual demographic data, height, weight, education, previous occupation, history of
previous confinement, mode of housing within the institution, pulse rate,
and blood pressure determinations. In Institutions B and C, data were also
collected concerning the amount of time an inmate was out of his cell or dormitory, whether or not he had a job detail (these items were inappropriate for
the inmates in Institution A), reported attitude toward guards, and subjective
attitude toward the size and crowdedness of the institution. In Institution C
only, data were collected of furlough history as well as on specific complaints
of inmates about the institution. One to 3 days at each institution were required to obtain all relevant data.

BLOOD PRESSURE AND PULSE RATE
DETERMINATIONS

Blood pressure and pulse rate determinations in all institutions were made
by an investigator "blind" to all other data collected on each participant. Before the study began in each institution, reliability studies were conducted
comparing the values obtained by a physician and by the four nurses who
were to perform blood pressure determinations. Blood pressures were measured in random order and about 3 or 4 minutes apart of 24 individuals.
Pearson r's between the physician and each of the nurses' readings ranged

from .82 to .89 for systolic pressures and .82 to .91 for diastolic pressures. At the end of the brief interview, blood pressure determinations were made in the left arm at the level of the right atrium after the participant had been seated for a minimum of 5 minutes and without cigarettes for at least 40 minutes. Phase I and Phase V Korotkoff sounds were recorded. There was no evidence of alcohol or drug use at the time of blood pressure measurement. When hypertensive range blood pressures were found, the participant was notified and, with his permission, so were the institutional health care providers.

RESULTS

The Effect of Housing on Blood Pressure

In Institution A, mean systolic and diastolic blood pressures in both black and white inmates were higher for those housed in the dormitory than for those housed in either a single- or double-occupancy cell. It should be noted, however, that the number housed in dormitories is very small. Table 4.1 indicates that mean systolic and diastolic pressures are significantly higher for those housed in a dormitory versus those housed in a single-occupancy cell and shows that the only significant differences in all variables compared for the total population are those found in systolic and diastolic pressures. Such factors as age (which has a fairly narrow range in all three institutions),

TABLE 4.1
Institution A: Single-Occupancy Cell vs. Dormitory, Total Population
(White and Black Inmates Combined)

Variable	Housing Mode	Number of Cases	Mean	Standard Deviation	T Value	2-Tail Probability
Systolic BP	Single cell	27	109.63	17.70	3.37	0.005
	dormitory	7	133.57	11.80		
Diastolic BP	Single cell	27	67.78	9.84	2.86	0.01
	dormitory	7	79.29	7.87		
Height	Single cell	27	69.00	3.63	0.48	NS
	dormitory	7	68.29	2.75		
Weight	Single cell	27	168.04	24.27	1.11	NS
	dormitory	7	157.29	14.76		
Age	Single cell	27	29.44	11.91	0.27	NS
	dormitory	7	28.00	15.98		

height, and weight might have accounted for blood pressure differences but no such effect was noted here.

Table 4.2 displays data from the single-occupancy cell and dormitory (both dormitories combined) groups in Institution B and indicates that mean systolic and diastolic blood pressures are significantly higher for those inmates housed in dormitories as compared to those housed in single-occupancy cells.

Table 4.3 shows the corresponding data for Institution C. The results again reveal that men living in the dormitory have higher systolic and diastolic blood pressure than do the men living in single cells. An additional finding not seen before, is that the men in the dormitory have also significantly higher pulse rates. The Institution C data also reveal that men in the dormitory were significantly older and heavier than men in single cells. The known influences of age and obesity on blood pressure thus produce a confounding which will be removed statistically in multivariate analyses discussed later.

Further breakdowns by race of inmate revealed that in all three institutions, both groups of white and black inmates showed the expected differences in blood pressure due to housing mode. However, the effects on diastolic blood pressure on black men were somewhat weaker which, together with the smaller numbers of blacks involved in the analysis, led to a significant difference only for systolic blood pressure among the black inmates.

A stepwise multiple regression technique was used to assess the significance of housing mode, height, weight, age, duration of confinement, and

TABLE 4.2
Institution B: Single-Occupancy Cell vs. Dormitory A and Dormitory B
Combined, Total Population (White and Black Inmates Combined)

Variable	Housing Mode	Number of Cases	Mean	Standard Deviation	T Value	2-Tail Probability
Systolic BP	Single cell	52	112.11	12.38	4.98	0.001
	dormitory	39	127.31	16.73		
Diastolic BP	Single cell	52	68.65	7.42	4.94	0.001
	dormitory	39	76.79	8.23		
Pulse	Single cell	52	76.04	9.29	1.43	NS
	dormitory	39	79.08	10.94		
Height	Single cell	52	69.61	2.83	0.46	NS
	dormitory	39	69.33	3.05		
Weight	Single cell	52	163.29	22.81	0.22	NS
	dormitory	39	164.44	26.87		
Age	Single cell	52	26.04	6.78	0.99	NS
	dormitory	39	27.92	11.38		

TABLE 4.3
Institution C: Single-Occupancy Cell vs. Dormitory, Total Population
(White and Black Inmates Combined)

Variable	Housing Mode	Number of Cases	Mean	Standard Deviation	T Value	2-Tail Probability
Systolic BP	Single cell	97	114.90	11.88	5.83	0.001
	dormitory	29	131.03	16.55		
Diastolic BP	Single cell	97	69.54	11.37	2.78	0.01
	dormitory	29	76.55	13.63		
Pulse	Single cell	97	71.09	9.78	3.58	0.001
	dormitory	29	78.28	8.34		
Height	Single cell	97	69.23	3.11	0.27	NS
	dormitory	29	69.41	3.69		
Weight	Single cell	97	160.57	21.34	3.08	0.01
	dormitory	29	176.93	35.06		
Age	Single cell	97	23.14	7.21	2.17	0.05
	dormitory	29	27.03	11.77		

skin color in their association to systolic and diastolic blood pressure within each of the three institutions. In all regressions, systolic and diastolic blood pressures, age, height, weight, and institutional confinement are continuous variables, whereas skin color and mode of housing (dormitory is always $+1$, whereas the other comparison groups, such as single occupancy cells, are -1) are always dichotomous.

Institution A. The results of the stepwise multiple regressions for systolic and diastolic blood pressure show quite clearly that the only variable that is significant in its association with systolic and diastolic blood pressure is housing mode, single occupancy versus dormitory. The association of housing mode with systolic blood pressure is significant at the .001 level, with a simple correlation of .51; the association of housing mode with diastolic blood pressure is significant at the .001 level, with a simple correlation of .45.

Institution B. The results of stepwise multiple regressions for systolic and diastolic blood pressure in Institution B again show that housing mode is significant at the .001 level in its association with systolic blood pressure, with a simple correlation of .47; the association with diastolic blood pressure is also significant ($p < .001$), with a simple correlation of .46. In addition, weight also found to be a significant influence ($p < .005$) on diastolic blood pressure. However, the contribution of housing mode on blood pressure is above and beyond any separate effects weight was observed to have.

Institution C.   The results of the stepwise multiple regression once again revealed a strong effect of housing mode on systolic blood pressure ($p <$ .001, represented by a simple correlation of .46). The association with diastolic blood pressure, however, failed to reach statistical significance. This was because age and weight were found to be associated both with housing mode and with diastolic blood pressure, and the removal of their confounding influence brought the association between housing mode and diastolic blood pressure into non-significance.

The Effects of Personal Attitudes and Perceptions on Blood Pressure

Table 4.4 shows mean blood pressures by inmate perception of available space based upon the data collected in Institutions B and C combined. No data were collected on perception of available space or inmate perception of guards' attitudes in Institution A because the concept had not yet occurred to us. For white inmates, there is a suggestive but not significant linear associa-

TABLE 4.4
Perceptions of Available Space and Mean Blood Pressures in
Institutions B and C Combined All Inmates

Perceived as Very Crowded			
Systolic		Diastolic	
all 121.43 ± 9.45 (N = 7)		all 74.29 ± 5.35 (N = 7)	
Whites (N = 4)	Blacks (N = 3)	Whites (N = 4)	Blacks (N = 3)
121.25 ± 10.31	121.67 ± 10.41	73.75 ± 6.29	75.00 ± 5.00

Perceived as Crowded			
Systolic		Diastolic	
all 119.20 ± 14.74 (N = 69)		all 71.52 ± 9.67 (N = 69)	
Whites (N = 53)	Blacks (N = 16)	Whites (N = 53)	Blacks (N = 16)
119.81 ± 15.84	117.19 ± 10.48	71.41 ± 10.07	71.87 ± 6.80

Perceived as Quite a Bit of Room			
Systolic		Diastolic	
all 118.20 ± 16.41 (N = 111)		all 71.31 ± 12.35 (N = 111)	
Whites (N = 87)	Blacks (N = 24)	Whites (N = 87)	Blacks (N = 24)
118.68 ± 16.13	116.46 ± 17.66	71.61 ± 13.08	70.21 ± 9.38

Perceived as a Lot of Room			
Systolic		Diastolic	
all 118.17 ± 13.86 (N = 30)		all 72.00 ± 9.52 (N = 30)	
Whites (N = 15)	Blacks (N = 15)	Whites (N = 15)	Blacks (N = 15)
115.67 ± 5.63	120.67 ± 18.79	69.67 ± 9.35	74.33 ± 9.42

tion between blood pressure levels and degree of perceived crowding, with higher blood pressure in those who perceive their environment as very crowded and lower blood pressure in those who perceive their environment as offering a lot of available space. For black inmates, this association appears to be curvilinear in nature, but is not significant.

Table 4.5 shows blood pressure levels for those inmates in Institution B and C combined by perception of guards' attitudes. White inmates who viewed the guards as "very harsh" and as "very easygoing" had higher blood pressures than inmates who viewed the guards in an intermediate way. The data for the black inmates do not show this same relationship perhaps, in part, because of small numbers. Black inmates tended to view the guards as considerably harsher than did white inmates. Most guards were white.

When the relationship of institutional confinement to perception of guards' attitudes was examined for the data collected in Institution B and C combined, it showed that the longer the inmate was confined, the less apt he is to view the guards in a positive manner (Gamma = − .272 significant at the .001 level).[1] This relationship was somewhat stronger in the data collected from Institution C, (Gamma equaling − .302) than in Institution B (− .248).

When Gamma was calculated utilizing the data collected in Institutions B and C to assess correlation between perception of available space and perception of guards' attitudes, it was found to be .195, significant at the .005 level revealing that perceptions of greater availability of space were associated with more positive perceptions of guards. When the data from Institutions B and C were examined separately, Gamma was found to be .363 for Institution C, significant at the .001 level, but was not significant for Institution B (Gamma = .143).

Other Factors Examined for Their Effect on Blood Pressure

Black recidivists tended to have slightly but not significantly lower blood pressures than first-time offenders; there was no difference for white inmates.

Table 4.6 shows mean blood pressure levels by size of community lived in most of the inmate's life. There is a significant non-linear negative correlation (significant at the .001 level) between the size of community lived in and systolic blood pressure. Diastolic blood pressure also shows this relationship, but it is not statistically significant.

---

[1]Goodman and Kruskal's (1953) Gamma is a measure of the strength of an association for ordinal scaled data. Ths statistic ranges from 0.0, when there is complete independence, to 1.0, or − 1.0 for positive and negative associations respectively.

TABLE 4.5
Perceptions of Guards' Attitude by Mean Blood Pressures in
Institutions B and C Combined All Inmates

Perceived as Very Harsh

Systolic		Diastolic	
all 125.45 ± 17.39 (N = 11)		all 77.73 ± 9.05 (N = 11)	
Whites (N = 6)	Blacks (N = 5)	Whites (N = 6)	Blacks (N = 5)
129.17 ± 19.85	121.00 ± 14.75	78.33 ± 8.16	77.00 ± 10.95

Perceived as Harsh

Systolic		Diastolic	
all 122.81 ± 16.93 (N = 16)		all 71.25 ± 8.27 (N = 16)	
Whites (N = 6)	Blacks (N = 10)	Whites (N = 6)	Blacks (N = 10)
120.83 ± 18.28	124.00 ± 16.96	68.33 ± 10.33	73.00 ± 6.75

Perceived as Somewhat Harsh

Systolic		Diastolic	
all 118.92 ± 19.58 (N = 37)		all 71.08 ± 12.14 (N = 37)	
Whites (N = 23)	Blacks (N = 14)	Whites (N = 23)	Blacks (N = 14)
121.30 ± 20.01	115.00 ± 18.91	71.30 ± 13.16	70.71 ± 10.72

Perceived as Fairly Easygoing

Systolic		Diastolic	
all 117.43 ± 13.90 (N = 107)		all 70.65 ± 10.03 (N = 107)	
Whites (N = 81)	Blacks (N = 26)	Whites (N = 81)	Blacks (N = 26)
117.78 ± 14.01	116.35 ± 13.75	70.62 ± 10.73	70.77 ± 7.57

Perceived as Easygoing

Systolic		Diastolic	
all 116.45 ± 12.46 (N = 38)		all 70.53 ± 11.26 (N = 38)	
Whites (N = 36)	Blacks (N = 2)	Whites (N = 36)	Blacks (N = 2)
116.53 ± 12.30	115.00 ± 21.21	70.41 ± 11.55	72.50 ± 3.54

Perceived as Very Easygoing

Systolic		Diastolic	
all 125.62 ± 15.91 (N = 8)		all 83.12 ± 14.62 (N = 8)	
Whites (N = 7)	Blacks (N = 1)	Whites (N = 7)	Blacks (N = 1)
124.29 ± 16.69	135.00	82.86 ± 15.77	85.00

OVERVIEW OF THE FINDINGS

The major research hypothesis that dormitory housing in a prison setting is associated with higher levels of systolic and diastolic blood pressures was substantiated by showing a significant association between housing and those physiological measurements. The relationship was evident in all three institutions studied, and the relation of housing mode to blood pressure was about the same magnitude in all study sites.

The expectation that men who had lived much of their lives in larger and probably more crowded and complex communities would have adapted to some extent to crowding and therefore would exhibit lower blood pressures in a prison setting than men from small cities or towns is substantiated (Table 4.6). However, the fact that men who lived most of their lives in a country or rural setting did not have lower blood pressures than those from a small city or town is unexplained.

In collecting data dealing with the perception of available space and the attitude of guards, it would be expected that some inmates would have negative attitudes but report positive ones to protect themselves from anticipated problems that might arise if their attitudes were made known. This factor may have operated to reduce differences in blood pressure comparisons made along these dimensions.

The relationship between blood pressure levels and perception of guards' attitudes (Table 4.5) for white inmates suggests the possibility that some men who reported the guards as "very easygoing" are those repressors of aggressive, hostile feelings who are hypothesized by some observers to have high

TABLE 4.6
Mean Blood Pressures by Type of Area Lived In:
All Institutions Combined

Large City

Systolic		Diastolic	
all 114.46 ± 15.45 (N = 270)		all 69.89 ± 10.67 (N = 270)	
Whites (N = 140)	Blacks (N = 130)	Whites (N = 140)	Blacks (N = 130)
117.71 ± 14.31	111.15 ± 13.87	71.68 ± 10.45	67.96 ± 10.62

Small City

Systolic		Diastolic	
all 117.47 ± 17.34 (N = 81)		all 71.36 ± 12.30 (N = 81)	
Whites (N = 55)	Blacks (N = 26)	Whites (N = 55)	Blacks (N = 26)
118.18 ± 18.01	115.96 ± 16.06	71.82 ± 13.72	70.39 ± 8.71

Town

Systolic		Diastolic	
all 121.96 ± 14.93 (N = 46)		all 71.74 ± 9.56 (N = 46)	
Whites (N = 35)	Blacks (N = 11)	Whites (N = 35)	Blacks (N = 11)
121.86 ± 14.61	122.27 ± 16.64	70.71 ± 9.41	75.00 ± 9.75

Country, Rural

Systolic		Diastolic	
all 113.67 ± 12.46 (N = 15)		all 71.67 ± 5.88 (N = 15)	
Whites (N = 9)	Blacks (N = 6)	Whites (N = 9)	Blacks (N = 6)
110.56 ± 6.82	118.33 ± 17.80	70.00 ± 3.54	74.17 ± 8.01

blood pressures (Alexander, 1939; Ayman, 1933; Berkowitz, 1962; Harburg, Erfurt, Hauenstein, Chape, Schull, & Schork, 1973; Wurtz, 1960).

A significant association between the duration of confinement and the perception of available space, as well as the perception of guards' attitudes was found. This association indicates that the longer an inmate is confined, the less likely he is to view his environment as spacious or the guards' attitudes as satisfactory. An alternate explanation is that inmates with longer sentences who have committed more serious crimes are less likely to view the guards and environment as satisfactory.

It should be kept in mind, however, that Institution C (from which the data were collected on tier level) was an example of a relatively "open" system. The men, when not on a job detail or in school, were allowed out of their cells during their free time for recreation. Those on the first tier level had an option of easy access to the outside area, which offered them additional opportunities for recreation. Those on the second tier also had this option but, because of the level, may have found it more inconvenient to make use of it.

Based on the conceptualization that the previous experience would mediate blood pressure response to the prison environment, one would hypothesize that recidivists would have lower blood pressures than first-time offenders. This was true for the black inmates but was not true for the white inmates. A more detailed analysis, controlling for mode of housing and type of area previously lived in, may prove useful in illuminating the effect of previous institutionalization.

There are major limitations to this study. For example, inmates were not assigned in a random fashion to a housing mode within an institution. Although available space at the time of confinement usually determined whether a prisoner was sent to a dormitory or a single cell, other factors were operating. Dormitory housing is considered to be preferred housing by some, and the attitudes of the administration as well as guards' feelings may also have influenced assignment of housing modes. If men were assigned to a dormitory as "preferential treatment," then ironically, what may have been thought to be preferential housing may have been less than preferential with respect to some of its psychological effects. There is another possible source of bias in the data. Chapter 3 has indicated that there may be an inverse relationship between expression of anger and aggression and blood pressure. The guards may have decided to keep more violent aggressive men in cells and send the quieter repressors and suppressors of anger and aggression to the dormitories. Such an arrangement might make the guards' life easier but could make our blood pressure results an artifact of assignment of housing mode. For the resolution of this issue, consult chapter 8.

The intriguing results and methodological limitations of these pilot studies prompted us to carrying out a more definitive longitudinal effort described in the following chapters.

5 Middlesex County House of Correction and Jail

THE SETTING FOR THE LONGITUDINAL STUDY

The purpose of this chapter is to provide a comprehensive description of the physical and the social environment of the institution in which the longitudinal study was carried out. The chapter provides background for understanding how the prison environment may have affected the perceptions, behavior, questionnaire responses, and blood pressure changes in inmates as they went through the duration of their sentences. The description characterizes the institution during the period 1974–1983.

The Middlesex County House of Correction and Jail (Billerica) is a medium security correctional facility 30 miles northwest of Boston, in Billerica, Massachusetts. The complex consists of a main building (Fig. 5.1), a dormitory, two work release buildings and a Personnel and Payroll Building. The main building is a four-story structure containing housing and visiting areas for both pre-trial detainees and sentenced men. Most of the administrative and other staff offices are located in this building. Except for the infirmary and photography unit, all admission and release procedures take place on the first floor of the south wing of the building. This area holds the records of inmates collected during the booking procedure as well as data on warrants and reports, schedules, and records of court appearances, prison behavior of inmates and parole eligibility. Adjoining the record keeping area are two holding cells and a holding room 20′ × 18′ where inmates are temporarily held during the booking process. The main administrative building has two visiting rooms to accommodate the two types of inmates housed in Billerica. The jail men utilize a visiting room on the first floor adjoining the jail courtyard.

FIG. 5.1.   Main building.

No contact between jail men and visitors is possible in the visiting room. For the sentenced men, there is a visiting room on the first floor, across from the central control room that regulates all admission to the building. The room is 34'8" × 18' and can accommodate up to 48 inmates and 48 visitors at one time (Fig. 5.2).

The visiting room is plainly furnished, neat, and clean. No barriers separate visitors and sentenced men. The chairs for inmates and visitors are contiguous and arranged in rows. When the room is filled or nearly so, the inmates and visitors sit cheek by jowl and private conversation is difficult.

Lower Report

This is a separate isolation unit on the first floor of the west wing of the main building. The unit consists of 10 single occupancy cells 7'9" × 5'8". The area is designed to confine inmates for disciplinary reasons. Each cell contains a toilet, sink, and cot. There are no windows, no lights, and no ventilation in the cells. The toilets and sinks are cracked, the floors of the cells are covered with filth, and refuse is often heaped in the corridor in front of the cells. The walls of the cells are covered with graffiti. An inmate may be confined to one of these cells for a maximum of 10 days on any single charge. He must be removed from the cell for 24 hours before being returned to it on another charge.

FIG. 5.2.   Visiting room.

Infirmary

The infirmary or medical unit serves both jailed and sentenced men and is located on the second level of the south wing of the main building directly above the admissions and release area. The unit has 1 locked ward 40' × 18'6" containing 16 cots and 16 night tables, 10 windows, 1 radiator, and 1 ceiling light controlled from outside the room. There are also four private rooms 11' × 6'1" containing a bed, bedside table, radiator, window, and ceiling light controlled from outside the room. A seclusion room similar to the cells in lower report is used for inmates considered dangerous. The medical area has one bathroom 12'6" × 4'6" with one toilet and a wash stand. Adjacent to the bathroom is a shower 12' × 6'6" with a tub and a shower. This unit has one central locked storage room for medical supplies and drugs and a treatment room 12' × 12' in which the county physician examines inmates.

The infirmary is clean, tidy, and uncluttered. The floors are usually polished and the walls recently painted. The office and medical equipment are in good condition. There are standard hospital beds, metal bunks, and examining tables.

Dining Area

The central dining area is located at the east side of the main building courtyard on the second level. It measures 73' × 38'. The meals are served cafeteria style and scheduled so that sentenced and jailed inmates eat separately. The dining area is usually neat, clean, and well lighted.

Recreation Areas

The day room, 83'6" × 38', is located on the second level between the infirmary and the tier. In the room are a television set and areas for playing cards, talking, or use of a telephone. Only sentenced men use this room.

The gym, 60' × 32', is located on the third level and is usually neat, clean, and well lighted. It is equipped with a basketball court, a stage for weight lifting and entertainment, and several pieces of equipment for exercise. Jailed men and sentenced men may also use the outside courtyard completely surrounded by the walls of the main building. The courtyard is sometimes cluttered with rubbish. The sentenced men may also use a large ball field enclosed by a wire fence topped with a razor ribbon. The yard is little used because of several escapes from it.

Counseling services for inmates are available in the Human Service Department housed in a series of offices on the second level of the main building.

Inmate Living

The house of correction consists of two tiers of cells on the second and third levels of the main building. Each cell measures 8'6" × 6'2" and is equipped with a cot, toilet, and sink. There are small windows covered on the outside with heavy wire mesh. The doors to the cells are made of steel with a 12" × 2" grate at each cell. The doors are electronically controlled from the correctional officer's station. There are 98 cells on the first tier (second level) and 99 cells on the second tier (third level). There is an open shower area behind the officers' station that has not been used in recent years. Eleven of the 99 cells on the second tier are used for administrative segregation. On the second tier there is a shower area with nine stalls that is in regular use (Fig. 5.3).

Twenty-seven of the cells on the first tier are used for the protective custody unit. The unit houses inmates who, because of the nature of their crime or their behavior, might be potential victims if housed with other inmates. If these men are reassigned to other housing, they sometimes encounter difficulty with other inmates because they have been labeled as "in protective custody."

In the house of correction, some cell walls are peeling. The sinks are dirty and graffiti covers the walls (see Fig. 5.4 and 5.5). The showers are often filthy and in poor repair.

FIG. 5.3.　Shower room adjoining cell tiers.

FIG. 5.4.　Inmate housing.

FIG. 5.5.   Inmate housing.

The Jail

The fourth floor of the main building houses those men awaiting trial who are kept separated from the men under sentence. Administrative policy prohibits the entire jail population from being outside their cells at one time. One side is always locked in, whereas the other side has the opportunity to shower, socialize, and exercise. For jailed men, outside activity is restricted to the jail yard and for only small numbers of men for short periods.

The Dormitory

The dormitory is a two-story brick building north of the main building (Fig. 5.6). The first floor controls two areas for inmate activities, and shower and toilet facilities, as well as a 40′ × 50′ dining area also used as a day room for watching television. Visiting also occurs in this room. The officers' station is centrally located on this level so that both areas where inmates congregate are immediately accessible to the officers. On the other side of the first floor is a gym where inmates can lift weights and play active games. Behind the officers' station and adjacent to the gym is the shower and toilet area that includes six showers, four urinals, four toilets, one washer, and one dryer (Fig. 5.7).

The second floor of the dormitory is the main area for housing inmates. The west wing consists of 10 rooms 15'11" × 10'2" usually housing four inmates each. Each room is equipped with one double bunk bed and two single beds, one locker, one night table, one window, and a wall lighting fixture that usually does not work. Each room is freely accessible from the other rooms and the remainder of the dormitory. The east wing of the dormitory is divided into two open bays divided by a cement wall. Each bay is 67'6" × 20' and holds 44 inmates in single beds. Between the east and west wings is an open toilet area containing two sinks, two toilets, two mirrors, and one window. There is no door to the open toilet area.

In the dormitory, the rooms are cluttered with wash drying on the lines (Fig. 5.8). Some bunks are neat and others messy. The urinal and showers are dirty and the sinks are grimy. In contrast to the gym in the main building, the dormitory gym is usually so poorly illuminated that it is hard to use.

The dormitory was designed to house 50–75 inmates and during the period of our study housed 80–90 men. In early 1982 it held 110–120 men.

FIG. 5.6.   Inmate dormitory.

FIG. 5.7.   Inmate facilities in dormitory.

FIG. 5.8.   Cluttered dormitory.

Work Release Buildings 1 and 2

Work Release 1 is a three-level single family multi-occupancy dwelling (Fig. 5.9). The first floor has a day room 22' × 15' with three windows, one radiator, a television set and three chairs for inmate viewers. The remainder of the first floor contains four bedrooms 14'10" × 14'11", each bedroom holding four single beds, one bureau, one closet, and one night stand. Three windows in each room provide light and ventilation. The second floor holds four bedrooms containing a total of 16 single beds as well as a bathroom, shower, tub, and toilet. The third floor contains two bedrooms housing six inmates. In the basement is a recreation and weight-lifting room.

Work Release 2 is a two-level brick house built originally to house the sheriff of Middlesex County. The first floor contains five bedrooms housing 10 inmates. These bedrooms are a little smaller than the ones in Work Release 1. Work Release 2 also holds a dining room 23'6" × 9'5" used by all men housed in Work Release 1 and 2. A small kitchen 8' × 7'4" with refrigerator, stove, and sink is available to inmates wishing to prepare their own meals. A bathroom 12'10" × 5'9" containing one urinal, one toilet, one shower and two sinks is located on the same floor. An officers' station is located at the front entrance of Work Release 2. The second floor of Work Release 2 housed no inmates and was used as a storage area during the period of our study.

The work release dormitories resemble private housing. The windows have blinds and flowered curtains, and the kitchen and dining areas are clean and

FIG. 5.9.   Work release building 1.

brightly lit (Fig. 5.10). In the rooms, clothes are usually scattered on the floor and beds. The TV room has large upholstered comfortable chairs. There are prints of nude women on the walls, and calendars with each past date carefully marked off.

PROCEDURES AND PROGRAMS IN THE HOUSE OF CORRECTION

Billerica is a medium security institution. The majority of offenses are larceny, petty theft, drug violation, breaking and entering, assault and battery, and manslaughter. Persons sentenced to Billerica receive sentences of 3 months to 2 years. There are occasional exceptions, however. A few men serving sentences of up to 10 years in a state institution may be transferred to this county facility. The inmates believe that such transfers are the result of political favoritism or plea bargaining.

Admissions Procedures

Upon admission to the Middlesex County House of Correction, the inmate is required to remove his clothing and he and his clothing are searched. The prisoner showers and is issued prison clothing, bed linens (when available),

FIG. 5.10.   Housing in work release dormitory.

and toilet articles. He is escorted to the infirmary on the second floor. Staff nurses take a medical history using standard printed forms, and blood pressure, pulse rate, respiratory rate, height, and weight are recorded. Urine for routine urinalysis and blood for a serological test for syphilis are obtained. The inmate is escorted to a gate that leads into the day room and told to find an officer who will give him directions to his tier and cell. The new inmate, alone, carries his linens and toilet articles through groups of established inmates to locate the guard. The new inmate and the resident prisoners look each other over carefully, but there is usually little verbal communication. When the new inmate finds the guard, the guard gives him his cell assignment and the inmate goes off to find it, thus ending the first day's orientation. All new inmates are placed in single occupancy cells.

The following morning, the new inmate is awakened at 7 a.m. when the electronically controlled cells are opened. He follows the men to the inmates' dining room for breakfast. After the meal he is returned to his cell and locked in while jail inmates awaiting trial go to the dining room.

At about 9:30 a.m., the new inmate is summoned to the infirmary where he is examined by the single county physician with that responsibility. The physical examination is recorded on a standard printed form. The inmate is then moved to a nearby area where he is photographed and fingerprinted. Then he returns to his cell from 11 a.m. until noon, for the counts of inmates. At noon, the cells re-open for lunch. Twenty minutes are allowed for the meal. After lunch, the new inmate is locked in his cell while the jailed men have lunch. From 1 p.m. until 4 p.m., he is allowed out of his cell and may choose to go to the day room for television, cards and other games, to the gym, the library or (weather permitting) the outside enclosed courtyard.

During the 1 p.m. to 4 p.m. period, the inmate may be called to see a counselor who obtains a brief psychosocial history, as well as information that should be helpful in determining the kind of work the inmate does while in the house of correction. The counselor also explains the contract system to the new inmate. The contract system is a set of guidelines that permit the cooperating inmate certain freedoms and privileges. The system is explained a little later in this account.

Job Assignment

Within his first few days, the inmate is given a job assignment. Although the counselor has discussed job interests and skills with the inmate, this information does not usually reach the assignment officer and has no effect on the work assigned. The assignment officer usually sends the inmate to a site and job at which additional workers are needed. The inmate may refuse the job assignment but seldom does. The prison grapevine has it that inmates who refuse job details are confined to their cells and are required to eat meals in their cells; after 1 to 2 days of being locked in his cell, the inmate is usually willing to accept the job assignment he initially spurned.

About 15 days after the first job is assigned, the work performance of the inmate is reviewed and sent to the Intake Worker. This staff member reviews the work evaluation and the counselor's report and makes a report and recommendation to the contract officer. The report includes recommendations on whether the inmate should be moved to the dormitory, when work release or educational release might be appropriate, and whether or not the inmate requires treatment for alcohol or drug addiction. With these recommendations, but without direct input from the inmate, the contract officer puts together the plan for the inmate. When the definitive contract is written, the inmate is called in to review and sign it. Should the inmate refuse to sign the contract, he will lose all the privileges and freedom he has obtained.

After about 30 days, some inmates in cells are transferred to a dormitory. Men assigned to the dormitory usually sleep and spend their leisure time in the dormitory, although the programs and activities of the dormitory men are the same permitted those men who are housed in cells. Transfer to dormitory is dictated in large part by space requirements. For instance, if a large number of new inmates is admitted, cell space is freed up for them by transferring men housed in cells to the dormitory. The dormitory is considered preferred housing by prison staff and that factor has some effect on inmate housing.

The transfer of men to the work release program is usually made according to seniority and good behavior. Men on work release are housed in separate buildings. At the start of our study, all men on work release were housed in this building. However, as the work release program expanded to include about one fourth of the inmate population, additional housing was needed. The need for increased space was met by the construction of a cell block to house only men on work release. This cell block was sectioned off from the older cell blocks housing other inmates.

Medical and Dental Care

Requests for medical and dental care or for counseling services are made in writing by inmates and placed in a box in the day room where they are collected daily for scheduling. Medications are dispensed at the gate to the day room at 8 a.m., noon, 4 p.m., and 8 p.m. daily. If an inmate requires X-rays or special short-term treatment he is moved to a community hospital and guarded around the clock. If long-term treatment is required, the inmate is transferred to Lemuel Shattuck Hospital, a state chronic care facility. The Middlesex County House of Correction must provide guard coverage 24 hours a day in these hospitals.

Inmate Privileges

Inmates whose behavior is viewed favorably by the prison staff may earn certain privileges. These include daily visits by family or friends, use of the prison canteen if family or friends have deposited money for canteen purchases by the inmate, special recreational facilities provided by outside agencies, weekend movies, pizza on Friday nights, housing in the dormitory, and participation in work release or educational release programs. The term *release* means outside the prison. Other things being equal, inmates with longer sentences are more likely to be rewarded with privileges.

A number of inmate behaviors cause withdrawal of some or all privileges. They include lateness or absence from work, poor work performance, refusing an officer's direct order, being insolent to an officer, missing counseling appointments, defacing property, and possession of contraband items. Stealing food from the kitchen, especially the theft of raisins or sugar to make home brew, also results in loss of privileges.

Prison Staff

At Billerica, during the period of our study, there were 59 correctional officers (guards) who had daily direct contact with inmates. During the same period, the inmate population ranged from about 300 to 330, creating an inmate/guard ratio of about 1:5. There were also approximately 31 to 35 other prison staff including correctional treatment, service, and clerical personnel. The prison master was responsible for the day by day administration, and the sheriff for policy, overall direction, and communication with the public.

Inmate Socialization

This qualitative account of inmate socialization is based on the observations of our senior interviewer, Eleanor Eliopoulos during 1974–1980. Its relevance to other institutions cannot be specified. The socioeconomic status of most inmates outside the house of correction is such that the prison food, clothing, and shelter do not usually induce feelings of material deprivation.

Beginning in the dining room and increasingly in the day room, dormitory, and work detail, the inmate begins to find his place among the hierarchy of inmates and staff. An inmate's status appears to be determined largely by the type of crime he has committed and the length of sentence. For example, an armed robber or bank robber may develop high social status whereas the rapist or child molester is scorned and may receive abuse from many inmates. It is an interesting paradox that inmates deny they have committed crimes to prison staff and to our interviewers but assign and accept prison status based on the crimes they deny committing. The effect of length of sentence on inmate status may be a result of the fact that inmates with longer sentences will compete more readily for that status than someone whose sentence is 3 months.

Obviously, inmate social status is more evident and more important in the dormitory, where groups of inmates interact, than in the cell. The low status inmate in the dormitory may receive daily abuse. The abuse may range from being forced to serve higher status inmates to beatings, sexual assault, and, rarely, death. An inmate who feels threatened by dormitory life may ask to return to a cell. Such a request is viewed as cowardly by the inmates but is usually effective in obtaining the change in housing.

Once social status levels are assigned and accepted by the inmate, some cohesiveness develops among the inmate population and can be threatening to the daily routine and to the prison staff. The guards may receive taunts, curses, and revilement from cohesive groups of inmates that do not occur when there is no group adherence. Once the privileges and length of sentences of individual group members are threatened the cohesiveness falls apart, although there have been exceptions. In a county prison like Billerica where sentences are shorter and achieving freedom is a matter of weeks or months, inmates may be less likely to jeopardize their release by aggressive behavior toward the guards than they are in institutions where sentences are longer.

The relationships that develop between the prison personnel and the inmates can also influence the inmate's status among the other prisoners. For example, an inmate who is favored by the guards may lose status because the inmates usually feel enmity toward the guards. On the other hand, a good relationship with the counselor does not threaten an inmate's status and may result in more privileges. If a counselor does not believe that an inmate is adjusting adequately to prison life, he or she may refer the inmate for psychiatric evaluation. A commonly applied psychiatric diagnosis is that of sociopath or psychopath. Although prison staff appear to accept these diagnoses, the inmate sometimes feels that he is now called crazy, in addition to being viewed as evil and criminal.

Inmates who have the highest status do not usually get much attention from the guards. This occurs because high status inmates usually do not themselves break any rules or verbally abuse guards. The guards know who the inmate leaders are and know that they determine the behavior of lower status inmates, but their manifest behavior is not a direct challenge to the guards or to the system.

6 The Methods of the Longitudinal Study

The longitudinal study to which most of the remainder of this book is devoted took place at the Middlesex County, Massachusetts House of Correction and Jail (Billerica). Only inmates already sentenced and in the House of Correction were eligible to participate. The institution was selected for several reasons:

1. Its inmate population size was such that all new inmates could be enrolled in the studies and followed over time by a research staff commensurate with our resources.
2. It was geographically accessible to us.
3. It had a history of successful collaboration in previous studies.
4. The modes of inmate housing there enabled us to test our central hypothesis relating housing mode to blood pressure.
5. The administration and inmates accepted our invitation to participate.

Selection of any single site for a study such as this imposes certain penalties on the research. Any single institution may differ from some or most other institutions in important ways, and what is found in one may not be generalized to others. Billerica is a medium security institution with an inmate population that is largely white and with relatively short sentences. Although housing more inmates than it was built to accommodate, it is not nearly so overcrowded as many others. Research results at Billerica may not be relevant to high security, vastly overcrowded institutions, with high proportions of black or Hispanic inmates in other parts of the United States, or to institutions housing female prisoners. What we have learned about relationships between housing mode, psychosocial stress, and blood pressure in Billerica cannot be applied without question to other institutions.

INFORMED CONSENT PROCEDURES

It is appropriate to begin this account with a description of the procedures for informed consent that were employed in the study.

After three meetings between the sheriff and the investigators during which the study was described in detail, the sheriff agreed that he comprehended the purposes, methods, and significance of the research and gave us permission to meet with the five-member Inmate's Council, a group elected by inmates and concerned with self-government. The study was presented to the Inmate's Council a week later. At the end of the meeting, the Inmate's Council unanimously recommended that the study be permitted to begin. A few days later, however, the Council changed its mind, required that the study be described in detail to the entire inmate body and that the view of the latter group should determine the inmates' position on participation. David D'Atri met with almost the entire inmate population in the cafeteria and explained the study. About 210 inmates, a large majority of those present, voted in favor of participation and 3 voted against it. Ten to 15 inmates abstained.

The inmates understood the purposes of the study and the risks and benefits of participation. They were informed that participation was voluntary and that those agreeing or refusing would be treated equally by the institution. They were told that if they started in the study they could drop out at any time. Inmates were aware that all data would be given code numbers, names removed from forms and that no participant would be identified by name in any oral or written account of the study. Health data were to be provided to the prison health personnel only after written consent of the inmate. Data on other than health matters were not to be transmitted to anyone under any circumstances. Data collection forms were not stored in the prison. Our staff, at the end of each work day, took with them all data collected that day and mailed it to the investigators at the Yale School of Medicine where the forms were kept locked. Inmates were paid $3 to $5 by check from Yale University for each session of data collection.

The question asked by inmates most often about participation was whether blood or urine specimens would be requested in the study, probably reflecting their concern about chemical tests for drugs and alcohol. Assured that we needed no blood or urine specimens, the inmates were generally quite favorably inclined to participation. We observed no evidence that some inmates coerced others into either participating or not participating but we cannot be certain that no coercion existed.

The central difference between the initial study (D'Atri & Ostfeld), 1975) and the one described here is that the former was cross sectional, the latter longitudinal. In cross-sectional studies, it is usually not possible to know clearly the chronology of events. In the longitudinal method, the serial standard collection of data provides that chronology.

SUBJECTS

The study cohort consisted of 568 male inmates of the Middlesex County House of Correction in Billerica, Massachusetts. Six hundred and twelve men were eligible to participate during the 3-year study period; therefore the response rate was 93%. Because the Billerica facility is a medium security institution, the majority of offenses are minor, for example: larceny, petty theft, drug violations, breaking and entering, although more violent and aggressive crimes, including assault and battery and manslaughter, are not uncommon. Men were recruited into the study between March 1975 and May 1978 and followed for 18 months.

Men eligible for the study were all persons admitted to the House of Correction between the dates just specified and men who were imprisoned at the time the study began.

METHODS

Although it is customary to present the hypotheses of a study first and then methods, it is desirable for clarity's sake to reverse the order.

Data Collected Only Once

At the initial interview, data on those inmate characteristics that, for the most part, could not change during the study were collected only once. These included height, standard sociodemographic data such as age, race, religion, degree of religious interest, nativity, marital status, parenthood, education, history of residential moves, CIES scores (Moos, 1976) previous time in prison and whether it was spent in Billerica or elsewhere, and whether parents were in the home when the inmate was a child. Height was measured in inches by means of an upright steel tape fixed to the wall.

Data Collected at Each Interview

Physiological Data.   Weight was measured in pounds by means of a standard upright hospital scale whose calibration was periodically checked.

Pulse rate was counted at the left radial artery. Blood pressure was measured by means of upright mercury manometers whose zero set and free flow were checked daily. Pressures were measured in the left arm with the arm resting at heart level after the inmate had been without cigarettes for at least 40 minutes and after a minimum of 5 minutes of quiet sitting. Systolic and diastolic pressures were recorded at the first and fifth Korotkoff sounds. Our methods of measuring blood pressures were virtually identical with those of the Hypertension Detection and Followup Program (HDFP, 1979). First the cuff was inflated to identify the point at which the pulse at the wrist was obliterated. After deflating the cuff, it was again pumped to a pressure about 30 mmHg higher than that needed to occlude the brachial artery. The cuff was deflated slowly so that the column of mercury fell at the rate of 2 mm per second. Pressures were read to the nearest 2 mmHg. A second blood pressure reading was taken at the end of the interview; that is, about 30 to 40 minutes after the first blood pressure. All data on blood pressure presented here are the means of the two readings. A standard 12 lead electrocardiogram was also obtained at each interview.

Psychologic Data.   Affective states were assessed with anxiety, hostility, and depression scales that were based on multiple adjective checklists describing how the inmate recently felt (Zuckerman & Lubin, 1965; Appendix B). The anxiety scale included items like "afraid," "shaky," "worried," the hostility scale, "hostile," "mad," "furious," and the depression scale, "blue," "alone," "low." An index of psychophysiologic symptomatology (National Center for Health Statistics, 1970c; Appendix C), containing items such as, "In the past few years how often have you had headaches?" and "How often have you been bothered by your heart beating hard?" was also used as an indicator of psychologic distress.

The psychologic variables measured may be categorized into three major content areas: (a) relatively stable characteristics of the person, (b) perceptions of the physical and social environments of the prison, and (c) affective state. The first area focused on irritability threshold, specific coping style with respect to expression versus suppression of anger and irritability, and guilt over the expression of aggression. The following scales, with illustrative items were used: (a) frequency of feelings of anger and irritation (e.g., "How often do you have a feeling of being irritable?", "How easy are you to annoy?"), (b) frequency of feeling aggressive impulses (e.g., "How often do you *feel* like picking a fight with someone?", "How often do you feel like smashing things?"), (c) frequency of expression of aggression (e.g., "How often *do* you pick a fight with someone?", "How often *do* you smash things?"), (d) control of aggression, a derived scale representing the difference between scores on scales 2 and 3, (e) duration of anger (e.g., "When you are angry, how long does your anger last?", "When you get angry with someone you like, how long do you think about it?"), and (f) guilt over expression of aggression (e.g., "I feel it is wrong to pick a fight", "I feel it is alright to lose my temper.") These scales were obtained from epidemiologic studies of specific health conditions, including hypertension (Harburg et al., 1973; Appendix D; Kasl & Cobb, 1970, 1980).

Each item was rated from "1" ("nearly all the time") to "5" ("almost never"). The scores were added and divided by the total number of items to form a mean used as the scale score. The reliability coefficient alpha, used to assess interval consistency equalled .83 while the Spearman-Brown split half coefficient was .80 (Nunnally, 1978).

Subjective assessments of the prison environment were gathered through three instruments that measured perceptions of the institution, cell, and guards, respectively, and used the format of a Semantic Differential. For example, inmates were asked the extent to which they felt that the prison was "safe" (at one end of the rating scale) or "dangerous" (at the other end of the scale). Other items asked about their cell as "closed-in" or "open" and the guards as "harsh" or "easy." These scales were original efforts developed specifically for the purposes of this study and were constructed by selecting from a larger pool of adjectives or phrases the set of items which maximized the internal consistency (reliability) coefficient alpha (Nunnally, 1978). The values of alpha for these scales ranged from .72 to .90.

The social climate of the prison was assessed with the Correctional Institution Environment Scale or CIES (Moos, 1976; Appendix A). It is comprised of 12 subsets; e.g., autonomy, support and order. The subsets represents three conceptual dimensions: (a) personal development, (b) interpersonal relationships and (b) systems maintenance. Newly admitted men were administered a version dealing with their expectation. Items included: (a) "Staff do/will encourage residents to start their own activities," (b) "Staff do/will help new residents get acquainted on the unit," and (c) "Things are/will be sometimes very disorganized around here."

The Pre-Release and Community Interviews

The content of this interview was identical to the others with the addition of questions concerning expectations and plans for residence, employment and personal relationships. The community (post-release) interview contained most of the same items, adapted when necessary for non-institutional settings. For example, perceptions of the area in which the subject lived were obtained. They were given questions about problems in finding a job and about work. All data obtained from inmates are contained in Table 6.1.

Scheduling of Interviews

Each person admitted to the institution was interviewed for this study as part of his usual prison intake procedure. The interview was conducted in the

TABLE 6.1
Assessments Made on All Inmates

Physiologic Factors

Systolic and diastolic blood pressure**
Pulse**
Height*
Weight**
Electrocardiogram**

Socio-demographic Factors

Age*
Race*
Education*
Marital status**
Nativity*
Religion* and Religiosity*
Number of children**
Recidivism*
Residential history*
Parents alive and present when inmate was a child*

Current Situational Factors

Housing mode**
Work release**
Furloughs**
Number of inmates known well enough to talk to**
Frequency of talking to other inmates**
Frequency of visits from family and friends**
Recreational activities**
Family financial problems**
Smoking**
Self-perceived health**

Psychologic Factors

Relatively stable characteristics of person
    Frequency of feeling anger and irritation*
    Frequency of feeling aggressive impulses*
    Frequency of expressing aggressive impulses*
    Control of aggression*
    Duration of anger*
    Guilt over expression of anger*
Perceptions of physical and social environment of prison
    Perception of institution**
    Perception of residence**
    Perception of guards**
    Correctional Institution Environmental Scale*
Affect
    Anxiety Adjective Checklist**
    Depression Adjective Checklist**
    Hostility Adjective Checklist**
Psychophysiologic Symptom Checklist**

*Initial Interview only
**All interviews

infirmary wing by registered nurses. Persons taking blood pressures were trained by the principal investigator of the study. Training was completed when each trainee achieved results virtually identical with the principal investigator on ten rested tranquil subjects. Blood pressure technics were monitored periodically by the investigators. The collection of data was double blind in the sense that neither the nurse-interviewers nor the participants were told the research hypotheses. The interviewers, of course, became familiar with the content of the questions and in that sense knew what types of data the study was collecting.

Inmates were reinterviewed 2 weeks after the first interview and questioned a third time after another 2-week period. Subsequent interviews took place at monthly intervals and continued until the respondent left the institution. Inmates were given a schedule of dates after release at which time an interviewer would be in touch with him. These men were also informed as to how they would be able to contact the interviewer if an alteration in schedule was necessary. Meetings and data collection after release always occurred at neutral sites, such as motels. Inmates were not asked to meet in their homes or at work.

Figure 6.1 presents the disposition status of participants at the in-house stage of the project. The number of respondents decreased from the original 568 to 181 at the 6-month interview; attrition was primarily due to scheduled release of the inmates upon completion of their sentences (other inmates were transferred to another institution, escaped or died). Thirty-one of the original 568 (5%) refused to continue to participate at the in-house stage after initially agreeing to take part. Additional information regarding release was gathered from 380 (87%) of the 447 who were eligible for a release interview immediately before discharge from the institution. The remaining 57 men were released unexpectedly and interviews could not be rescheduled.

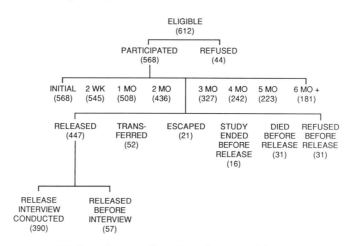

FIG. 6.1.   In-house disposition of study participants.

Intensive efforts were also made to locate inmates in the community after their release and to conduct follow-up interviews. Four hundred and forty-seven men were released into the community. Of this number, 158 (35%) were re-incarcerated soon after discharge. Those re-admitted to Billerica re-entered the study as if it were their first imprisonment and the same protocol followed as in their earlier sentence. After release, 17 men promptly relocated out-of-state and 8 died. The study ended when 16 men were still in prison and 8 men could not be seen for other reasons. Two hundred forty men were eligible for community interviews in Massachusetts. Of the 240 eligible for community follow-up, 213 (90%) were successfully interviewed at least once after release. The remaining 27 refused to participate at the follow-up stage. In-house data on the recidivists and follow-up data in the community were collected concurrently. Figure 6.2 presents the disposition of the men in the community after release.

Inmate Housing and Interview Schedules

New inmates were immediately placed in cells. However, after 14 to 30 days, some of these men began to be transferred to a dormitory. Men assigned to the dormitory slept and spent their leisure time there, although they were involved in the same programs and activities as were men who remained in the cells. Transfer of inmates from cells to the dormitory was dictated by space requirements (i.e., if space became a problem due to a large group of incom-

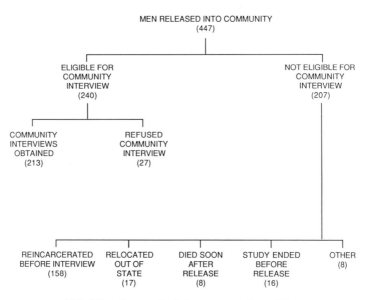

FIG. 6.2.   Community follow-up of study participants.

ing men, residents who had been in the institution for a month or more were then transferred to the dormitory). Officially, the choice of inmates to be transferred was "non-preferential," but in actuality, the presence of some selection bias cannot be ruled out. The administration was unable to make a commitment to us of random assignment of housing mode, and the investigators understood and accepted this limitation. The dormitory is considered preferred housing and administrative attitudes and correctional officers' feelings may have affected the assignment of housing modes by preferential assignment of favored inmates to the dormitory.

Determination of men to be transferred to the work release program was made according to seniority (i.e., length of stay in the prison and amount of "good behavior" on the part of the inmates). As described in chapter 5, the work release residence was a separate building on the prison grounds, separate from the dormitory with housing arranged in "open barracks" fashion, as was the dormitory). At the start of the study, all men on work release were housed in this residence. However, as the work release program expanded, additional housing was needed for men assigned to this program (about 20–25% of the men on work release). The need for space was met by the construction of a separate cell block allocated to those men.

Most of the initial interviews (73%) were collected within a week after the inmate's incarceration began. An additional 4% were conducted more than 7 days, but less than 2 weeks, after the intake date. The remaining 23% who were in prison at the start of the study were originally interviewed 2 or more weeks post-intake. Because many inmates were already living in the prison at the commencement of the study, their responses and measurements no longer represented the initial reactions to the prison environment. For these reasons, the analyses to follow were done only on those initially interviewed within 1 week of incarceration. The sample size was consequently reduced from 568 to 418 at the time of the initial interview.

HYPOTHESES

The central hypothesis of the study relating housing mode to blood pressure change is presented and tested in chapter 8. Other hypotheses concerning illness and illness complaints are also described and tested in chapter 11. The set of hypotheses described here relates to variables other than housing mode, illness, and illness complaints.

The hypotheses of major interest are described as either expected correlates of blood pressure (Stamler, Stamler, & Pullman, 1967) such as age, race, and ponderal index — which need to be included in the model so as not to confound the results — or those hypothesized by us to cause some type of change (increasing, decreasing, or having a mixed effect on the blood pressure levels). Ponderal index equals Height/$\sqrt[3]{\text{weight}}$ and is a measure of obesity. Lower levels mean more adiposity.

Table 6.1 displays the physiologic measures made as well as each of the independent variables incorporated into its appropriate category (i.e., sociodemographic and background variables), most of which represent known correlates of blood pressure. The social support indices, current situation variables, and psychological assessment scales are hypothesized to have a particular effect upon blood pressure.

At this point, we advance a bit beyond our story to explain further hypotheses. The distribution of sociodemographic characteristics in the inmate population defined a larger group who were young, white, unmarried, childless, with limited education, and without strong religious inclination, and a smaller group who were older, more likely to be black or foreign born, to be married and with children, with more education and stronger religious inclinations. The larger part of the inmate population (58%) was also recidivist. The smaller group of inmates were non-recidivists, had less prison experience and therefore were expected to feel more threatened by imprisonment. They were hypothesized to regard themselves as outsiders more vulnerable to the demands of inmate society, to come into conflict more often with the larger groups' views on appropriate inmate behavior, activities, and relationships with prison officers, and therefore to be subject to greater psychosocial stress.

The issues of larger group and smaller group status cannot be viewed in isolation from other variables, particularly housing mode. If an inmate spends 9 hours a day with other inmates, supervised at work, meals, and leisure, and 15 hours alone in a cell, he is less often likely to feel threatened by smaller group status than if he spends 24 hours a day largely unsupervised with other inmates who share a dormitory. Some inmates volunteered that they were more likely to get pushed around in the dormitories at night than at other times and places, but we have no systematic data on the issue.

Our first hypothesis is that each of the sociodemographic characteristics of smaller group status is positively and significantly associated with level of blood pressure in repeated cross-sectional analyses over the length of imprisonment.

Other sociodemographic characteristics were also hypothesized to be significantly related to blood pressure. Those inmates of urban origin and urban adult residence, and with more frequent changes in residence were expected to feel less threatened by another residential change to a crowded environment, the prison. Therefore, we expected that there would be a positive correlation between length of stay at last residence and blood pressure. Childhood and adult residence in a large city, more frequent residential change, and more prison experience were expected to be negatively correlated with blood pressure.

Inmates with both parents alive and at home during the inmates' childhood were expected to be more likely to view the environment as stable, predictable and non-threatening, and therefore to have lower pressures.

Current situation variables were also hypothesized to relate to blood pressure. Dormitory residence and self report of family financial problems were expected to be positively associated with blood pressure. Living in a cell, having a job detail, frequency of furloughs, time spent on work and leisure activities and time spent outside prison housing were expected to be negatively correlated with blood pressure.

Social support structures were also considered. Frequency of social interaction among inmates, number of inmates known well enough to talk to, frequency of visits by family members and friends and CIES scores were expected to be negatively correlated with blood pressure. Visitors who were neither family nor friends were expected to have an inconsistent effect. Such visitors were usually lawyers, former employers, social workers, and clergy. These visits sometimes provided emotional support and sometimes the opposite. A lawyer may bring good or bad news. A former employer may promise employment after release or deny it. Usually none of these people were as well known to the inmates as family or friends. Therefore, we expected a less predictable association between frequency of outside visitors and blood pressure, less predictable in terms of both magnitude and direction.

Psychological Assessment scale scores were also included in our hypotheses. Scores on measures of depression, anxiety, psychophysiological symptoms, and hostility were expected to be significantly and positively associated with blood pressure. Favorable perception of the prison environment was expected to be negatively associated with blood pressure.

Table 6.2 summarizes the hypotheses we tested. The same hypotheses are stated more precisely in Table 6.3.

DATA ANALYSIS

Several analytic methods were employed. Methods used in determining relationships between blood pressure and housing mode are described in chapter 8. Most of the remaining data were analyzed principally by multiple regression methods. The details of these method are provided in Appendix E.

The examination and interpretation of the data analyzed by multiple regression were primarily of a cross-sectional nature for each interview. The pre- and post-interview measurements of both systolic and diastolic blood pressure were averaged to obtain a mean reading; these two values were considered the dependent variables in a multiple regression analysis. A total of 46 sociodemographic, psychological scales, social support and current situation variables, and background characteristics were entered as independent varia-

TABLE 6.2
Hypotheses

	Effects on Blood Pressure		
	Increase	Decrease	Mixed
Sociodemographic factors:	Age Race (blacks) Marital status Children Education Religiosity Foreign born Length of stay at last residence	Number of times previously jailed Parents alive and present as a child Childhood residence (large city) Adult residence (large city) Previously in Billerica Length of time prison Number of residential changes since age 10	
Current situation variables:	Living in dormitory Financial problems Negative perceptions of institution and of residence Positive perception of guards	Living in cell Job detail Frequency of furloughs Recidivism Time spent outside residence Time spent on activities	
Social support indices:		Frequency of social interactions among inmates Number of inmates know well enough to stop and talk to CIES social support scale Frequency of visits by family members Frequency of visits by friends	Frequency of outside visitors (neither family nor friends)
Psychological assessment scales:	Depression Anxiety Hostility Psychophysiologic symptoms		Perceptions of environment

TABLE 6.3
Hypotheses

1. Anxiety scores will be positively associated with blood pressure.
2. Hostility scores will be positively associated with blood pressure.
3. Negative perception and reports on feelings toward the institution will be associated with higher blood pressure.
4. Positive perception and report on feelings toward guards will be associated with higher blood pressure.
5. There will be a negative association between time spent in recreation (TV, radio, hobbies, exercise, sports) and blood pressure.
6. Frequency of visits by family and friends will be negatively associated with blood pressure.
7. The frequency of social contact with other inmates will be negatively associated with blood pressure.
8. The greater the amount of time spent outside cells or dormitories in job details, furlough and work release, the lower the blood pressure.
9. The more previous time in prison, the lower the blood pressure.
10. The more time lived in cities, the lower the blood pressure.
11. The more frequent changes in residence outside prison, the lower the blood pressure.
12. Older men, married men with children, the foreign born, more educated men, and men with religious inclination differ from the majority of inmates who are younger, unmarried, childless, less well educated, and without religious orientation. Therefore, the former, a minority, will have higher blood pressures than the latter when age is controlled.

bles. Categorical factors like race, marital status, and housing mode were represented by dummy variables (Kleinbaum & Kupper, 1978).

The beginning of the analysis included computing univariate statistics, that is, frequencies and percentiles of the discrete variables, and frequencies, percentiles, and means of the continuous variable. There were 24 continuous variables and 22 discrete variables selected as independent variables, and 2 continuous variables (average systolic and diastolic blood pressure) selected as the dependent variables. Based on these statistics, error checks and transformations were made on the data to facilitate the analysis. Bivariate statistics were computed next, histograms, bar charts, and correlations were computed for the continuous variables. A general overview of the results from these computations was then made.

Two kinds of analyses were undertaken. The first included analyses of data for all men in prison less than 8 days at the time the study began plus all admitted between March 1, 1975 and May 31, 1978. The second analysis defined a core of men with complete data sets for a given time period. The core chosen had data sets from the initial interview through the 2–month point and numbered 165 men. The core was later extended to include men interviewed beyond the 3–month point, although the number declined sharply after that.

The variables chosen for study with the core group of men included all independent variables that were significantly related to blood pressure for the entire group at any of the time points analyzed cross-sectionally. In addition to these measures, initial (T_1) blood pressure was included in all computations as a covariate.

The results of these analyses are described in chapters 7 and 9.

7 Correlates of Blood Pressure at the Start of Imprisonment

This chapter complements chapter 8, which deals with the longitudinal association between blood pressure and housing mode in Billerica by examining the relationships of other environmental and personal characteristics to blood pressure early in the prison stay. These associations are examined first at the time of admission to the institution. Blood pressure was again measured after 2 weeks and factors associated with change in blood pressure over the first 2 weeks were also studied.

Analyses of relationships between blood pressure and personal and social characteristics were carried out separately for the first and second times of data collection for several reasons. All inmates were housed in cells during these times and the effects of housing mode on blood pressure do not confound relationships with other measures. The status of inmates shows less variation in other ways than housing. No work release or educational release assignments have been made yet and all inmates are less familiar with each other, with prison staff, and with the environment than they will be later in the sentence. Because the effects of housing, work, or educational release and general familiarity with the institution are either absent or reduced in this early stage of imprisonment, we believed that the relationships between blood pressure and characteristics of the inmates might be understood more clearly than at times later in the prison stay.

Although the hypotheses and approach to the data in these analyses of data early in the prison sentence are not identical with those carried out for the 1 month to release period, in chapter 9, they are quite similar.

The questions specifically addressed include those explored cross-sectionally in our first study described in chapter 4 (D'Atri & Ostfeld, 1975). For example, does the lack of experience with densely populated environments in general and correction institutions in particular result in higher blood pressure among men from more rural backgrounds and first-time offenders, and do these inmates experience an increase in blood pressure over time? This chapter also investigates other socio-demographic, background, situational, and psychologic variables to test hypotheses that were not examined in our earlier work. Psychosomatic theory, for instance, proposes a positive relationship between constructs like repressed hostility and anxiety on the one hand, and blood pressure and blood pressure change on the other (Alexander, 1939; Harburg, Erfurt, Chape, Hauenstein, Schull, Schork, 1973; Harburg, Erfurt, Hauenstein, Chape, Schull, & Schork, 1973; Kalis, Harris, Sokolow, & Carpenter, 1957). The prison environment provides an ideal setting for the examination of these hypotheses, because aggression and fear are pervasive elements, but their expression and resolution are institutionally inhibited (Toch, 1975).

It its important to note that no data were gathered before imprisonment. Relationships observed upon admission may therefore reflect baseline associations of blood pressure and the independent variables without implicating the environment. A positive relationship between age and blood pressure, for instance, would simply confirm the results of other studies (Stamler, Stamler, & Pullman, 1967) and not necessarily indicate an age-related effect of imprisonment per se. Previously unreported findings or those contrary to the findings of other investigators (e.g., greater blood pressure among first-time offenders or the highly educated) however, would suggest a specificity of findings among prisons and perhaps a role for the prison environment. An environmental influence would also be evident in the analysis of blood pressure change over the 2-week period. These types of results would offer important information concerning patterns of initial response and early adaptation to the prison environment.

ANALYSIS

Two multiple regression analyses were conducted. (For methodology see Appendix 5.) The first concerned blood pressure at T1. The average of the two blood pressure readings at the T1 interview was considered the dependent variable. The independent variables included body bulk, assessed as ponderal index, and the socio-demographic factors, background characteristics, situational variables, and psychologic scales listed in Fig. 6.1, chapter 6. Nominal factors like religion and marital status were represented as "dummy" variables.

The second multiple regression analysis focused upon change in blood pressure from T1 to T2, i.e., the difference between average blood pressure at T1 and average blood pressure at T2 (T2–T1) was used as the dependent variable. The following independent variables were entered in this analysis: (a) the socio-demographic factors and background characteristics assessed at T1, and (b) changes in body bulk, situational variables, and the psychologic scales over the two-week period, calculated as the differences between T1 and T2 values. To control for initial blood pressure level, blood pressure at T1 was incorporated as a covariate in the analysis of blood pressure change over time.

A three-stage process was employed in each of these analyses to accommodate the relatively large number of independent variables and to minimize the deletion of cases due to missing data (see Appendix E). The methods employed aimed at identifying those characteristics of inmates that were the most strongly predictive of blood pressure level at T1 and of change in blood pressure from T1 to T2 and at determining the statistical significance of changes in systolic and diastolic blood pressures associated with different levels of these predictors.

RESULTS

Correlates of Systolic Blood Pressure at T1

Table 7.1 presents the variables included in final regression model for systolic blood pressure at T1, the initial interview. This model was significant at the 0.0001 level and explained 22.4% of the variance. Age and body bulk were positively related to systolic blood pressure at T1. The mean T1 systolic blood pressure of non-whites was significantly higher than whites, and foreign-born inmates had a greater mean systolic blood pressure at T1 than American-born inmates.

Length of stay at last residence, whether an inmate's parents were alive and present when he was a child, and recidivism jointly explained 4.49% of the variance. The first variable was positively associated with T1 systolic blood pressure. The mean T1 systolic blood pressure of men whose parents had divorced or separated was significantly less than that for men with one parent who died or inmates with both parents alive and present. The mean systolic blood pressure at T1 for first offenders was greater than recidivists. Higher levels of T1 systolic blood pressure were also observed among inmates whose families had greater financial difficulties at T1. This situational variable accounted for 0.62% of the variance in systolic blood pressure at T1.

Four psychologic scales were correlated with T1 systolic blood pressure. Psychophysiologic symptomatology, perceptions of the guards, frequency of feeling aggressive impulses, and perception of the cell explained a total of 4.57% of the variance, adjusting for other factors. The first two were posi-

TABLE 7.1
Final Regression Models for Systolic Blood Pressure

	Increment in R^2 (%)	T_1 Coefficient	Mean BP mmHg	Increment in R^2 (%)	Δ BP Coefficient	Mean Δ in BP mmHg
T_1 Systolic Blood Pressure				****26.75	0.4397	
Physiologic						
Body bulk	****3.35	4.2039				
Socio-demographic						
Age	****6.78	0.4681		**0.79	0.1194	
Race	**1.09					
White		0.0000	120.03			
Non-white		4.7775	124.80			
Nativity	**0.90					
USA		0.0000	119.40			
Non-USA		6.0221	125.43			
Background						
Length of stay at last residence	***1.51	0.7578				
Parents alive and present as child	**2.35					
Yes		0.0000	121.45			
No, mother died		5.2005	126.65			
No, father died		2.3482	123.80			
Other		− 3.6861	117.76			
Recidivism	*0.63			***1.33		
Recidivist		0.0000	121.34		0.0000	− 1.95
First-time offender		2.1509	123.49		2.4186	0.46
Number of days in jail before conviction				**0.70	0.0321	
Situational						
Family financial problems	*0.62	1.0559				
Psychologic						
Psychophysiologic symptomatology	****2.91	0.3515				
Frequency of feeling aggressive impulses	0.85	0.3861				
Perception of guards	0.80	0.1182				
Perception of cell	0.60	− 0.1661				

*$p < .10$
**$p < .05$
***$p < .01$
****$p < .001$

tively related to T1 systolic blood pressure, indicating higher blood pressure among men who reported many psychophysiologic symptoms or who viewed the guards more favorably. The last two scales and systolic blood pressure at T1 were inversely associated, suggesting that men who seldom felt aggressive impulses or who perceived their cells negatively had greater blood pressure.

Correlates of Change in Systolic Blood Pressure from T1 to T2

Variables in the final regression model for change in systolic blood pressure over the 2-week period from T1 to T2 are also given in Table 7.1. The model was significant at the 0.0001 level and accounted for 30.27% of the variance. It was based on the 396 inmates who participated in the study at T1 and T2 and who had complete data regarding the variables. The grand mean was -0.91 mmHg ($p = .0370$), indicating that systolic blood pressure decreased slightly but significantly from T1 to T2 among this cohort.

Systolic blood pressure at T1 was negatively related to systolic blood pressure change from T1 to T2. It explained a relatively large proportion of the variance (26.75%) in systolic blood pressure change. Age and systolic blood pressure change from T1 to T2 were positively correlated, with age contributing an additional 0.79% of the variance: older inmates tended to show a larger increase (smaller decline).

Two background characteristics, recidivism, and the number of days spent in jail before conviction awaiting trial or bail, were also associated with systolic blood pressure change. A mean increase in systolic blood pressure was observed among first-time offenders, contrasted with a mean decline for recidivists. Systolic blood pressure decrease was greater for men who had spent a greater number of days in jail before conviction awaiting trial or bail. The two variables jointly accounted for 2.03% of the variance on systolic change from T1 to T2.

Correlates of Diastolic Blood Pressure at T1

Variables included in the final regression model for diastolic blood pressure at T1 are shown in Table 7.2. The model was significant at the 0.0001 level and accounted for 17.73% of the variance. It was based on 334 inmates with complete data concerning the nine included variables. The grand mean was 72.90 mmHg.

Concordant with the findings for systolic blood pressure at T1, T1 diastolic blood pressure was positively related to age, body bulk, length of stay at last residence, psychophysiologic symptomatology, and perception of the guards. First-time offenders also had a greater mean diastolic blood pressure than recidivists at T1, higher diastolic blood pressure was also associated

TABLE 7.2
Final Regression Models for Diastolic Blood Pressure

	Increment in R^2 (%)	T_1 Coefficient	Mean BP mmHg	Increment in R^2 (%)	Δ BP Coefficient	Mean Δ in BP mmHg
T_1 Diastolic Blood Pressure						

Physiologic

Body bulk	**1.44	2.0259				

Socio-demographic

Age	****8.86	0.3823		***.156	0.1211	
Nativity				***1.75		
USA					0.0000	−2.19
Non-USA					4.5512	2.36
Education	**1.39	1.1785				

Background

Length of stay at last residence	*0.85	0.4135				
Parents alive and present as child				*1.83		
Yes					0.0000	1.79
No, mother died					−4.2614	−2.47
No, father died					−2.5404	−0.75
Other					0.0314	1.76
Recidivism	*0.76					
Recidivist		0.0000	72.16			
First-time offender		1.7206	73.88			
In jail before conviction (awaiting trial or bail)				*0.48		
No					0.0000	0.59
Yes					−1.0131	−0.42

Situational

Job detail				*0.84		
No					0.0000	0.79
Yes					−1.4047	−0.62

Psychologic

Psychophysiologic symptomatology	**1.34	0.1674				
Perception of guards	**1.33	0.1086				
Perception of cell	**0.97	−0.1489				
Hostility checklist				**0.90[a]	0.2968	
Support subscale of CIES	*0.79	1.7206				

*$p < .10$
**$p < .05$
***$p < .01$
****$p < .001$

[a]The two psychologic scale score levels in the column labeled Δ BP, increment in R^2 (0/0) represent changes from T1 to T2.

with more negative perceptions of the cell at T1. Age and body bulk jointly accounted for 10.30% of the variance, length of stay at last residence and recidivism 1.61%, psychophysiologic symptomatology, perceptions of guards and cell 3.64%.

Two additional variables emerged in the model for diastolic blood pressure at T1 that were not observed with systolic blood pressure. Diastolic blood pressure at T1 varied directly with education, and the support subscale of the Correctional Institutions Environmental Scale (CIES) was positively correlated with T1 diastolic blood pressure. These two variables respectively explained 1.39% and 0.79% of the variance. The latter finding indicates that expectations of social support from fellow inmates were associated with higher blood pressure.

Correlates of Change in Diastolic Blood Pressure from T1 to T2

Table 7.2 also presents variables in the final regression model for change in diastolic blood pressure from T1 to T2. The model was significant at the 0.0001 level and explained a total of 39.66% of the variance. It was based on a cohort of 359 men who participated in the study at T1 and T2 and who had complete data concerning the eight included variables. The grand mean was -0.78 mmHg ($p = .0074$), which indicates that diastolic blood pressure also decreased slightly but significantly over the 2-week period among this cohort.

As was noted with systolic blood pressure change, T1 diastolic blood pressure was inversely associated with diastolic blood pressure change from T1 to T2. Diastolic blood pressure change also increased as age increased. The two variables jointly accounted for 30.05% of the variance. Nativity was associated with change in diastolic blood pressure from T1 to T2, accounting for 1.74% of the variance. Foreign-born men had a mean diastolic blood pressure increase, compared to a diastolic blood pressure decline for native-born inmates.

Change in diastolic blood pressure also varied by the several background characteristics. Pairwise, contrasts showed that the adjusted mean decreases in diastolic blood pressure for those whose mother or father had died were significantly different from the mean increases for men whose parents were alive and present and those whose parents were divorced or separated. Men who had been in jail before conviction awaiting trial or bail had greater diastolic blood pressure declines than men who had not been in jail prior to their conviction. These two variables jointly accounted for 2.31% of the variance.

The situational variable job detail explained 0.84% of the variance. Inmates who were first assigned to a job detail by T2 had a mean diastolic blood pressure decrease, whereas men who remained without jobs had a mean diastolic blood pressure increase. As seen in Table 7.2, changes in two psychologic scales from T1 to T2 were correlated with diastolic blood pressure change, explaining 2.25% of the variance. Diastolic blood pressure increased as inmates reported more hostility over time.

Residuals were calculated and plotted against predicted blood pressure and against values of the independent variables. Normal probability plots were also graphed. No unusual patterns were noted, supporting the contention that the final regression models for systolic and diastolic blood pressure at T1 and change in systolic and diastolic blood pressure from T1 to T2 adequately described the data.

DISCUSSION

Sociodemographic Characteristics

Systolic and diastolic blood pressure were found to correlate positively and significantly with age and body bulk at T1, a finding that concurs with data for many United States and other populations (Ostfeld & D'Atri, 1977; Stamler, Stamler, & Pullman, 1967). Age and blood pressure change, however, were also positively related. This finding suggests an environmental influence and may indicate that older inmates adapt less readily to the prison environment than younger men. (This effect of age is independent of the effect of recidivism, discussed later.)

The mean systolic blood pressure at T1 of non-whites was significantly higher than whites. Because most of the non-whites in this study were black, this relationship could be assumed to reflect the well-known fact that blacks in the general United States population have higher blood pressure and a greater prevalence of hypertension than whites (Comstock, 1957; Stamler, Stamler, & Pullman, 1967). This black–white difference did not persist in later interviews and so must be interpreted differently. It probably indicates initial apprehension among blacks in an institution in which most of the inmates and guards were white.

Foreign-born inmates exhibited significantly greater mean systolic blood pressure at T1 than native-born inmates, and they also experienced a diastolic blood pressure increase over the 2-week period. This relationship also disappeared later in the sentence. These findings indicate that the experience of confinement in its early stages may be particularly difficult for men from a foreign background. The absence of ethnic ties probably evokes loneliness and fear, compounded by possible language and cultural barriers that contribute to communication problems. A diversity of ethnic backgrounds and variation in length of time lived in the Unites States preclude a less general explanation of their adverse initial reaction and lack of adaptation.

Education was found to be positively correlated with diastolic blood pressure at T1. This finding is of interest because it contrasts with other data that demonstrate that, in the United States, the poorly educated have higher blood pressure (Dawber, Kannel, Kagan, Donabedian, McNamara, & Pearson, 1967; Harburg, Erfurt, Chape, Hauenstein, Schull, & Schork, 1973; Harris, 1982; James & Kleinbaum, 1976; Lee & Schneider, 1958; Metropolitan Life Insurance Co., 1967). Its explanation may therefore be environmental. Those inmates who have attained a higher level of education will likely find that their educational achievements do not afford them the status they would have in the outside world, and, in fact, they may be at a disadvantage in that they lack the "street-wise" coping skills that will serve them in the prison environment. More highly educated inmates may also experience discordance in accepting the authority of guards, who probably have less formal education. Conversely, guards may have acted in a more threatening way toward inmates with education exceeding theirs.

Background Variables

As expected, recidivists were found to have significantly lower mean systolic and diastolic blood pressure at T1 than first-time offenders.[1] The initial experience of confinement probably has all of the situational characteristics associated with increased blood pressure, e.g., uncertain outcome, possibility of bodily harm, need for vigilance (Ostfeld & Shekelle, 1967), whereas for recidivists, past experience in the prison environment may reduce apprehension. The finding that recidivists had a mean decrease in systolic blood pressure from T1 to T2, whereas first-time offenders showed an increase indicates that the former group also adapted more easily. The decline among recidivists is especially notable because their T1 values are already lower to start with, and one would not expect them to decline further.

 The length of time an inmate spent at this last address may also be a useful predictor of blood pressure and blood pressure change, because prior experience with residential change may be conducive to a less drastic initial response and to easier adaptation. This belief was confirmed at T1 because length of stay at last residence was positively correlated with systolic and diastolic blood pressure. Experience with change in early family structure may have a similar effect, as inmates whose parents divorced or separated when they were children had significantly lower systolic blood pressure at T1 than inmates whose parents were alive and present. Inmates whose mother or father died demonstrated blood pressure levels at T1 that were significantly higher than the other groups, but they adapted readily to the prison environment because they experienced greater diastolic blood pressure decreases

---

[1]About 60% of the recidivists had been in Billerica previously, the others in other jails or prison.

from T1 to T2. Correlations between blood pressure and parental status changed later in the sentence requiring reinterpretation.

Confinement in jail awaiting trial or bail before conviction, sentencing, and incarceration in prison can be a time of extreme stress due to the uncertainty of the length of confinement, potential threat of fellow inmates, lack of control over decisions affecting ones fate, and the process of losing familiar social roles (Toch, 1975, 1977). The results showed that most of the inmates (62%) had not spent time in jail; those who had spent some time in jail showed larger declines in both systolic and diastolic blood pressure from T1 to T2. The experience may have facilitated adjustment to the prison because the two environments share a number of characteristics.

Situational Characteristics

Factors in the inmates' current situation were also found to be related to blood pressure. The degree of family financial problems, presumably exacerbated by the inmate's confinement, was a variable that contributed to higher systolic blood pressure at T1. Change in diastolic blood pressure between T1 and T2 differed significantly by job detail, with a decrease in blood pressure for those with a job detail compared to an increase for those without employment. Although the work assignments of inmates may not necessarily be meaningful or directed toward rehabilitation or vocational training, they undoubtedly break the monotony of an otherwise very routine day. They may also reduce the number of potentially threatening interactions between inmates and guards and lead to a more comfortable orientation toward the institution.

Social Contact

Ties to significant others are considered a resistance resource in resolving tension (Kosa, Antonovsky, & Zola, 1969). It was therefore hypothesized that a higher frequency of social interaction with family and other inmates would be associated with lower blood pressure. The lack of significant findings may be attributed to the probability that a pattern of visits by family and friends was not yet established at the early stages of confinement, and that initial wariness of the new environment and other inmates had a deterrent effect on social interaction. Other data on social interaction in the prison suggest a pattern of relationships frequently based on mutual need rather than attraction; thus, social interaction may also be a source of stress (Brodsky, 1977) if higher levels of social interaction mean more demands from those with whom one is interacting. Analysis of data from later interviews offers clarification of the type and frequency of social interaction in the prison and its relationship to other variables; these findings are presented in chapter 9.

Psychologic Characteristics

The frequency of feeling aggressive impulses was inversely related to systolic blood pressure at T1, i.e., inmates who seldom reported aggressive feelings had higher T1 systolic blood pressure. This finding supports the notion that suppression of aggression is associated with elevated blood pressure (Alexander, 1939; Harburg, Erfurt, Hauenstein, Chape, Schull, & Schork, 1973), if one makes the assumption that not reporting aggressive feelings is primarily the result of repression. The other scales assessing coping style, anger-in versus anger-out, and guilt over the expression of anger, however, were not significant correlates of blood pressure, so the results of the study in this content area remain inconclusive.

Perception of the guards was positively associated with systolic and diastolic blood pressure at T1, whereas perception of the cell was negatively related to T1 blood pressure. In other words, T1 blood pressure was higher among men who viewed the guards *more* favorably or the cells *less* favorably. This apparent contradiction of effects may reflect differential processes of reporting, with the possibility of denial, given a powerful and dominant person as the object of perception, compared to inanimate objects like the cell. An alternative and equally plausible interpretation is that a more positive attitude toward guards may represent suppression of aggression and thus higher blood pressures. The CIES subscale dealing with the expectation of social support from fellow inmates was positively associated with T1 diastolic blood pressure, suggesting that men expecting more social support react more stressfully to the prison environment.

The only other psychologic variable related to blood pressure was the frequency of psychophysiologic symptoms. Men who reported many psychophysiologic symptoms had higher systolic and diastolic blood pressure at T1. This finding may indicate either that men who feel threatened by imprisonment respond with psychologic distress and elevated blood pressure, or it may represent stable pre-prison characteristics. Change in psychophysiologic symptoms from T1 to T2, however, was not associated with corresponding change in blood pressure. This lack of temporal concordance may be an artifact of the instrument used to assess psychophysiologic symptoms. The inmates were queried about a broad timeframe, including present and past, so the scale may not be a sensitive measure of change in psychophysiologic symptomatology over brief periods of time. The possibility also exists that the inmates who reported many psychophysiologic symptoms and had high blood pressure at T1 maintained their levels of symptomatology and blood pressure at T2, thereby resulting in a "steady-state" situation that would not be detected in an analysis of change.

Anxiety and depression were not related to either blood pressure at T1 or blood pressure change from T1 to T2. Depression has been proposed as an affective indicator of a conservation/withdrawal response, so the lack of a positive finding for that variable was not unexpected (Henry & Stephens, 1977). A positive correlation between anxiety and blood pressure, however, has been reported by a number of investigators (Davies, 1971; Wolf, Cardon, Shepard, & Wolff, 1955). Denial may be involved, since Toch (1975) has emphasized that inmates are likely to repress feelings of fear and anxiety, given their belief that the expression of such feelings is incongruent with the image of manliness necessary to survive the prison experience. Hostility was not related to blood pressure at T1, but change in hostility from T1 to T2 and blood pressure change were positively correlated. An earlier finding showed that men who seldom felt aggressive impulses had higher initial systolic blood pressure; this result suggests that men with an increase in hostile feelings also have a corresponding increase in diastolic blood pressure.

FURTHER INTERPRETATIONS, IMPLICATIONS, AND CONCLUSIONS

Because T1 data were collected within a week of imprisonment, they provide information regarding initial response to the prison environment (i.e., the acute effects of a stressful life event). The results demonstrate that the greatest impact is among several specific subgroups. These include men who before their imprisonment had relatively few changes of residence. These inmates may therefore be less familiar with environmental change and less able to meet its demands. Previous experience with imprisonment is also important, because first-time offenders had higher blood pressure than recidivists. Those who were socio-demographically "deviant" when compared to the majority of prisoners (e.g., the foreign-born and the college educated) had greater blood pressure, indicating that cultural familiarity and status congruity may lessen initial adverse reactions. The interplay between the experience of imprisonment and other aspects of the inmates' lives was reflected in the finding that the initial impact was greatest among men whose families were suffering from financial problems.

Some concordance was observed between physiologic response (blood pressure) and psychologic reaction (psychophysiologic symptomatology). Inmates who repressed the feeling of aggressive impulses responded to imprisonment, a potentially dangerous situation laden with physical and psychologic threats, with greater blood pressure. Men who viewed aspects of the physical environment negatively (e.g., cell), or exhibited positive attitudes toward guards also reacted with higher blood pressure. These perception scales may be operating as intervening variables and link the objective environment with physiologic and psychologic responses.

Change in blood pressure over the 2-week period may be a partial indicator of adaptation to imprisonment. Although blood pressure decreased significantly from T1 to T2, the magnitude of this change was small (less than 1 mmHg). This finding may reflect the fact that the T1 interview was not conducted on the day of admission for every inmate; in fact, for a few inmates the length of time between admission and the T1 interview was as much as 8–14 days. Men in prison more than 2 weeks before we began the study were excluded from all analyses. The following deals with this issue.

Recall that blood pressure was taken once by the prison nurses usually on the first day of imprisonment. Sometimes the prison nurses' readings preceded ours by only an hour or two and sometimes the interval was as long as 14 days. For about two thirds of inmates the interval was 1 to 3 days. We decided to examine the differences in blood pressure between our readings and the prison nurses' reading as a function of the time interval between the two. We postulated that in many cases some adaptation to the prison began as early as the first day and increased thereafter. Therefore, we expected that the longer the interval between our readings and theirs, the greater would be the difference.

In constructing Tables 7.3 and 7.4, we subtracted a single pressure taken by prison staff from the mean of our two blood pressures. Table 7.3 concerns systolic pressure and Table 7.4 diastolic pressure. The tables indicate the number of men for each category of time interval between our and their readings and the mean difference in blood pressure at each time interval.

The relationship for diastolic pressures showed smaller differences and a similar but less consistent relation between blood pressure differences and the interval between readings.

When the same tabulations were carried out for the prison medical staff's single blood pressure reading and our first blood pressure, rather than the

TABLE 7.3

Relationship Between Systolic Blood Pressure Obtained by Prison Nurses and Those Obtained by Us as a Function of the Time Interval Between the Two[a]

N	Interval in Days	Mean Systolic Blood Pressure Difference in mmHg
26	0	−3.15
183	1	−4.34
105	2-3	−5.17
56	4-7	−5.73
24	8-14	−9.17

[a]The prison nurses always measured blood pressures first. A negative sign means that the prison nurses' readings were higher.

TABLE 7.4
Relationship Between Diastolic Blood Pressure Obtained
by Prison Nurses and Those Obtained by Us as a Function
of the Time Interval Between the Two[a]

N	Interval in Days	Mean Systolic Blood Pressure Difference in mmHg
26	0	−0.46
182	1	−0.23
105	2-3	0.70
56	4-7	−2.30
24	8-14	−3.54

[a]The prison nurses always measured blood pressures first. A negative sign means that the prison nurses' readings were higher.

mean of our two readings, the results were much the same in direction and size.

The data indicate that some inmates begin adapting to the prison environment very early in the prison stay. Even when prison nurses measured pressure on the same day and only an hour or two before we did, our readings were lower. In general, the longer the interval between readings, the larger the difference. Thus, our T1 pressures already were influenced by some degree of adaptation to imprisonment.

Many of the variables related to blood pressure at T1 were also associated with change in blood pressure from T1 to T2. Recidivists, for example, not only had lower blood pressure initially but also experienced a blood pressure decrease over time. Their greater familiarity with the prison setting may facilitate coping and lead to more rapid adaptation. A similar finding was found for men who spent time in the jail before imprisonment awaiting trial or bail. Native-born men had a blood pressure decline, whereas those who were foreign-born had a blood pressure increase, suggesting that acculturation reduces vulnerability. Blood pressure change and age were positively associated, indicating that younger men may also be more adept with new environments and more familiar with attitudes and behaviors characteristic of prison life. Inmates who parent(s) died when they were children may have reacted negatively to imprisonment initially, but they rapidly adjusted, because their blood pressure from T1 to T2 declined. On the other hand, an increase in specific emotional arousal, as noted by an increase in hostility from T1 to T2, was associated with an increase in blood pressure.

The data are relevant to theories linking psychosocial factors and blood pressure. They also have implications for prison design and administration. They indicate that individual inmates react differently to their situation during the first few weeks of their imprisonment. The physiologic effects were greatest among men who were the least familiar with environmental change and the prison environment, and those who were socially and culturally the most atypical. Job details may be useful because they were associated with a blood pressure decrease over time, and work release programs may be helpful in reducing an inmate's concerns over the financial condition of his family. Caution should be exercised in the extrapolation of these results to other environments, and the interpretation of some findings may be limited by the fact that pre-imprisonment blood pressure was not available as a baseline measurement. These results nevertheless aid in understanding the noxious effects of the prison environment on various types of inmates, and help suggest ways of remedying the situation or proposing alternatives to current methods of confinement.

8

Changes in Housing Mode: Effects on Blood Pressure, Perceptions, Mood, and Symptoms

This chapter focuses on changes in housing mode and on the associated consequences: changes in blood pressure and in various psychological outcomes, including perceptions, indices of mood, and symptoms. The analysis concentrates on data based on the first six interviews. For our purposes, the interviews are designated T1, the initial interview, through T6, the 4-month interview. Figure 6.2 in the methods chapter (chapter 6) outlines the interview status of inmate participants during this period. The number of inmates remaining in the institution decreased from 568 to 224 after 4 months. The primary reason for the decline was scheduled release from prison.

As noted in previous chapters, all inmates were placed in single cells. After 14 to 30 days, however, some began to be transferred to a dormitory. Inmates assigned to the dormitory slept and spent their leisure time there, but they were involved in the same programs and activities as were men who remained in cells. Other inmates were placed in a work release program usually after 1 month or more of imprisonment. These men were employed outside the prison during normal working hours but returned to their assigned living quarters in the prison by evening. For some inmates, these quarters were a separate work release dormitory, whereas others were housed in a special work release cellblock.

The study institution therefore employed four modes of housing: cell (C), dormitory (D), work release dormitory (WR-D), and work release cell (WR-C). The transfers from C to D and from C to WR-D provided two examples of change from a less dense to a more dense residence, whereas the change from C to WR-C served as an example of transfer from one residence of low density to another of low density. Although assignments from C to D, WR-D, and WR-C began at T3, 1 month after admission, it continued from

T4 through T6, 2 months through 4 months postintake. Retransfer from D, WR-D, or WR-C to C also occurred during the period, as did change from D to WR-D or WR-C.

Space requirements dictated the transfer from C to D: When space became a problem due to a large number of incoming men, some cell residents were transferred to D. Assignment to WR was dependent on an inmate's conduct while in prison and was also more likely to be granted as completion of sentence drew near. These men were usually placed in WR-D, but WR-C was used if WR-D was fully occupied. Inmates were not selected for transfer from C to D, or placed in WR-C instead of WR-D, according to any specific criteria; however, assignment was not truly random in the experimental sense. Attempts were made to detect selection bias, assess its importance, and control for it when necessary in the analysis.

ANALYSIS

The relationship between change over consecutive interviews in average blood pressure and corresponding change in mode of housing was investigated among the 418 men who had been in the institution for 1 week or less at T1. The 150 inmates who were first interviewed after they had spent more than 1 week in the prison were not included in this analysis. Many of these men had already transferred from C by T1, thereby precluding the assessment of baseline blood pressure[1], and their responses may have been influenced by their longer stay in the institution.

The first set of analyses dealt with the initial effects of transfer from C to D, WR-D, or WR-C. It focused upon the comparison of blood pressure, measured during the scheduled interview that was closest in time just before the transfer (pretransition pressures) with blood pressure measured during the next scheduled interview that fell after the event (post-transition pressures). As an example, consider inmates who were housed in cells at T1 and T2, and were then assigned to either D, WR-D, or WR-C sometime after T2 and before T3. Their blood pressure at T2 was defined as pre-transition pressure, their T3 value as post-transition pressure, and the difference between them as blood pressure changes. Similar procedures were followed for inmates who transferred from C to D, WR-D, or WR-C between T3 and T4, T4 and T5, and so on.

Instead of studying the association between change in residence and change in blood pressure at each time point separately, however, the data were collapsed over time. In other words, blood pressure changes among inmates who transferred from C to D, WR-D, or WR-C between T2 and T3 were pooled with data for inmates who made a similar change between T3

---

[1]The issue of baseline blood pressures is considered in more detail in chapter 7.

and T4, T4 and T5, and so on. This method avoided the limitations that small cell frequencies would impose if each time point was analyzed separately and simplified the presentation of results.

Two-tailed t-tests for paired samples were used to determine if the mean change in blood pressure for each group that changed housing modes differed from zero at the 0.05 significance level. The mean blood pressure changes of the three groups were also compared simultaneously in a one-way analysis of variance (ANOVA). Pairwise contrasts between the groups were performed with t-tests for independent samples after the ANOVA to determine which mean changes were different. SAS and BMDP computer programs were employed.

The "control" group consisted of men who remained in C for the 4-month period from T1 through T6. Mean blood pressure changes among these inmates were calculated from T2 to T3, T3 to T4, T4 to T5, and T5 to T6, to contrast with mean changes in blood pressure among men who changed residences. These four differences corresponded to the time periods when the other groups were changing modes of housing and were examined to determine if any blood pressure change took place in the absence of residential transfer. Each mean change was first tested with a t-test for paired samples. The four mean changes were then tested with Hotelling's T2, the exact multivariate extension of the paired t-test, to determine if they differed from each other or if they constituted an overall trend (Morrison, 1976).

Additional analyses examined change in blood pressure among inmates who were transferred from C to D and then retransferred to C. Blood pressure change associated with continued stay in D or WR-D was also investigated by studying inmates who remained in D or WR-D for more than 1 month.[2] Methods similar to those discussed earlier were used to pursue these issues, i.e., pre-transition blood pressure and readings corresponding to the first and second time periods post-transition were obtained, change in blood pressure were calculated, and paired t-tests were performed after the data were collapsed over time.

RESULTS

Change in Systolic Blood Pressure (SBP) by Change in Housing Mode

Of the 418 inmates, 128 were transferred from C to D during the first 4 months of the study. Table 8.1 shows that this change in residence was associ-

---

[2]Unfortunately, the number of men who resided in WR-C for more than 1 month was too small to permit additional analysis. This problem also arose with other subgroups (i.e., C to WR-D to C).

TABLE 8.1
Mean Change in Systolic Blood Pressure (mmHg) by Change in Mode of Housing[a]

Change in Mode of Housing	N	$\bar{x}$	S.D.	Range	t	p
Cell to dormitory	128	2.64	9.75	− 18 to 30	3.05	0.003
Cell to work release dormitory	37	3.78	9.97	− 20 to 28	2.35	0.020
Cell to work release cell	19	− 3.79	9.80	− 19 to 18	− 1.69	0.094

[a]$F(2,181) = 4.16: p = 0.017$

ated with a statistically significant mean increase of 2.64 mmHg in SBP. A statistically significant mean increase in SBP of 3.78 mmHg was noted among the 37 inmates who went from C to WR-D. The 19 men who changed from C to WR-C experienced a mean SBP decline of 3.79 mmHg, a decrease that did not achieve statistical significance at the 0.05 level. The one-way ANOVA indicated that these mean changes differed from each other ($p = 0.017$). Pairwise contrasts showed that the change for the C to WR-C group differed from that for the C to D ($p = 0.008$) and C to WR-D ($p = 0.007$) groups, whereas the mean changes for the latter two were not statistically different from each other.

Table 8.2 displays mean change in SBP over consecutive interviews among the 99 inmates who remained in C for the 4-month period (one additional inmate had a couple of missing values). These values ranged from a decrease of 0.95 mmHg to an increase of 1.55 mmHg, and none differed statistically from zero. The simultaneous comparison of these changes, with Hotelling's T^2 was also nonsignificant, indicating that they did not differ statistically from each other nor was there a reliable long-term trend. In contrast with the data for men who were transferred to D, WR-D, or WR-C, this pattern of results suggests little reliable variation in SBP over time.

Of the 128 inmates who were transferred from C to D, 31 were retransferred to C. For this subset of 31 men, their original change from C to D was accompanied by a mean increase of SBP of 3.26 mmHg, whereas their retransfer from D to C was associated with a mean decrease of 0.90 mmHg. This finding supports the notion that the critical factor influencing systolic

TABLE 8.2
Mean Change in Systolic Blood Pressure (mmHg) by Time Period
Among Men Who Remained in Cells[a]

Time Period	N	$\bar{x}$	S.D.	Range	t	p
T2 to T3	99	1.55	9.45	− 19 to 33	1.60	0.111
T3 to T4	99	− 0.95	8.55	− 25 to 19	− 1.01	0.314
T4 to T5	99	0.31	9.53	− 25 to 26	0.32	0.748
T5 to T6	99	1.14	9.60	− 25 to 24	1.17	0.244

[a]$T^2 = 5.78, p = .240$

blood pressure is the number of persons per housing mode, and also suggests that the effect is reversible. Another 42 men were transferred from C to D and remained in D for more than 1 month. These men had a mean increase in SBP of 2.62 mmHg when they were first transferred. After they had been in the dormitory for more than 1 month, however, SBP declined by a mean of 1.31 mmHg. This finding indicates that adaptation or accommodation to crowding may occur over time. In addition, there were 17 men who lived in WR-D more than 1 month; they had an initial mean increase of 2.65 mmHg and a subsequent mean decline of 1.59 mmHg. Collectively, these three groups of 90 men showed a significant increase of 2.85 and a decline of 1.22, with the latter change being reliably different ($p < .01$) from the former.

Table 8.1 also shows that the 19 men who were transferred from cell to work release cell experienced a mean decline of -3.79 mmHg, statistically significant at the .10 level. In spite of the small numbers involved, this finding is important because it demonstrates that the increases for the dormitory and work release dormitory groups cannot be explained as a simple function of change in residence independent of crowding. The cell to work release cell group was transferred from one type of cell to another, and they did not experience a mean increase in systolic blood pressure.

The control group of men who remained in cells for their first 4 months in prison had little change in systolic blood pressure, as Table 8.2 shows. Group average systolic blood pressure remained relatively stable over time if housing mode did not change.

Changes in Perceptions, Mood, and Symptoms by Change in Housing Mode

At this point we wish to turn to some of the psychological variables in order to understand better some of the consequences of the housing mode changes. Table 8.3 shows the mean changes in the perception of three features of the prison environment: the institution, individual housing, and the guards. The three groups of men are those that were described for the analysis of systolic blood pressure changes (Table 8.1). In discussing the results, we also refer to separate analyses done on the 100 men who remained in cells for the whole 4 months and who are described in connection with Table 8.2.

Table 8.3 shows that all three groups had a more positive view of the institution following the housing mode change. The effect is strongest in the C to WR-D group, but the three groups are not reliably different from each other. The 100 men staying in cells showed virtually no changes and Hotelling's T^2 was clearly not significant.

Perceptions of individual housing also became more positive in all three groups as a result of the housing mode change. The C to WR-D group again shows the strongest effect and it is reliably different from the other groups.

TABLE 8.3
Mean Changes in Perceptions of Environment (Summary Scales) by Change
in Mode of Housing*

Change in Mode of Housing	N^{**}	Institution		Housing Mode		Guards	
		$\bar{x}$	$P_x = 0$	$\bar{x}$	$P_x = 0$	$\bar{x}$	$P_x = 0$
Cell to dormitory	128	3.18	.001	3.68	.001	−2.60	.006
Cell to work release dormitory	37	6.06	.001	7.50	.001	2.62	.145
Cell to work release cell	19	2.84	.188	2.68	.146	−6.68	.019
		$F = 1.88$		$F = 5.49$		$F = 5.07$	
		N.S.		$p < .005$		$p < .007$	

*Positive score indicates more favorable perception, negative score indicates less favorable perception.
**The N's may be slightly smaller due to occasional missing data on one subject or another.

The 100 men staying in cells showed some fluctuations — first toward more positive, then toward more negative perceptions — but Hotelling's T^2 revealed that they were not reliably different from each other.

The data on perceptions of the guards show a different pattern in two ways. First, the 100 men remaining in cells do show a significant overall trend ($p < .03$): with each occasion, their perceptions of the guards become somewhat more negative. Second, the three groups in Table 8.3 no longer show the same changes: the C to D and C to WR-C show more negative perceptions, whereas the C to WR-D show more poositive perceptions. The negative changes can no longer be interpreted as due to housing mode change because the 100 men remaining in cells show the same trend (albeit a somewhat weaker one). However, the positive change among the C to WR-D is genuinely due to housing mode change and is reliably different from the negative trend seen in the 100 men remaining in cells or the other two groups who change housing mode.

It might be noted that in the above analyses, pre-transition values on the three variables analyzed in Table 8.3 were not significantly different from each other. When the pre-transition values are introduced as covariates in the change analysis, the findings are essentially the same. There appears to be no confounding between perceptions of the institutional environment and being selected for one or another housing mode change.

The total scale, perception of housing mode, consists of individual items, some of which did not show changes that paralleled the total scale scores. Table 8.4 presents the data for six selected items in an attempt to pinpoint the perceptual changes that followed the housing mode changes. The most important finding is with respect to privacy: those making the C to D move experienced a substantial loss in privacy, compared to no change for the C to WR-C group and small increase in perceived privacy for the C to WR-D

TABLE 8.4
Mean Changes in Perceptions of Housing Mode (Selected Items) by Change in Mode of Housing*

Change in Mode of Housing	N**	Very Private vs No Privacy		Safe vs Dangerous		You Can do What You Like vs Cannot		Spacious vs Crowded		Big Enough vs Too Small		Open vs Closed In	
		$\bar{x}$	$P_{\bar{x}}=0$	$\bar{x}$	$P_{\bar{x}}=0$	$\bar{x}$	$P_{\bar{x}}=0$	$\bar{x}$	$P_x=0$	$\bar{x}$	$P_x=0$	$\bar{x}$	$P_{\bar{x}}=0$
Cell to dormitory	128	−1.59	<.001	0.40	<.005	−.25	N.S.	0.02	N.S.	0.60	<.006	1.91	<.001
Cell to work release dormitory	37	0.42	N.S.	0.68	<.027	.87	.025	−0.32	N.S.	0.66	N.S.	1.92	<.001
Cell to work release cell	19	0.00	N.S.	0.37	N.S.	−.32	N.S.	0.26	N.S.	0.74	N.S.	0.74	N.S.
		$F = 13.39$		$F = 0.58$		$F = 6.41$		$F = 0.75$		$F = 0.08$		$F = 1.88$	
		$p < .001$		NS		$p < .005$		NS		NS		NS	

*Positive score indicates more favorable perception, negative score indicates less favorable perception.

**The N's may be slightly smaller due to occasional missing data on one subject or another.

group. Another important finding concerns perceived control ("you can do what you like"): the C to WR-D experienced a significant increase in perceived control, whereas the other two groups experienced a small decrement. On three other items—safety, size and openness—the three groups did not differ from each other, and all showed more positive perceptions, the same as the total scale scores. On perceptions of crowdedness, the group changes were somewhat more variable, but these changes were not reliable or reliably different from each other.

The group of 100 men who remained in cells during the first 4 months showed no significant changes (as tested by Hotelling's T^2) on the six individual items just discussed, with one exception: on the item "Big enough vs. too small," there was a tendency to rate the housing mode increasingly more negatively (as too small) over time ($p < .01$).

The next set of changes that we examine in relation to housing mode changes concern mood and symptoms. The relevant data are given in Table 8.5. The findings are pretty straightforward: Men in all three groups show decreases in anxiety, hostility, depression, and psychophysiologic symptoms. The magnitude of these declines is not significantly different across the three groups, but there is some tendency for the C to WR-D group to show the biggest benefits of the change in housing mode.

The data on the 100 men who remained in cells showed no significant changes for hostility and depression. On anxiety, Hotelling's T^2 was significant, but this was due to changes both up and down, rather than a single trend over time. Only on psychophysiologic symptoms was there a steady trend (downward) that was reliable. However, the average mean decline between a pair of interviews was only -0.35, or about one fourth of the average change seen in Table 8.5.

Intercorrelations among change scores for the seven variables presented in Tables 8.3 and 8.5 (collapsed over the three groups) were also examined. Change scores on the three perception scales were moderately intercorrelated (average $r = .32$), as were the four mood and symptom scales (average $r = .35$). The average correlation of scales in one cluster with scales in the other cluster was only .16.

Selected Correlates of Systolic Blood Pressure Change Primarily Among Men Going from Cell to Dormitory

In Table 8.1 we saw that the 128 men who made a change in mode of housing from cell to dormitory increased their systolic blood pressure an average of 2.64 mmHg. This small, reliable change hides behind it a good deal of individual variability in actual blood pressure changes, as can be seen from the high range and large standard deviation, also given in Table 8.1. It is the purpose of this section to attempt to understand more about the magnitude of

TABLE 8.5
Mean Changes in Affective States by Change in Mode of Housing*

Change in Mode of Housing	N^{**}	Anxiety		Hostility		Depression		Psychophysiologic	
		$\bar{x}$	$P_{\bar{x}} = 0$	$\bar{x}$	$P_{\bar{x}} = 0$	$\bar{x}$	$P_{\bar{x}} = 0$	$\bar{x}$	$P_{\bar{x}} = 0$
Cell to dormitory	128	-.31	.027	-.70	.001	-1.05	.001	-1.24	.001
Cell to work release dormitory	37	-.84	.007	-1.05	.004	-2.13	.001	-1.31	.030
Cell to work release cell	19	-.37	.331	-.16	.721	-.58	.404	-2.11	.013
		$F = 1.15$		$F = 1.32$		$F = 2.21$		$F = 0.34$	
		N.S.		N.S.		N.S.		N.S.	

*Positive score indicates increased negative affect or increase in symptoms, negative scores indicates decreased affect or decrease in symptoms.
**The N's may be slightly smaller due to occasional missing data on one subject or another.

this change: why some men showed a particularly large increase, whereas others showed no change at all, or possibly even a decline in blood pressure. We concentrate on this group because it is by far the largest one and is of central interest to this entire volume. If we collapsed all three groups experiencing housing mode change, we would have a much too heterogeneous group, both with respect to type of housing mode change as well as blood pressure change. Nevertheless, we pay attention to any interesting correlates of blood pressure change in the other two groups and note them as appropriate.

The results in Tables 8.3, 8.4, and 8.5 suggested an admixture of effects of the C to D move: negative mood and psychophysiological symptoms declined and perceptions of institution and housing mode became more positive. On the other hand, perceptions of guards became more negative and the men experienced a striking loss in privacy; there was also some decline in sense of control. The dormitory was seen as more open and somewhat safer, with no change in perception of crowding. Against this summary of psychological effects, let us now look at some correlates of the magnitude of systolic blood pressure change.

Table 8.6 shows the effects of age on magnitude of systolic blood pressure change. Younger men tend to show a larger increase than older men; however, the non-linear trend is also significant, showing that the highest increase is in the 20- to 22-age grouping. This effect of age is difficult to interpret but it may indicate that older inmates are better able to adapt to the housing mode change (given their broader and more extensive life experiences) that involves loss of privacy. The effect of recidivism was not significant, suggesting that previous imprisonments do not affect the response to the C to D move.

Table 8.7 shows that men whose pre-imprisonment residence was more urban had virtually no change in systolic blood pressure, whereas the increase was larger among men from more rural places of residence. Because the data on childhood residence were nearly identical, we are probably dealing with a fairly stable residential history variable. This effect of childhood and present residence suggests that extensive experience with the large urban environment facilitates adaptation to the dormitory setting.

TABLE 8.6
Age Correlate of Systolic Blood Pressure Change for Inmates
Moving from Cell to Dormitory

Age Grouping	N	Mean Change in SBP	Significance
≤ 19	37	2.38	Linear Trend $p < .05$
20-22	32	5.72	Quadratic Trend, $p < .05$
23-29	39	2.56	
≥ 30	20	− 1.65	

TABLE 8.7
The Influence of Place of Residence on Systolic Blood
Pressure Change for Inmates Moving from Cell to Dormitory

Present Residence	N	Mean Change in SBP	Significance
Large city	49	−0.14	$p < .01$
Small city, rural	74	3.95	

An examination of the influence of level of education revealed virtually no association with magnitude of systolic blood pressure change among the C to D change group. Interestingly, the men in the two work release groups showed a substantial association ($p < .001$). Men with at least some college education showed a decline of −4.17, whereas men with only grammar-school education showed a large increase of 12.00; men with intermediate education had an intermediate change (−0.77). This effect among the work release men is reliably different ($p < .02$) from the absence of effect for the C to D group (i.e., the interaction is significant). It may be speculated that lower level of education portends a greater difficulty in adapting to the work demands of the work release program; the men in the C to D group are not working and education level is thus not salient.

Table 8.8 shows the association between systolic blood pressure change and amount of change in leisure activity. Specifically, men who after the move to the dormitory showed an increase in "withdrawal" had a larger increase in systolic blood pressure than did men who showed a decrease in just sitting around and instead became more active. This suggests that coping style may be important; men who dealt with the situation passively by "sitting around and thinking" reacted to a greater extent than those who participated in athletics, hobbies, or other activities.

Table 8.9 shows some of the psychological correlates of the magnitude of systolic blood pressure change; these psychological correlates are themselves changes associated with the move from cell to dorm. It will be recalled that the move resulted in loss of privacy (adverse change) and reduction in perceived danger and in psychophysiologic symptoms (beneficial change). The findings indicate, for all three variables, that the more adverse the psychological change, the larger the blood pressure increase; conversely, inmates who had positive changes in the psychological variables showed the smallest increase (or a decline) in blood pressure. In short, individual differences in the psychological reaction to the move do explain some of the individual differences in systolic blood pressure reactivity to the same move.

The three scales examined in Table 8.3 — perceptions of institution, housing mode, and guards — did not show that individual differences in such perceptions were significantly related to individual differences in blood pressure change. The lack of a significant relationship with the perception of guards

TABLE 8.8

Systolic Blood Pressure Change for Inmates Moving from Cell
to Dormitory in Relation to Change in Leisure Activity

Change in Leisure Pattern of Activity After Move*	N	Mean Change in SBP	Significance
Relative Increase in "Withdrawal"*	70	4.55	p < .01
Relative Decrease in "Withdrawal"*	57	0.14	

*Based on inquiry "How many hours a week do you sit around thinking?"

TABLE 8.9

Psychological Correlates of Systolic Blood Pressure Changes
Among Inmates Moving from Cell to Dormitory

Psychological Changes Due to Move	N	Mean Change in SBP	Significance
Perceived loss in privacy			
Large	59	4.14	p < .007 for
Medium	54	2.48	Linear Trend
Small, or gain	15	− 2.67	
Perceived change in danger			
Increase	28	3.71	p < .10 for
Small decrease	50	3.36	Linear Trend
Large decrease	47	0.94	
Change in psychophysiologic symptoms			
Increase	61	4.71	p < .006 for
Small decrease	26	1.35	Linear Trend
Large decrease	38	− 0.16	

was particularly surprising and we pursued it further by examining interactions with the three variables seen in Table 8.9. One interaction effect did stand out: Change in perception of guards in the more negative direction was associated with a higher blood pressure increase but only among inmates who at the same time had a more negative change in their views of privacy ($p <$ .008).

Changes in perceptions of the institution did prove to be significantly related to blood pressure changes, but only among inmates making the change from cell to the work release program. The results are given in the top of Table 8.10. It can be seen that in both groups of inmates, changes in perceptions

TABLE 8.10
Some Correlates of Systolic Blood Pressure Changes Among Inmates Going from
Cell to Work Release

Correlate of SBP Change	Residential Change	Change in Correlate	N	Mean Change in SBP	Significance
Perceptions of the institution	Cell to work release dorm	More negative	9	−2.11	
		Less negative	10	−5.30	Main effect due to change in
	Cell to work release cell	More negative	7	12.57	correlate
		Less negative	28	1.54	$p < .005$
Frequency of telephone contacts	Cell to work release dorm	More frequent	6	−6.50	
		Less frequent	13	−2.54	Main effect due to change in
	Cell to work release cell	More frequent	6	−3.17	correlate
		Less frequent	31	5.13	$p < .005$

of the institution in the negative direction were associated with a larger increase (or smaller decline) in systolic blood pressure. In a more complete analysis that included the C to D groups as well, the interaction term was significant ($p < .03$), confirming the observation that the association between change in perception of the institution and blood pressure change is specific to the type of housing mode change being made. We might speculate that for men who enter the work release program, perceptions of the larger setting, the institution itself, become more salient and perceptions of the immediate residential setting, the housing mode, become less salient. On the other, Table 8.9 suggests that those who have not yet taken the first step toward release (the work release program), but do make a residential move from cell to dormitory, certain specific dimensions of the perceptions of housing mode (i.e., privacy and safety) become highly salient.

Table 8.10 also shows that when the cell to work release move is associated with a relative increase in telephone contacts, there is a greater likelihood of a decline in blood pressure than when there is a relative decrease in such telephone contacts. Because this association was not observed for the C to D group, we may again speculate that for those who have made the step toward rejoining the society outside of the prison, frequency of telephone contacts becomes salient and a higher frequency appears to facilitate adaptation.

EXPLORATORY ANALYSES

In this section we describe the results of an analysis that we consider as preliminary or exploratory. Essentially, we asked ourselves: what more can we learn about the relationships between prison events and blood pressure change if we select out for attention inmates who show the largest increases in systolic blood pressure between any two readings coming from any pair of consecutive (time-adjacent) interviews? The computer identified 20 individuals ("cases") who had the largest increases. Then, for each case, the computer selected at random from the remaining pool of subjects a "control" who was matched on interview number (i.e., stage in the imprisonment process in order to control for the duration of confinement at the time of the blood pressure change). The process was then repeated by selecting the next 20 highest blood pressure increases and a random drawing of another 20 controls from the remaining pool.

The interviews of these 40 cases and 40 controls were then examined for events that might have happened during the time bracketed by the two interviews and the two blood pressure readings that yielded the change scores. Specifically we looked for: (a) any change in residence, including moving from one cell to a different cell; (b) two forms of punishment involving housing: individual lockup (inmate not allowed to get out of his cell) and "lower report" solitary confinement; (c) interviewer notations about drugs and alcohol abuse (actually being caught).

The limitations of this kind of an analysis must be noted because the cases are being selected for extreme values on the dependent variable. One limitation is the possible exploitation of chance results. However, this concern is pretty much removed if the results on the first 20 cases are similar to the data on the next 20. Thus, an association can be reliably established, but the magnitude of the relationship cannot be estimated: the actual blood pressure changes on the 40 cases exaggerate the true effect, and the contrast between cases and controls is a comparison of one extreme group against a sample of the remainder (but not a contrast of extremes from both ends of a distribution).

Table 8.11 presents the results of this analysis. The two groups of cases are kept separate so that consistency of findings can be assessed; the two groups of controls are combined because they are randomly selected and there is no need to keep them separate. It can be seen that the cases and controls are fully comparable on age. The controls show an average change in blood pressure that is close to zero; this is as expected, because they are randomly selected from a whole spectrum of blood pressure increases and decreases. The average blood pressure increase for cases is simply the 40 highest values; it cannot be used to estimate magnitude of effect.

Table 8.11 shows that the cases with large blood pressure increases are more likely to have had the selected events, for which the interviews were searched, than are the controls who are unselected for blood pressure change. Table 8.11 also shows that both groups A and B — that is, the cases with the first 20 and next 20 highest blood pressure increases — show this excess of events, compared to controls. The slightly higher prevalence of events in

TABLE 8.11

Events Experienced by Inmates Showing Highest Systolic BP Increases
Between Two Consecutive Interviews, and by "Controls"

| | | Groups | | | | | | Groups | | | |
		A	B	C				A	B	C	
	2+	3	2	1			2+	2	1	1	
Events						Events					
	1	11	8	14			1	8	6	5	
"A"						"B"					
	0	6	10	25			0	10	13	34	
		20	20	40	80			20	20	40	80

Gamma = .42   Gamma = .52
    p < .01   p < .002

Group A: "Cases" who showed highest SBP increase
Group B: "Cases" with the next 20 highest SBP increases
Group C: "Controls", randomly selected from remaining inmates,
matched on interview no. (i.e., control for duration of confinement at time
of SBP change)
  Cases: Age X = 25.55   SBP X = 24.5 (±3.82)
  Controls: Age X = 25.41   SBP X = −0.6 (±9.74)
  Events "A": 1. All changes in residence, including cell to different cell
              2. Individual lockups and "lower report" (punishments)
              3. Interviewer Notations on drugs and alcohol (being caught)
  Events "B": Delete cell to dormitory changes

group A, compared to B, is entirely compatible with the notion of an overall
linear association between event frequency and magnitude of increase: in
group A the average increase (27.65) is somewhat higher than for group B
(21.35).

The data in Table 8.11 are presented in two ways, with the second way
(right side of table) deleting from the events those that were specifically C to
D changes. This was done because early in this chapter we already established
the impact of C to D changes on blood pressure and in Table 8.11 we wish to
show new, or additional, relationships. The findings in Table 8.11 closely
support the notion that inmates showing large increases in blood pressure
within a period of time bracketed by two consecutive interviews are at considerably greater risk for experiencing various prison events that may be deemed
to be of a stressful nature.

Table 8.11 (left side) also shows that 16 of the 40 men with highest blood
pressure increases did not experience any of the listed events. This failure to
identify stressful prison events for the men showing the largest blood pressure increases may well be related to the limitation of the data we collected.
For example, we have information on the frequency of phone use and of
prison visits by family, friends, and others. But we have no data on what hap-

pened during the visits or phone calls. Did a wife or girlfriend express a desire to leave the inmate? Did a past employer refuse to rehire the man after release? Did a family member complain of financial problems or a friend refuse to help? We do not know. Certainly communications of this kind could have caused blood pressure changes as well as changes in affect and perceptions.

The relationship between these prison events (solitary confinement, cell lockups, being caught with illicit drugs or alcohol, and movement from cell to dormitory) and the increase in systolic blood pressure serves to confirm the usefulness of employing blood pressure change as a measure of the stressful effects of these events in the prison environment. It also enabled us to pursue further some of the relationships suggested by Table 8.11. One area we pursued was the effect of being placed in protective custody (PC). Preliminary conversations with the prison master after the study was underway indicated that some men asked for PC and presumably welcomed it, whereas others who may have needed protection sought to avoid it. We collected no data on why the men were given PC and about their attitudes toward it. Ten men were involved in 24 transfers into or out of protective custody. No significant changes in mean pressures were noted on moves either into or out of PC.

Another event, suggested by Table 8.11, which was chosen for closer scrutiny was "lower report" solitary confinement (or, as the inmates called it, "the hole"). A systematic search of prison records for the period during which the study was conducted showed 31 inmates had been sent to solitary confinement for disciplinary reasons, and we had blood pressure data on them from one interview sometime before the offense and from a second interview after the offense. Because we had exact dates for the two interviews and the offense in between we chose to test a more refined hypothesis than the simple prediction that the second blood pressure value would be higher than the first.

The reasoning behind the more refined hypothesis is presented schematically in the top of Fig. 8.1. The basic assumption we make is that the actual offense and the subsequent punishment are but the end stage of a perturbation or episode in the inmate's life. The beginning of such an episode may come well before the actual date of the offense and thus the inmate's blood pressure may begin to rise away from baseline before the offense. At the same time, we assume that following punishment, blood pressure may remain elevated for some time but then begins to decline and return to normal. If this reasoning is correct, then the hypothesis that the second blood pressure will be higher than the first because the inmate experienced solitary confinement has a best chance of support if the first interview is well before the date of the offense and the second interview is shortly after the offense. Conversely, when the first interview is just before the offense and the second one is well after it, the chances of finding support for the hypothesis is small and, in

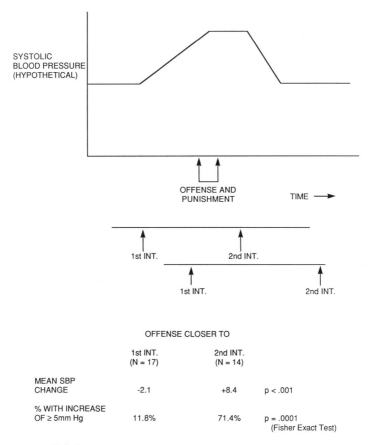

FIG. 8.1.   Solitary confinement and systolic blood pressure.

fact, a decline in blood pressure may be observed. Given this reasoning, we divided the 31 inmates into two groups, one where the offense was closer to the first interview and the other, where it was closer to the second interview. The results are given at the bottom of Fig. 8.1. The findings provide clearcut support for the above reasoning: solitary confinement does lead to a temporary elevation of blood pressure and the timing of the two interviews in relation to the confinement does strongly influence the chances of detecting this effect.

THE IMPACT OF RELEASE FROM PRISON

In this section we describe briefly some selected findings on changes from before release to after release. The core analysis involved 145 men for whom data were examined for three interviews: the next to the last one before release, the one just before release, and the one just after release. Data were examined for perceptions of the institution, anxiety, hostility, depression, psychophysiological symptoms, and systolic blood pressure. Perceptions of guards and of the housing mode were, understandably, not administered after release and thus these two scales were not involved in the change analysis. The inmates length of confinement (under vs. over 6 months) was used as a stratification variable.

There were two significant changes in anticipation of release, that is, from the next to the last to the last interview before release: hostility and psychophysiological symptoms declined somewhat ($p < .04$ for both). Length of confinement made on important difference: the men with a stay of less than 6 months had a large decline in psychophysiological symptoms ($\bar{x} = -1.69$, $p < .001$) in anticipation of release, whereas the men with a longer imprisonment had a small increase in such symptoms ($\bar{x} = 0.32$, N.S.). The difference between the two groups was highly reliable ($p < .001$).

The changes associated with release from the prison — that is, differences between the last interview in prison and the first interview after release — may be summarized as follows: (a) There was a substantial improvement in the evaluation of "the area you are living in now," compared to their evaluation of the institution; the mean value went from 28.82 to 42.77, which is a change of about 1½ standard deviations ($p < .0001$). This finding, of course, carries little surprise. (b) The mood and symptom checklists all showed significant declines, the largest was for depression (about ½ of a standard deviation, $p < .0001$) and the smallest was for psychophysiological symptoms (about 1/5 of a standard deviation, $p < .04$). (c) Inspection of the results by length of confinement revealed generally comparable changes, with somewhat larger declines in the group with longer confinement.

Examination of the systolic blood pressure data revealed no significant change in anticipation of release, that is, from the next to the last to the last interview before release. However, the change from before to after release was associated with a significant change, a mean decline of -2.0 mmHg ($p < .01$). This is certainly compatible with the interpretation that release into the community represents a reduction in environmental stress. However, because the magnitude of the change is small, we must further speculate that either (a) the adjustment to community living has its own difficulties and thus the net decrease in environmental stress is relatively small, or that (b) there are many other unmeasured influences on the blood pressure change that attentuate the magnitude of the impact of the release itself; for example, gain in weight and increased alcohol consumption.

Confounding Variables and Alternative Explanations

To assess the role of confounding variables and the possibility of alternative explanations, men who were assigned to D, WR-D, or WR-C and those who remained in C were compared in regard to SBP at T1 and SBP immediately before transfer, socio-demographic characteristics, and other important factors. The first of these analyses showed that the four groups defined by residential change did not differ significantly in mean SBP at T1. SBP at T1 was also not related to later changes in SBP over time, and adjusting for it with analysis of covariance did not alter the change in housing mode change in SBP association.

There were no significant differences among men who changed modes of housing in mean SBP immediately before transfer, and these readings were comparable to the mean values at T2 through T6 of men who remained in C. Level of SBP before transfer was inversely related to change in SBP. When it was controlled for with covariance analysis, however, the differences among housing modes in regard to SBP change were not reduced.

One-way ANOVA indicated that the four residence groups differed significantly in age and body bulk. The mean age of inmates who remained in C was lower than that of men who were transferred to WR-C, and the former group was leaner than the C to D and C to WR-D groups. The mean age of the C to WR-C group was also greater than the mean age for the C to D group. Cross-sectionally, SBP was higher among older men and those with greater body bulk, but these factors were not related to change in SBP. Adjusting for age and body bulk with analysis of covariance did not affect the comparison of mean SBP change among residence groups, and SBP at T1 and SBP immediately before transfer did not differ by housing mode when these variables were controlled for.

Changing housing mode was also significantly related to length of confinement. Inmates who remained in cells stayed in the institution for a greater period of time than men who were transferred to D, WR-D, or WR-C. Length of confinement, however, was not related to SBP at T1, SBP immediately before transfer, or change in SBP, and when length of confinement was used as a covariate, the results concerning SBP change and residential transfer did not change.

There were no differences in the proportion who transferred from C to D, WR-D, or WR-C by race, education, religion, nativity, recidivism, and length of stay at last address. All men ate the same diet and little change in weight over time was noted. Alcohol and drug abuse did occur during the study period but the frequency of this behavior did not appear to differ by housing mode. These variables therefore do not confound the relationship between SBP change and residence group.

Analyses were also conducted to determine if the association between change in housing mode and change in SBP differed according to time of transfer. Forty-eight men went from C to D between T2 and T3, 32 between T3 dnd T4, 30 between T4 dnd T5, and 18 between T5 and T6. Each of these groups showed an increase in SBP accompanying the change in residence, an effect that varied in magnitude from a mean of 1.59 mmHg before T4 to a mean of 4.56 mmHg before T6, but they did not differ statistically from each other. Fifteen men were transferred from C to WR-D before T3, 10 before T4, 7 before T5, and 5 before T6. An increase in SBP ranging from a mean of 0.29 mmHg before T5 to a mean of 6.47 mmHg before T3 was also evident for each of these groups, and these changes were not statistically different from each other. The C to WR-C transition was made by 5 men before T3, 5 before T4, and 9 before T5. Each group had a decrease in SBP, varying from a mean of − 1.00 mmHg before T5 to a mean of − 8.00 mmHg before T4. They too did not differ statistically from each other. These findings indicate that inmates who made similar residential transfers experienced similar changes in SBP, regardless of when the transfer occurred, and they support the use of pooled data to summarize these associations.

Other statistical techniques were employed to determine if different methods would yield different results. Four ANOVAs with repeated measures were undertaken, using the pre- and post-transition SBP for the C to D, WR-D, and WR-C groups and the T2 and T3, T3 and T4, T4 and T5, or T5 and T6 SBP, respectively, for those inmates who remained in cells. A multivariate ANOVA was also conducted (Morrison, 1976). The findings were compatible with the analysis of change in SBP, i.e., the C to D and C to WR-D groups had significant increases, whereas the readings of the C to WR-C group declined and the SBP of those who stayed in C remained stable.

Change in Diastolic Blood Pressure (DBP) by Change in Housing Mode

Change in DBP among residence groups was also analyzed. Unlike its counterpart, no statistically significant findings emerged. The general pattern of results, however, paralleled SBP.

DISCUSSION

The data support the contention that aggregation of humans may elevate SBP, and they longitudinally confirm our earlier cross-sectional findings. Inmates who were transferred from C to either D or WR-D experienced a statistically significant mean increase in SBP. Men who remained in C, however, showed little mean change in SBP over time. Mean level of SBP among these groups at entry to prison and immediately before transfer were not statistically different. With the exception of housing mode, these men were subject to the same conditions, e.g., type of diet and leisure activity, and adjustment for potentially confounding variables did not alter the findings.

The results cannot be explained as a simple function of any kind of change in residence, whether or not it also might involve change in aggregation.

A third group was transferred from C to WR-C, and these men did not experience a mean increase in SBP. In fact, this transition from one type of cell to another was associated with a mean SBP decrease significant at the 0.10 level. Another finding which suggests that aggregation is the causal factor is the fact that SBP decreased on the average among men who were retransferred from D to C. This mean reduction in SBP upon a rapid return to C was not statistically significant, but it does indicate that the effect of aggregation may be reversible in its early stages, an observation similar to that of Henry, Stephens, and Santisteban (1975) in their studies of mice.

The data on perceptions and mood revealed that reductions in negative mood and in psychophysiological symptoms accompanied the housing mode changes. In addition, overall perceptions of the institution and of the housing mode became more positive. Perceptions of the guards tended to become more negative, but this was also true of the C to C group as they continued to stay in the cells. Additional analyses revealed that, in spite of these positive changes, the C to D move was also accompanied by a striking decline in sense of privacy and some loss of perceived control.

A number of characteristics among the C to D men were observed that were associated with a particularly large increase in systolic blood pressure as a response to the housing mode change: they were younger, had lived in rural settings, and responded to the housing move with greater withdrawal. Furthermore, those inmates who after the move had a greater perceived loss in privacy and safety and had an increase in psychophysiological symptoms, were the inmates who also showed a larger increase in blood pressure.

Among the inmates who moved from C to the work release program, lower levels of education were particularly predictive of a larger increase in systolic blood pressure. Other changes, such as more negative perceptions of the institution and a reduction in frequency of telephone contacts, were also associated with larger increases in blood pressure.

Exploratory analyses of inmates who experienced the 40 largest systolic blood pressure increases (at any time) revealed that, compared to unselected "controls," these inmates were at greater risk for other types of prison events, including individual lockups, solitary confinement, and being caught abusing drugs or alcohol. Independent analyses of all men subjected to solitary confinement confirmed the exploratory analyses. Incidentally, the data on the impact of solitary confinement represent evidence regarding other types of prison stresses and cannot be easily subsumed under the concept (or interpretive framework) of crowding or aggregation.

The term *crowding* has been used in this study to conveniently describe aspects of the prison environment and to provide theoretical linkage with other relevant work. It refers to the number of persons per housing mode but has no preeminent status, and we have not tried to develop an elaborate model of crowding. We do believe, however, that crowding is a complex phenomenon, and that it implies more than the physical limitation of space. The subjective dimension, represented by a perceived discrepancy in the amount of space an individual requires and the amount of space available, is of great importance (Stokols, 1972). Social and personal factors interact with physical parameters to mediate this experience (Stokols, Rall, Pinner, & Schopler, 1973), and loss of privacy (Altman, 1975) and lack of personal control (Proshansky, Ittelson, & Rivlin, 1970) may be intervening variables. In the prison environment, aggregation may be associated with increases in the number of threatening interactions among inmates and between inmates and guards, and leading to states of vigilance and arousal. Also pertinent to this discussion are the concepts of personal space (Hall, 1966; Sommer, 1969) and sensory overload (Lipowski, 1974; Milgram, 1970). Crowding or aggregation may impinge on the area immediately surrounding an individual, space he or she regards as an extension of self. It may also serve as an additional burden to individuals already overtaxed by the demands of his or her environment.

Although they were not statistically significant, the findings regarding continued stay in D or WR-D indicate that some adaptation to crowding may occur. Individuals who spend more than 1 month in D or WR-D had an initial mean increase in SBP, but they subsequently experienced a mean SBP decline as they remained in these housing modes. Their mean blood pressure after more than 1 month in D or WR-D was nevertheless higher than their mean SBP before transfer.

Caution should be exercised in the interpretation and extrapolation of these results for several reasons. First, prison inmates represent an unusual sample of men studied under atypical circumstances. The extent to which these findings can be generalized to other persons in other environments is therefore limited. Although explicit criteria were not employed in determining which inmates were to be transferred from C to D or placed in WR-C instead of WR-D, assignment was not random. A number of potential confounders were examined and controlled for in the analysis, but the possibility remains that some undetected selection bias explains the relationship between housing mode and SBP change. Furthermore, one cannot infer from these data that crowding is causing hypertension in this population of young men because the average magnitude of the effect regarding SBP was relatively small, and no statistically significant increase in DBP was observed.

We observed greater differences in SBP and a statistically significant DBP effect in our previous cross-sectional work (D'Atri & Ostfeld, 1975). In this earlier study, we were able to interview the inmates and measure their blood pressure in their usual mode of housing. Unfortunately, this procedure was not feasible in the current longitudinal study. Assessments were made in the prison infirmary, which consisted of several rooms located outside the main residential and work-related areas of the prison and was staffed by medical personnel with few guards present. The relatively benign atmosphere of this setting may have lowered blood pressure, especially among men who lived in D or WR-D. Differences in blood pressure change by residence group consequently may have been reduced.

These findings nevertheless have important implications. They support the theory that crowding may operate as a stressor in man and may influence cardiovascular activity. They may have relevance for prison design and policy. For example, the disadvantages of the dormitory may outweigh its efficient use of space, and work release programs may be beneficial only if employed in conjunction with assignment to a cell. The results concerning blood pressure levels must be integrated with data regarding affect and behavior to yield a comprehensive picture of response to a prison environment.

9 Correlates of Blood Pressure Throughout the Sentence

Chapter 7 has dealt with an analysis of the associations between blood pressure and other variables at the first interview and the changes between the first and second interview. The purpose of this chapter is twofold: (a) to continue the correlational analysis begun at T1 by extending it to all interviews; and (b) to test the hypotheses about relationships between blood pressure and the other data collected as specified in chapter 6.

The methods of analysis are described in Appendix 5. The analyses were carried out in two ways. First, associations were identified at each interview for all inmates who contributed data at that interview ("entire group"). In these analyses, the numbers of inmates decrease with each interview. Second, similar analyses were made only on those men who contributed complete data at each of the first four interviews, i.e., through 2 months ("core group"). This involved 165 men. (This "core group" analysis was also extended through 3 months; now the number with complete data was reduced to 116 men.) The first analysis ("entire group") uses all the data, but because a diminishing set of inmates is involved in analysis, temporal trends might thus become obscured (men with shorter sentences are released). Hence the second analysis ("core group") deals with results, through 2 months, on an unvarying group of men with complete data. For this latter core group analysis, initial systolic and diastolic pressures were included as covariates in the analysis. In an unchanging group of men this provides us not only with a definition of blood pressure correlates at each interview, but also some understanding of how other variables relate to blood pressure over time, adjusting for initial blood pressure levels. The summary tables are contained in Appendix E: Table E.1 — entire group, systolic blood pressure; Table E.2 — entire group, diastolic blood pressure; Table E.3 — core group, systolic blood pressure; and Table E.4 — core group, diastolic blood pressure.

In the presentation of results, details for the entire group analysis are presented first, followed by a comparison of the results of the core group analysis to that of the entire group.

There are at least two reasons why there could be differences between the entire group and the core group besides their different numbers and composition: (a) only for the core group was the initial blood pressure included as a covariate and (b) on the average, the men in the core group were in prison 2 to 3 weeks longer.

Because chapter 8 dealt with the relationships between housing mode and blood pressure, no further presentation of such material is made in this chapter.

TWO-WEEK INTERVIEW

Systolic Blood Pressure

Entire Group.   The final model contained terms for age, ponderal index, recidivism, religiosity, education, and hours per week spent sitting and thinking. The final model was significant at the $< .0001$ level $(F = 10.65, df = 10)$ and explained 22.17% of the variance in mean systolic blood pressure. The model was based on 385 of the 402 men in the sample at this time, men who had complete data regarding the six variables of interest. The grand mean was 114.96 mmHg.

As expected, age was positively related to systolic pressure $(p < .0001)$, while ponderal index was negatively associated with the dependent variable $(p < .005)$; i.e., older men and those who were short and heavy had higher systolic pressure on the average. Two other socio-demographic factors, religiosity and education, were also correlated with systolic pressure. Men who reported themselves as being deeply religious had mean systolic pressures 5.85 mmHg greater than those who reported more neutral feelings about religion $(p < .001)$. The blood pressure data in relation to education revealed a somewhat non-linear positive association $(p < .05)$; the contrast was largest between those with eighth-grade education and those with some college, with the latter being 5.71 mmHg higher $(p < .005)$. First-time offenders were observed to have higher systolic blood pressure compared to recidivists — a difference of 4.18 mmHg $(p < .001)$. Finally, the results showed that men who spent more hours per week sitting and thinking had higher blood pressure levels $(p < .05)$.

Core Group.   This analysis involved the 165 men who had complete data through the 2-month stage of interviewing. As was seen in the analysis of all men, age and recidivism were significant predictors of blood pressure. The scale that assessed perception of individual residence also entered in the model. These variables were important in addition to initial systolic blood pressure which was included in the model as a covariate. The final model was significant at the < .0001 level ($F = 42.54$, $df = 4$) and explained 51.54% of the variance in mean systolic pressure. Each variable was significant ($p < .10$) and adjusted simultaneously for the effects of all others in the model. The grand mean was 114.80 mmHg.

Given the known temporal stability of blood pressure, it was completely expected that initial mean systolic blood pressure would make its strongest contribution to systolic blood pressure levels at the 2-week stage. The other two correlates, age and recidivism, represent repetition of the results from the entire group. However, because initial blood pressure is used as a covariate, this would suggest that older men and first time offenders are showing a greater increase (or smaller decrease) between initial and 2-week blood pressure values. Conversely, because the contribution of education and religiosity is no longer seen, this would suggest that these two variables did not influence change between initial and 2-week blood pressure values. The new variable entering the prediction is perception of residence: those inmates who have more negative perceptions of their housing mode (still the cell at this time) have higher blood pressure levels ($p < .03$).

Diastolic Blood Pressure

Entire Group.   The summary analysis for mean diastolic pressure developed a significant final regression model ($F = 11.72$, $p < .0001$). The model contained three terms that were noted earlier with systolic pressure (age, education, and ponderal index). Additional variables were also observed: job detail, frequency of visits by friends, frequency of social contact among inmates, and anxiety, as measured by the adjective checklist. The model was based on 355 men for whom a complete set of data concerning the seven variables of interest was available, and explained 27.32% of the variance in mean diastolic pressure. The grand mean was 72.41 mmHg.

Concordant with the cross-sectional findings for systolic pressure, diastolic blood pressure was higher among older men and those who were heavier. The data on education were also similar in that the men with some college education had higher mean levels. The additional variables contributing to diastolic blood pressure levels are of some interest: (a) the men who had a job by the second week had significantly lower blood pressure, compared to men without a job (difference of 1.94 mmHg, $p < .03$); (b) high frequency of social contacts with other inmates was related to lower blood pressure ($p < .05$); (c) compared to inmates reporting no visits by friends, those reporting monthly visits had lower values (a difference of 3.37 mmHg), as did the inmates reporting weekly visits (0.44 mmHg). This suggests a curvilinear relationship ($p < .02$) with moderately frequent visits by friends being "optimal," representing neither abandonment nor excessive pressure and attention; (d) higher levels of reported anxiety were associated with higher blood pressure levels ($p < .07$).

Core Group.   Based on 165 men, the final regression model contained terms for initial mean diastolic pressure, age, ponderal index, frequency of social contact among the inmates, hours per day spent outside the residence, perception of this residence, hours per week spent exercising, frequency of phone use, and childhood residence. The model, significant at the $< .0001$ level ($F = 24.71$, $df = 11$), explained 63.98% of the variance in mean diastolic blood pressure, and the grand mean was 72.35 mmHg.

The associations with age ($p < .03$), ponderal index ($p < .03$), and frequency of social contacts with other inmates ($p < .03$) are like those seen for the entire group analysis. However, because the initial mean diastolic blood pressure is entered as a covariate, this suggests that older, heavier men with few social contacts in prison show a greater increase between initial and two week interviews. Correlations significant for the core group only revealed the following determinants of higher diastolic blood pressure levels: (a) rural setting of childhood residence ($p < .05$); (b) fewer hours spent outside of the inmates' residence ($p < .04$); (c) fewer hours per week spent exercising ($p < .002$); (d) lower frequency of telephone use ($p < .01$); and (e) negative perceptions of the residence (i.e., still individual cells at this time) ($p < .01$).

In the remainder of this chapter, significant associations between blood pressure and age or ponderal index, found in the entire group analyses — those not including initial blood pressure values as covariates — are no longer discussed. They are entirely commonplace associations meriting no further attention. The contributions of initial blood pressure values in the core group analyses are also ignored from now on because they only reflect temporal stability.

ONE-MONTH INTERVIEW

Systolic Blood Pressure

Entire Group.   The final regression model for average systolic blood pressure after 1 month of incarceration contained terms for age, ponderal index, length of stay at last residence, number of residential changes since age 10, frequency of visits by friends, financial problems related to the inmate's incarceration, and the multiple adjective checklists assessing anxiety and hostility. The model, significant at the $< .0001$ level ($F = 7.50$, $df = 14$), explained 25.00% of the variance in mean systolic pressure, and was calculated

on data from 330 men with complete data on the aforementioned eight variables. The grand mean was 115.87 mmHg.

History of high residential mobility was originally hypothesized to be negatively related to blood pressure levels: We thought that men who had experienced a lot of moves would find it easier to adapt to the prison environment.
The 1-month systolic blood pressure data support this expectation with two
variables: (a) men with a greater number of residential changes since age 10
had lower blood pressure ($p < .05$), and (b) men whose length of stay at last
residence was more than 5 years had higher blood pressure (a difference of
5.67 mmHg, $p < .005$) than those who spent 3–5 years at last residence before incarceration. However, because those with less than 3 years at last residence had intermediate values (but closer to the 5 + years group), an overall
curvilinear relationship seems to be present: higher blood pressure levels are
associated with both very high and very low mobility.

Other determinants of higher systolic blood pressure levels were: existence
of more severe financial problems ($p < .003$), higher levels of anxiety ($p <
.04$) and higher hostility ($p < .005$). The observed association with frequency
of visits by friends was again a curvilinear one, the same as already seen for
diastolic blood pressure at two weeks (entire group): lower blood pressure
was seen among those receiving monthly visits, in contrast to either those receiving weekly visits or no visits.

The residual analysis between residual and predicted values of systolic
blood pressure as well as between the residuals and the observed values of
each of the continuous independent variables in the model showed no unusual patterns. The normal probability plot also indicated that the model adequately fit the analyzed data. Similar analyses were carried out on all additional data with similar results.

Core Group.   The analysis based on the 165 men in the cohort revealed
somewhat different results from those seen with the entire group. The final
model contained terms for initial mean systolic pressure, housing mode, frequency of phone use, frequency of visits by friends, and whether the inmate
had any children. Significant at the $< .0001$ level ($F = 18.67$, $df = 9$), this
model explained 52.02% of the variance in the dependent variable and each
variable in the model was significant at the $< .10$ level, adjusted for the effects of all others. The grand mean was 115.07 mmHg.

The results show that men with children have higher blood pressure levels
than men reporting no children (a difference of 2.77 mmHg, $p < .05$). Another association observed in this analysis is the higher systolic blood pressure seen for men reporting more frequent use of the telephone (a mean difference of 1.45 mmHg, $p < .06$, between weekly or daily use vs. no use). This
would appear to be, at best, a serendipitous finding that can receive only a
post hoc, tentative interpretation. Depending on the stage of adaptation to

the prison environment and on the actual nature of such telephone contacts (with whom, concerning what issues, etc.), one would expect that such contacts can either be a source of increased pressure and tension, or can be instrumental in facilitating adaptation and reducing tension. Thus level of telephone contacts would show variable associations with blood pressure. In fact, we saw earlier in the core group analysis at 2 weeks that higher diastolic blood pressure was associated with lower frequency of telephone use.

The analysis showed, once again, the curvilinear association with frequency of visits by friends: monthly visits were associated with lower blood pressure than either weekly visits or no visits. The final set of significant relationships involves housing mode: compared to men in single cells, those housed in dormitory, protective custody and infirmary, and work release dormitory have higher blood pressure means (3.85 mmHg, 16.53 mmHg, and 10.25 mmHg, respectively; all $p < .05$ or less). This is in agreement with the major hypothesis that inmates in cells would have lower blood pressure. These findings have been more fully explored in chapter 8 dealing with housing mode and utilizing longitudinal, change score analysis strategy.

Diastolic Blood Pressure

Entire Group.   For mean diastolic blood pressure at the 1-month period, terms for age, ponderal index, financial problems, education, frequency of social contact among the inmates, and the scales assessing perception of residence and anxiety were included in the final regression model. The model was calculated using the 366 men with complete data for these seven variables and explained 25.53% of the variance in diastolic pressure. A grand mean of 72.66 mmHg was computed, and the final regression model was significant at the $< .0001$ level ($F = 11.03$, $df = 11$).

Higher diastolic pressures were observed among more anxious men ($p < .02$), men who perceived their individual residence in a more negative manner ($p < .06$), and men having less frequent social contact with other inmates in the prison ($p < .04$). The remainder of significant associations in this analysis is also familiar to us: higher blood pressure levels for those with some college education, and those who have some financial problems.

Core Group.   The analysis based on the 165 men resulted in a model significant at the .0001 level ($F = 12.03$, $df = 18$), that accounted for 59.74% of the mean diastolic pressure variation. The final regression model includes terms for initial diastolic blood pressure, education, age, ponderal index, length of stay at last residence, childhood residence, hours per day spent outside the inmate's residence, hours per week spent going for walks, and the multiple adjective checklists assessing anxiety and hostility. The grand mean was 71.84 mmHg.

As with the entire group, mean diastolic blood pressure was observed to be positively related to anxiety ($p < .0001$) and hostility ($p < .01$), and negatively with hours per day spent outside the residence ($p < .05$). Longer stay at last residence still appears related to somewhat higher blood pressure. However, the variable of childhood residence shows a reversal of association, compared to the results of core group analysis of diastolic blood pressure at 2 weeks: now the group of inmates raised in a rural setting shows the lowest blood pressure, compared to the 2-week data when they showed the highest blood pressure mean. Remembering that these core group analyses utilize the initial blood pressure level as covariate, this reversal of association may be interpreted as follows: inmates from rural backgrounds had initially a greater difficulty in adapting to the prison environment and tended to show a greater increase between initial and 2-week data. By 1 month, however, the data may begin to reflect longer term adaptation and the men of rural background appear to be adapting better: their blood pressure levels at 1 month are lower than the men's from more urban background. Later analyses (described later) show that the differences between urban and rural men get even bigger with longer stay in prison.

TWO-MONTH INTERVIEW

Systolic Blood Pressure

Entire Group.   The analysis was based on 314 men with complete data for those variables of interest. The final regression model, significant at the $< .0001$ level ($F = 15.72$, $df = 4$), accounted for 16.91% of the variance in systolic pressure, and contained terms for age, recidivism, hours per week spent exercising, and CIES social support scale scores. The grand mean was 116.00 mmHg.

First time offenders continue showing higher blood pressure means than recidivists (a difference of 3.30 mmHg, $p < .01$). In addition, higher systolic blood pressure levels were seen among inmates who: (a) spent fewer hours exercising per week ($p < /001$), and (b) had stronger initial expectations of social support from fellow inmates ($p < .07$).

Core Group.   The final model was computed for the 165 inmates of the core group. The only variable significantly predicting systolic pressure that was seen in both this and the associated entire group analysis was time spent each week exercising. Additional significant variables included: whether or not the inmate had any children, smoking history, housing mode, and hours spent "taking it easy." The model accounted for 50.86% of the variance in mean systolic pressure and was significant at the $< .0001$ level ($F = 15.94$, $df = 10$). The grand mean was 115.84 mmHg.

Men who spent more time exercising and less time "taking it easy" had lower blood pressure ($p < .01$ and .10, respectively). Systolic blood pressure continued to be higher for men who had children. The current smoking history data showed that non-smokers had higher blood pressure values. Because several other analyses (discussed later) persist in showing the non-smokers to have somewhat higher blood pressure values, we may assume that this is not a chance relationship. Because ponderal index is always entered in the prediction, the possibility that smokers weigh less is not a tenable explanation. A tentative suggestion of this association is that smoking is an additional source of tension reduction in the prison setting, but it is obviously a coping mechanism only available to the current smokers. Cigarettes are also used as the medium of the inmates informal barter system and may facilitate communication and personal relationships between inmates. The data on housing mode continue to show the same relationship seen at 1 month: men remaining in individual cells have lower blood pressure values, particularly so in contrast to the results on men in protective custody and in the work release dormitory. The longitudinal analyses of blood pressure changes with respect to housing mode have already been presented in chapter 8.

Diastolic Blood Pressure

Entire Group.   The final model for mean diastolic pressure at two months was significant at the $< .0001$ level ($F = 27.88$, $df = 3$) and explained 20.52% of the diastolic pressure variability. Terms for age, recidivism, and hours per week spent exercising were included in the model. The grand mean was 72.89 mmHg, and the analysis was conducted using the 327 men with complete data for the variables of interest.

These findings are by now familiar to us. First time offenders and those who spent fewer hours exercising continued to show higher blood pressure levels ($p < .03$ and $p < .04$, respectively).

Core Group.   When the independent variables were evaluated on the core of 165 men, a more complex model emerged that was quite different from the entire group analysis. It contained age, smoking history, frequency of furloughs, number of residential changes since age 10, perceptions of the inmate's residence, time spent outside of residence and on reading books and magazines, and anxiety measured by the adjective checklist. The final regression model was significant at the $< .0001$ level ($F = 12.02$, $df = 12$) and accounted for 48.68% of the variance in diastolic pressure. The grand mean was 72.33 mmHg.

Higher diastolic blood pressure was observed to be related to: (a) fewer residential changes since age 10 ($p < .04$), (b) fewer hours spent each day outside the inmate's residence ($p < .06$) and lesser frequency of furloughs ($p <$ .001), (c) fewer hours spent reading books and magazines ($p < .04$), (d) more negative perceptions of residence ($p < .05$), and (e) self-reports of higher anxiety on the adjective checklist ($p < .01$). In addition, current non-smokers were again observed to have higher blood pressure, compared to all other groups of smokers ($p < .01$).

THREE-MONTH INTERVIEW

Systolic Blood Pressure

Entire Group.   The final regression model was based on 297 of the available 299 inmates for whom complete data existed regarding the variables of interest. The grand mean was 116.48 mmHg and the final model, significant at the $< .0001$ level ($F = 11.94, df = 6$), explained 19.80% of the variance in systolic blood pressure at the 3-month stage.

Housing mode continued to make a strong impact on blood pressure levels: men in single cells had, on the average, 6.98 mmHg lower blood pressure compared to men in protective custody, dormitory and work release combined ($p < .0001$). Negative perceptions of residenced also continued to have a strong impact on raising blood pressure levels ($p < .0001$). In addition, blood pressure levels were somewhat lower among those who spent more time listening to the radio ($p < .03$).

Core Group.   The analysis was based on the 116 men with complete sets of data from the initial interview through the 3-month stage. The regression model was significant at the $< .0001$ level ($F = 6.32, df = 12$) and explained 42.42% of the variance in systolic pressure. Terms were included for length of stay at last residence, childhood residence, whether the inmates had any children, hours per week spent exercising, perception of the inmate's residence and hours per week spent reading books and magazines. The grand mean was 115.67 mmHg.

The findings here are mostly those we have already encountered. Higher levels of systolic blood pressure were found associated with (a) longer stay at last place of residence ($p < .05$), (b) having children ($p < .05$), (c) spending fewer hours exercising ($p < .03$) or reading books and magazines ($p < .09$), and (d) reports of more negative perceptions of residence ($p < .006$). In addition, the more urban the place of childhood residence, the higher the blood pressure ($p < .05$). This last finding was first noted in the 1-month core group analysis of diastolic blood pressure and represents a reversal of association observed for the 2-week diastolic blood pressure data.

Diastolic Blood Pressure

Entire Group.   At 3 months of incarceration, the final model explaining 25.19% of the variance in diastolic pressure, contained terms for age, ponderal index, perception of the correctional institution, housing mode, childhood residence, and whether the inmate's parents were alive and present when he was a child. Two hundred and ninety-five men had complete data for these six variables of interest at this time, and the grand mean was 72.86 mmHg. The overall model was significant at the $< .0001$ level ($F = 7.91$, *df* $= 12$).

Concordant with the previous findings, mean diastolic pressure was higher with more negative feelings about the prison environment ($p < .01$). Other familiar findings include the lower blood pressure means for inmates staying in single cells ($p < .01$) and those whose childhood home was in a rural setting ($p < .01$). The new association observed in this analysis involves presence of parents in the home when the inmate was growing up: In comparison to men whose parents were both alive and present, men whose fathers had died had lower diastolic blood pressure and men whose mothers had died had higher blood pressure. Because this is an association which is both difficult to interpret and not seen in any other analyses, it is possible that it represents a random relationship; the overall association is of borderline significance ($p = .06$).

Core Group.   Based on the 116 men with complete data for all variables of interest from the initial interview through the 3-month stage of the study, a final regression model was obtained that contained terms for initial mean diastolic pressure, childhood residence, and hours per week spent exercising. This model, significant at the $< .0001$ level ($F = 11.41$, *df* $= 5$), accounted for 34.16% of the variance in mean diastolic pressure at this time point. The grand mean was 71.55 mmHg.

The associations with childhood residence and exercising are now familiar and need no additional comment.

FOUR-MONTH INTERVIEW

From the 4-month interview on, only analyses based on the entire group of men are presented. The size of the core group had become so small by 4 months that further analyses were not justifiable.

Systolic Blood Pressure

The final regression model obtained for mean systolic pressure was significant at the $< .0001$ level ($F = 8.33$, *df* $= 6$) and was based on 220 men with complete data for the variables of interest. Age, number of times previously in jail, smoking history, and whether the inmate had any children were included in the final model. The grand mean was 117.83 mmHg, and the correlates observed to be significantly associated with mean systolic blood pressure together explained 19.01% of the variance in the dependent variable.

Mean systolic pressure was observed to be inversely associated with the number of times the inmate had previously been imprisoned ($p < .0005$). This is, of course, consistent with the previously noted higher blood pressure levels among first-time offenders. The other two findings are also replications: the higher blood pressure values for men who have children ($p < .0001$) and who are currently non-smokers ($p < .05$).

Diastolic Blood Pressure

The model contained three terms that were just noted with systolic pressure: age, smoking history, and whether the inmate had any children. Significant associations with education, and frequency of outside visitors were also observed. The model was based on 222 men with complete data concerning these six variables of interest, and accounted for 33.7% of the variance in diastolic pressure. The model itself was significant at the $< .0001$ level ($F = 8.84$, $df = 12$). The grand mean was 73.68 mmHg.

The already familiar findings are those involving education, smoking history, and presence of children. The new finding involves frequency of outside visitors, that is, visitors who were neither family nor friends: the greater the frequency of such visits, the higher the diastolic blood pressure observed ($p < .007$). It may be supposed that although visits by family or friends can be either a source of additional pressures or a source of support and relief, visits by those who are neither friends nor family are likely to be mostly an additional source of pressure and tension. Such visitors were usually attorneys, clergy, former employers, or social workers. The fact that this relationship was not observed until the fourth month may suggest both that such visits are very infrequent earlier and that not until close to release do they come to represent a new source of tension.

FIVE-MONTH INTERVIEW

Systolic Blood Pressure

At this late stage, data on only 164 men were available for analysis. The final model included only three variables and accounted only for 8.79% of the variance ($F = 3.05$, $df = 5$, $p < .02$). The grand mean was 117.09 mmHg. The findings continued to show that men in single cells had lower blood pressure levels than men in all the other housing modes ($p < .01$). Two other, marginally significant ($p < .10$), associations showed higher blood pressure levels to be associated with more negative perceptions of the residence and with fewer hours spent sitting and thinking.

Diastolic Blood Pressure

Only three variables entered the final model, and two of these were age and ponderal index. The analysis on 163 men accounted for 15.28% of the variance and the grand mean was 72.78 mmHg. The one finding of potential interest was the somewhat lower blood pressure for inmates reporting frequent (i.e., daily) use of the telephone ($p < .06$). We have noted earlier, however, that the association between blood pressure levels and telephone use seems to flip-flop, suggesting either a chance (unreliable) association, or some complex dynamics that change over time.

SIX-MONTH INTERVIEW

Systolic Blood Pressure

At this point, the final regression model was based on data from 142 inmates. The model accounted for 8.26% of the variance ($F = 4.14, df = 3, p < .008$) and included only two variables: negative perceptions of the residence and reports of "desperate" financial problems were associated with higher blood pressure levels.

Diastolic Blood Pressure

The final regression model accounted for 37.34% of the variance ($F = 7.15, df = 11, p < .0001$) and included, in addition to age and ponderal index, six variables of interest. The grand mean was 73.57 mmHg.

Diastolic blood pressure was higher among men who (a) had been fewer times previously in jail ($p < .0001$), (b) viewed their residence more negatively ($p < .04$), (c) reported less depression ($p < .02$), and (d) spent fewer hours exercising ($p < .04$) and more hours taking it easy ($p < .02$). Weak associations with death of mother versus father during childhood and adolescence were also observed, the same as for the 3-month data.

The negative association with depression is of some interest. Even though anxiety, hostility, and depression are all moderately strongly positively intercorrelated, anxiety and hostility are positively related to blood pressure levels, whereas depression is negatively related. Unfortunately, the 6-month data on diastolic blood pressure are the only ones showing the significant association with depression (in contrast to the associations with anxiety and hostility, which were obtained several times), and it is thus possible that we are dealing only with a chance finding.

RELEASE INTERVIEW

Systolic Blood Pressure

Entire Group.   The release interview was similar to the monthly interviews, except for the addition of questions concerning future expectations and plans for residence and employment. As indicated in chapter 6, release interviews with 390 men were conducted; however, only 281 of these were men who had been initially interviewed as part of the usual intake procedure (i.e., between 1 and 7 days after their incarceration began). It should be obvious that because of the variable lengths of prison stays, the release interview is standardized with respect to the coming release but variable with respect to the initial interview. However, there are relatively few release interviews that come earlier than the schedule of 2-month interview.

The final model explained 21.68% of the variance ($F = 5.50$, $df = 8$, $p <$ .0001) and the grand mean was 116.41 mmHg. The three significant correlates (in addition to age) are rather difficult to interpret and the associations are somewhat at variance with previous results. Smoking history shows an overall association with blood pressure ($p < .02$), but the association now reveals the moderate smokers (< ½ packs/day) to have above average blood pressure, with the heavier smokers continuing to be below average. No satisfactory interpretation of this curvilinear association can be offered. The second blood pressure correlate shows that inmates who were growing up in families where at least one parent was missing (due to death or divorce/ separation) had higher blood pressure than those from intact families ($p <$ .003). This result is in agreement with the general hypothesis that growing up in a broken family setting renders one more vulnerable to later stresses of adulthood. However, earlier findings with diastolic blood pressure were somewhat different and seemed to call for a more complex interpretation. Finally, the results show a negative association ($p < .03$) between hours spent going for walks and blood pressure; this is in agreement with previous results showing the benefits of one or another form of physical activity.

Diastolic Blood Pressure

Entire Group.   The final regression model was significant at the .0001 level ($F = 12.23$, $df = 7$) and explained 24.01% of the variance in mean diastolic blood pressure. Terms for the National Center for Health Statistics psychophysiologic symptom checklist for anxiety, amount of time spent listening to the radio, and childhood residence were included in the final model (in addition to age and ponderal index). The grand mean was 73.05 mmHg.

Inmates who grew up in a rural setting continue to show increasingly lower diastolic blood pressure than the other groups of inmates ($p = .05$). In addition, the men who spent more time listening to the radio had somewhat lower blood pressure ($p < .02$). The one new finding, which is highly significant ($p < .0001$) and accounts for about 6.0% of the variance, is the association with the NCHS scale measuring psychophysiological symptoms of anxiety, such as headaches, sweaty palms, and sleeplessness. Men who are more anxious just before release (and whose anxiety manifests itself in psychophysiological symptoms rather than mood and affect) show higher diastolic blood pressure. We have previously seen that among men who change residence from cell to dorm, an increase in psychophysiologic symptoms of anxiety is associated with an increase in systolic blood pressure.

10 Time Trends in Inmate Activities and Perceptions

INTRODUCTION

This chapter describes over time the trends in inmate activities and relationships, perceptions, leisure, housing, job details and work release programs, and communications with persons outside the prison including family, friends, and others.

A few points should be repeated to orient the reader about the content and organization of the relevant data: (a) The chapter does not concern itself with data from the first interview. That information is contained in chapter 7. Furthermore, nothing can be said about inmate activities, leisure, work, and communication because, at the first visit, no such events have occurred. (b) Both the number and composition of the inmate body were somewhat different at each time of data collection. Thus the results presented here indicate trends in mean values over time and do not provide specific data on changes in a single inmate or in an unchanging group of inmates in prison for the same length of time. Such data are considered in chapter 9. (c) The release interview comes at the end of a stay of variable length and cannot be placed in any particular temporal sequence with respect to the other interviews. However, only a very few release interviews were conducted before the 2-month interview.

The results described here are all tabulated in Appendix E.

Inmate Activities and Relationships

Early in the prison stay, at the 2-week interview, the men spent an average of 9.4 hours per day outside their cells or dormitories. This period includes meal times, time spent with visitors or counsellors, leisure, and in a few cases, work release programs. Almost all work release experience began later. The daily average of time spent outside the cells declined somewhat through the first 4 months and rose slightly at the fifth- and sixth-month interviews with a small drop at the release interview. Familiarity with other inmates showed a somewhat different trend, beginning with a mean of 21 other inmates known well enough to talk to at 2 weeks, rising steadingly through the fifth month, and dropping a bit thereafter. This change is what one would expect. The longer one remains an inmate, the more fellow inmates one knows until, as release draws near, attention begins to be directed toward the outside and inmate relationships become less important. Because some inmates have sentences of only 3 or 4 months, those with longer sentences are likely to show a drop in number of inmates known toward the end of their sentence.

Frequency of social contact among inmates is highest at 2 weeks, drops down somewhat and then varies little after that. This may reflect the fact that early in the sentence, an inmate makes a number of contacts, then selects his friends and has more stable relationships with these friends thereafter. Toward the end of the sentence, the number of inmates known falls as friends are released, but the frequency of social contact changes little. This suggests more frequent contact with friends as release draws near.

Mood, Symptoms, and Perceptions of the Prison Setting

The mean anxiety self-report is relatively high at 2 weeks, falls rather regularly thereafter, and increases at the release interview, presumably as thoughts being to be redirected toward home, family, friends, jobs, and the problems of dealing with them all again. Hostility scale scores are relatively constant from 2 weeks to 5 months and rise a little at the 6-month and the release interviews. Presumably, an inmate gets angrier and more impatient at the prison and its personnel or feels freer to admit it as a release approaches. The depression scale score means are lowest at 2 weeks, a little higher but rather constant from the first to the fourth month and increase slightly at the fifth, again at the sixth month, and at the release interview. The changes in mean scores on the NCHS symptoms of psychophysiological distress scale show a somewhat different pattern increasing by small amounts from 2 weeks to 6 months with a slight drop at release.

Thus, there is a similarity in time trends on measures of anxiety, hostility, and depression and a reciprocal change in number of inmates known well enough to talk to. At the sixth-month interview, measures of hostility and depression have increased a little and number of inmates known has decreased. These trends all continue at the release interview at which time the anxiety score increases moderately. NCHS scale scores have a different trend perhaps because the symptoms associated with anxiety that it assesses are differentially perceived or reported than feelings of being worried or anxious.

Perceptions of the institution become somewhat more positive, going from the 2-week to the 3-month interview. After that, they seem to stabilize at a somewhat more negative level. Perceptions of residence become considerably more positive between the 2-week and 1-month interviews; beyond that, no specific trend is discernible. Perceptions of the guards show a rather steady decline toward more negative views: The 5-month interview data are an unexplained interruption of this overall trend. In general, it should be remembered that because housing and the guards encountered changed for most inmates at different times, it probably should not be expected that consistent group trends would be noted.

Leisure Activity

Changing patterns of leisure activity are clearer for some pursuits than for others. Hours per week spent watching television, hours per week listening to the radio and time working on hobbies show no consistent patterns or long-term trends. Hours per week reading books or magazines are highest at 2 weeks and generally decline thereafter. Hours per week "sitting and thinking" peak at the fourth month and decline after that. Hours per week taking it easy and hours per week going for walks in the enclosed prison courtyard show no pattern but there is a suggestion of diminution in amount of time spent exercising over the period of imprisonment. Overall there is a decline over time in the sum total of hours devoted to leisure pursuits, most notably in the latter half of the sentence and most clearly for reading, sitting, and thinking and exercising.

Housing

Changes in the proportion of inmates in the different housing modes shows a consistent and expected pattern. The proportion of inmates in cells is almost 100% at 2 weeks and about half that at time of release. Not unexpectedly there are reciprocal changes in occupancy of the other kinds of housing. The proportion of men in dormitories, about 1% at 2 weeks, rises to near 20% at 6 months, and drops a little by the release interview. The proportion of men in the work release dormitory, 0% at 2 weeks, climbs to nearly one third at release. There is an increase in proportion of men in protective custody and in the infirmary from the second week to the fifth month with a drop at the sixth-month and the release interviews. The proportion in protective custody and the infirmary never exceeds 11%. Men abused by other inmates because of the nature of their crime or their behavior are placed in protective custody, usually for their own safety.

Jobs

The proportion of men with a job detail ranges from about 64% to 81% but there is no specific pattern of change over time. The proportion of men on furlough increases regularly at each successive time of data collection, rising from less than 1% at 2 weeks to 66% of the men at release.

Communications with Family, Friends, and Others

Three categories of visitors were identified. The categories family and friends are self evident. Others or "outside visitors" in prison slang, are neither family nor friend but may be former employers, clergy, lawyers, social workers, or representatives of other agencies. The proportion of men with relatively frequent (weekly) family visitors was about 13% at 2 weeks, rose to a peak of some 37% at 3 months and declined steadily after that. At 6 months and at release, only about one quarter of the men reported weekly family visitors. The proportion of men with no family visitors starts at 26% at 2 weeks, dips a little and remains near 40% at the 6-month and release interview. Some of the men received family visitors only at monthly intervals and the changes in proportion of these men is naturally the reciprocal of the combined proportion of men with weekly or no family visitors.

The proportion of men with weekly visits from friends showed a trend nearly identical to that for family visits, beginning at 13% at 2 weeks, rising to about one third at 3 months, fluctuating at slightly lower levels thereafter. The proportion of men with no visits from friends was about 30% at 2 weeks, fluctuated around this level until the third month, and increased thereafter to near 45% at release. As with family visits, some friends came at monthly rather than weekly intervals. The trends for outside visitors were not dissimilar, starting at about 18% at 2 weeks, peaking near 40% at 3 months, and generally falling thereafter. Some 10% to 20% of men had no outside visitors at each time of data collection.

Almost all the inmates who used the phone did so daily. Phone use at wider intervals was unusual. The frequency of daily phone use was about 82% at 2 weeks, dropped to about 70% at 3 months and remained relatively stable thereafter. About 18% to about 25% of the men reported no phone use at each of the time periods.

The only subject of communication with family, friends, and others we asked about was presence or absence of financial problems. The first question dealt with inmates' perceptions that confinement did, or did not, cause his family financial difficulties. About one third believed that it did, and there was some tendency for more of them to reply affirmatively during later interviews. The second question asked about extent of financial problems experienced by the inmate's family. About half of them described their family's financial situation as "desperate," and there was a slight increase in this response over time.

Overall, these results suggest that a substantial majority of the men have some telephone or direct contact with family, friends, or others. But at each period of data collection, nearly one quarter have no phone contacts, less than half have weekly visits by friends or family, and one third or more of the men in prison for 6 months have no visits at all by family or friends. It is noteworthy that about 1 man in 2 admitting to financial problems described his family's financial plight as desperate at any one point in time throughout the sentence.

It is useful to compare change in these measures of inmate attitudes and behaviors over time in conjunction with the observation of Miller (1973). Miller undertook an insightful description of the sequence of adaptive processes used by young men during their imprisonment. His observations were based on contact with inmates as a prison psychiatrist at a medium security prison housing 525 youthful inmates. This was supplemented by a series of interviews with inmates, many just prior to release, and by conversations with other prison psychiatrists. He divided the sequence of stresses and problems into phases, and identified various modes of coping.

The "Initial" phase, occurring during the first 4 to 6 weeks of confinement in prison, Miller believes can be characterized by feelings of denial, often followed by depression, anxiety, and even panic. The inmate must deal with the issue of forceable restraint, separation, feelings of abandonment, and interpersonal disruption. He then begins an initiation process, turning his attention to the prison community. He is tested, harassed and closely observed, and, in coping with this process, begins to establish a role for himself.

The next or "middle" phase is one in which the inmate focuses most of his interest and energy on the prison community itself. He is intent on securing self-esteem, and the goods and services he requires. He assumes certain kinds of role behavior in order to protect himself and secure a degree of individual power, while building alliances and friendships with other inmates or groups of inmates.

The final, or "terminal" phase varies in duration depending on when the inmate is released. If an inmate serves all of his sentence, this phase begins about 6 weeks before his release. This tension–anxiety syndrome is known as the "short-time syndrome." The inmate experiences a return to consciousness of memories, thoughts, and feelings associated with his home community, in addition to contemplating the aspects of the prison community that have had an important impact on him. He is severing ties developed in the prison while anticipating reunion with family and friends on the outside. Concern with sexual problems may complicate this phase.

There are several similarities between our data and those of Miller. Early in the prison stay we observed higher scores on measures of anxiety, reports of smaller numbers of inmates known well enough to stop and talk to, and more solitary use of leisure. In the middle phase, we noted lower scores on measures of anxiety, more frequent visits, increase in the number of inmates known, more use of leisure and an increase in group leisure activities coupled with decreases in solitary leisure pursuits. Toward the end of the sentence self-reports of anxiety, hostility, and depression increase while leisure activity and number of inmates known decrease.

11 Health Status of Inmates of Billerica

The availability of the medical record data collected by the prison physician and nurses provided us with an opportunity to compare the health of this inmate population with other groups of prisoners and with the general population. We were also able to examine the inmates' use of the local medical facilities.

MEDICAL RECORD DATA

Data regarding the medical variables were obtained from the records of the medical department of the prison. A part-time physician, a full-time head nurse, and several part-time nurses comprised the personnel of this department. They performed physical examinations and obtained health histories upon admission for all inmates, and provided care at the prison infirmary for most complaints and problems. They also coordinated consultations with specialists and monitored hospitalizations. They utilized standard forms and procedures to record this information for every inmate from date of entry to the prison to date of release. Sick call was conducted every morning except weekends and holidays, and all inmates were offered the opportunity to attend.

The physical examination was the physician's clinical assessment of the inmate's current state of health. It consisted of 21 items (e.g., chest, heart, and back) which reviewed the status of 10 organ systems. The physician used auscultation, palpation, and other routine techniques to conduct the examination. The organ system was classified as abnormal if one or more of the items describing it were assessed by the physician as abnormal. For the purpose of analyses reported in this chapter, a scale measuring "objective" health status at intake was then formed by additively combining with equal weighting the number of abnormal systems and dividing by the total number of systems reviewed.

The health history was a self-reported list of current or past medical complaints. In this section, the physician asked the inmate if he had had any of 68 health problems (e.g., chronic cough, heart murmur, or chronic back pain), which collectively described 16 organ systems. The organ system was rated as abnormal if one or more items describing it were considered by the inmate as abnormal. A scale assessing "subjective" health status was then constructed additively combining with equal weights the number of abnormal systems by history and dividing by the total number of systems reported.

A third scale was developed to assess concordance between subjective and objective health status. The eight organ systems common to the physical examination and the health history were examined, and the proportion of abnormal systems were calculated for each. The score on the objective index was then subtracted from the score on the subjective one to obtain the difference between self-rated health status and physician assessment. A positive score indicated that the inmate's perception of the number of his health problems exceeded the physician's estimate ("over-reporting"), whereas a negative score suggested that the inmate reported fewer health conditions than the physician ("under-reporting").

The International Classification of Diseases – Clinical Modifications (ICD-9-CM) was employed to code diagnosis and, when appropriate, the cause of injury (United States National Center for Health Statistics, 1978). The guidelines of the American Hospital Formulary Service (AHFS) were followed to code medications by their primary pharmacologic actions (McEvoy, McQuarrie, & Douglas, 1979). The NCHS reason for Visit Classification System was also used for coding other types of treatments or tests. Their definition of a chronic condition was adopted, i.e., a condition that has existed for 3 months or more, or one of a list of conditions (including heart disease, cancer, epilepsy, and mental illness) regardless of reported duration. Multiple reasons for visit, diagnoses, causes of injury, medications, and other forms of treatments or tests were coded in descending order to severity of the disorder.

Data on in-patient hospitalizations were recorded. Noted were date of admission, diagnosis, whether the hospitalization was initial or follow-up, whether the condition was acute or chronic and new or pre-existing, surgical or other procedures conducted, and date of discharge. The methods discussed in the coding of ambulatory care services were followed: (a) the

ICD–CM was used to code diagnosis and surgical or other procedures, (b) the NCHS definition of a chronic condition was employed, and (c) multiple diagnoses and multiple surgical or other procedures were coded in descending order of significance.

Prevalence estimates for conditions at intake, which are the initial focus of concern, were based on the physician's clinical assessment and the inmate's self-reported health history. An inmate may deny a health problem identified by the physician, or he may report a condition that had been resolved by the time of the examination. These concerns were minimized by eliminating from the health history problems that are unlikely to leave detectable residual effects and by eliminating from the physical examination conditions that are commonly asymptomatic. The result was a pragmatic attempt to ascertain a potentially important dispositional factor, reporting of health conditions.

The numbers of previous operations and hospitalizations were also ascertained upon admission. In addition, each inmate told the physician his family and social histories. The former dealt with the number of first-order relatives with specific diseases or conditions (e.g., tuberculosis, diabetes, and high blood pressure). Specific conditions included alcohol and drug use and smoking behavior.

The form that was developed to abstract information regarding infirmary visits and any other ambulatory-care service shows date of visit, reason for visit, diagnosis, whether the visit was initial or follow-up, whether the condition was acute or chronic and newly diagnosed or pre-existing, the cause of injury (if relevant), the number of days of bed disability, the number of days of restricted activity outside of bed, medication dispensed, and any other treatment provided or tests conducted.

Reason for visit was defined as the inmate's self-expressed complaint or problem, and was coded according to the Reason for Visit Classification System of the National Center for Health Statistics (NCHS, 1979). This system was developed for use in the National Ambulatory Medical Care Survey, and utilizes a modular format for classifying reasons for visit as symptoms, diseases, injuries, tests, or treatments.

The inmate was the unit of analysis for the study of prevalence of health conditions at intake. The analytic unit for the investigation of health problems presented during imprisonment, however, was the infirmary visit. In other words, each visit was tallied to determine the total number of visits made by the entire cohort during the study period, and these visits were partitioned according to the characteristic of interest. This procedure conforms to the methods used by NCHS to report the results of the National Ambulatory Medical Care Survey (NCHS, 1980).

A similar analysis of in-patient hospitalizations while incarcerated was conducted. The number of hospitalizations was examined by primary diagnosis, initial or follow-up, acute or chronic problem, newly diagnosed or pre-existing condition, therapeutic procedures administered, and length of stay.

The study population for this chapter consisted of the 366 inmates who were interviewed within a week of their admission to the prison, remained in prison for at least 1 week, and did not refuse to continue with the study after it began or die in prison. One-way frequency and percentage distributions, together with other descriptive statistics, were employed as the chapter's primary statistical techniques. Missing data may result in some tables totalling less than 366 inmates.

RESULTS

Health Conditions at Intake to the Institution

Table 11.1 presents the number and percent of inmates with selected abnormalities at intake according to the physician's assessment. The median number of organ systems with abnormalities was one. The range was from

TABLE 11.1
Number(N) and Percent(%) of Inmates
with Selected Abnormalities at Intake
According to Physician Assessment

	N	$\%$
Oral Cavity	115	31.7
Musculo-skeletal	28	8.0
Extremities	18	5.1
Joints	6	1.7
Back	4	1.2
Eyes, Ears	27	7.5
Eyes	20	5.5
Ears	8	2.2
Skin	23	6.5
Cardiovascular	17	4.7
Heart	16	4.4
Respiratory	14	3.9
Chest	5	1.4
Genito-urinary	11	3.1
Digestive[a]	10	2.8
Viscera	9	2.6
Neurologic	4	1.2
Other	4	1.2
None	170	48.3

[a]Other than oral cavity.

zero to three organ systems. Nearly one half had no health problems according to the physician, whereas 15.9% had abnormalities of two or more organ systems. Dental, gingival, peridontal, and other diseases of the oral cavity were the most prevalent disorders, with almost one third of all inmates suffering from these conditions.

The number and percent of inmates who reported a history of selected health conditions at intake are given in Table 11.2. The median number of organ systems with abnormalities was three. The range was from zero to 11 organ systems. Only 8.8% reported no health problems, whereas 28.4% had abnormalities of five or more organ systems.

Psychologic problems and trauma were the most frequently cited conditions. Each was reported by over one half of the inmates. More than one third had respiratory problems, 29% reported a history of serious infectious diseases, and musculoskeletal problems were noted by 26.4%.

The admission medical data also indicated that the median number of pre-

TABLE 11.2

Number(N) and Percent(%) of Inmates with Past History of Selected Health Conditions at Intake According to Self-Report

Health Condition	N	%	Health Condition	N	%
Psychologic	184	52.7	Frequent dizziness	30	8.5
Frequent anxiety	138	39.4	Epilepsy or seizures	19	5.4
Frequent insomnia	100	28.5	Digestive	86	24.4
Frequent depression	76	21.9	Frequent indigestion	27	7.8
Attempted suicide	27	7.8	Ulcers	24	6.8
Trauma	183	52.4	Cardiovascular	77	21.9
Broken bones	144	40.9	Frequent chest pain	25	7.1
Stab or gunshot wound	79	21.9	High blood pressure	19	5.4
Head injury	72	20.2	Heart murmur	18	5.1
Respiratory	126	35.8	Eyes, Ears	71	20.1
Pneumonia	42	11.9	Visual difficulties	33	9.4
Asthma	33	9.4	Hearing difficulties	30	8.5
Chronic cough	30	8.5	Allergies	71	20.1
Frequent difficulty breathing	27	7.8	Medication	52	14.3
Infectious	102	29.0	Food, dust, pollen	31	8.7
Hepatitis	67	18.9	Neoplasms	33	9.4
Gonorrhea	36	10.1	Genito-urinary	20	5.7
Syphilis	13	3.6	Kidney stones	11	3.1
Tuberculosis	10	2.8	Frequent skin problems	18	5.1
Musculo Skeletal[a]	93	26.4	Diabetes mellitus	12	3.4
Chronic back pain	33	9.4	Anemia	1	0.3
Frequent foot problems	23	6.6	Other	61	17.3
Arthritis	20	5.7	Large weight gain or loss	20	5.7
Neurologic	88	25.6	Nights sweats	10	2.8
Frequent headache	64	18.1	None	31	8.8

[a]Other than trauma.

vious hospitalizations per inmate was one. Values ranged from zero to 11 hospitalizations. Nearly 27% had never been hospitalized, and 16.8% were hospitalized three or more times before they were imprisoned. The median number of operations was also one per inmate, with 46.7% reporting none and 3.6% three or more operations. The maximum was 13 operations. Nineteen percent reported a family history of heart disease, 15.1% a family history of high blood pressure, and another 15.1% a family history of diabetes. Alcoholism was reported as a condition among family members of 14.5% of the inmates, cancer 11.0%, asthma 9.6% and psychologic disorders 9.3%. Almost 36% of the inmates were self-admitted alcoholics, and 8.1% of the others said that they were "heavy" drinkers. Over 85% were current cigarette smokers, and they had smoked an average of 1½ packs per day for 10 years. Barbiturates were used by 60.5%, amphetamines by 60.3%, heroin by 51.2%, and other narcotics by 50.0%.

Health Problems During Imprisonment

The cohort of 366 men visited the infirmary a total of 3,974 times. Two or more reasons were listed for 1,286 visits (32.4%), and three or more reasons were given for 348 visits (9.0%). The average was 1.41 reasons per visit.

The number and percent of these visits by NCHS module and primary reason for visit are displayed in Table 11.3. Over one half of the visits were for symptoms. The most common were respiratory symptoms (14.8%), including head cold (5.5%), nasal congestion (4.2%), and sore throat (2.4%). Injuries and adverse effects of medications was the second most frequent module (18.5%). Twelve infirmary visits were for injuries considered by the prison staff to be self-inflicted and suicidal. More than 15% of the visits were treatment-related. The most common of these therapeutic visits, and, in fact, the most frequent of all single reasons for a visit was "psychotherapy" (10.8%).[1] Specific diseases were the reason for 9.8% of the visits. They were most frequently infectious diseases (3.1%) of a fungal (1.5%) or parasitic (0.9%) nature. The Diagnostic, Screening, and Preventive Module was given as the reason for 4.3% of the visits. Less than 1% of the visits were classified under the Test Results Module.

The majority of visits (56.9%) were primarily initial visits for a given illness episode, compared to 43.1% for follow-up visits. Over 63% of the infirmary visits were primarily for acute conditions, and a similar proportion (64.7%) were primarily for newly diagnosed disorders. The great majority (96.8%) of visits were not associated with any bed disability. A similar finding was noted for number of restricted activity days outside the infirmary bed. Only 1.0% of the visits had 1 or more restricted activity days.

---

[1]These visits provided brief reassurance and an opportunity to ventilate but did not usually consist of a series of visits for psychiatric treatment.

TABLE 11.3
Number(N) and Percent(%) of Infirmary Visits by NCHS Module and
Primary Reason for Visit

Module and Primary Reason for Visit	N	%	Module and Primary Reason for Visit	N	%
Symptom module	2,043	51.4	Medication reaction	15	0.4
Respiratory	589	14.8	Treatment Module	609	15.3
Head cold	218	5.5	Pre- and post-operative		
Nasal congestion	167	4.2	care	20	0.5
Sore throat	96	2.4	Specific therapeutic		
Digestive	332	8.4	procedures	589	14.8
Toothache	68	1.7	Psychotherapy	430	10.8
Nausea	45	1.1	Dental procedures	86	2.2
Stomach	32	0.9	Suture insertion or		
Musculo-skeletal	237	6.0	removal	29	0.7
Backache	67	1.6	Dressing and		
Muscle pain, general or			bandaging	19	0.5
unspecified	66	1.6	Disease Module	392	9.8
Skin	212	5.3	Infectious	123	3.1
Rash	61	1.5	Fungal	59	1.5
Infection	39	1.0	Parasitic	37	0.9
Eyes, ears	135	3.4	Skin	74	1.9
Earache	61	1.5	Dermatitis	26	0.6
Earwax	28	0.7	Cellulitis	19	0.5
Eye infection	22	0.6	Psychologic	48	1.2
Psychologic	129	3.3	Alcoholism or drug		
Anxiety	54	1.3	addiction	43	1.1
Neurologic	85	2.1	Digestive	26	0.7
Headache	69	1.7	Ulcer	11	0.3
Genito-urinary	33	0.8	Neurologic	25	0.6
Infection	10	0.3	Migraine headache	16	0.4
Cardiovascular/			Respiratory	23	0.6
Lymphatic	11	0.3	Bronchitis	7	0.2
General	280	7.0	Hay fever	7	0.2
Infection, general or			Circulatory	20	0.5
unspecified	91	2.3	Hemorrhoids	15	0.4
Inflammation, general			Diagnostic, screening and		
or unspecified	45	1.1	preventive		
Pain, general or			Module	171	4.3
unspecified	32	0.8	Specific examination	88	2.2
Injuries and Adverse			Dental exam.	47	1.2
Effects Module	735	18.5	Eye exam.	33	0.8
Injuries	701	17.6	Diagnostic tests	83	2.1
Lacerations	130	3.3	Urinalysis	26	0.7
Sprains and strains	107	2.7	Blood tests	19	0.5
Contusions, abra-			X-rays	16	0.4
sions, bruises	91	2.3	Test Results Module	24	0.6
Burns	67	1.7	Tuberculosis test		
Suicide attempts	12	0.3	followup	15	0.4
Adverse Effects	34	0.9	Total	3,974	100.0

One or more medications were dispensed for more than three quarters of
the visits. Table 11.4 illustrates the number and percent of infirmary visits by
primary medication dispensed. Drugs with central nervous system effects
were the most frequently prescribed (23.0%). They included analgesics and
antipyretics (11.6%) like aspirin and other salicylates (8.0%), as well as
synthetic narcotics (2.3%). Psychotropic agents such as tranquilizers (5.4%),
antidepressants (4.7%), and sedatives (0.8%) were also dispensed. Anti-

TABLE 11.4
Number(N) and Percent(%) of Infirmary Visits by
Primary Medication Dispensed

Medication	N	%
Central Nervous System	915	23.0
Analgesics and antipyretics	459	11.6
Salicylates	317	8.0
Synthetic narcotics	91	2.3
Tranquilizers	216	5.4
Anti-depressants	185	4.7
Sedatives	32	0.8
Anti-infectives	632	15.9
Antibiotics (systemic)	601	15.1
Skin and Mucous Membrane	333	8.4
Antibiotics (topical)	114	2.9
Anti-inflammary (topical)	49	1.2
Fungicides	40	1.0
Antihistamines	304	7.6
Autonomic Nervous System	273	6.9
Skeletal muscle relaxants	199	5.0
Cholinergic blocking	53	1.3
Gastro-intestinal	150	3.8
Antacids	53	1.3
Emetics and anti-emitics	44	1.1
Cathartics and laxatives	30	0.8
Hormones	134	3.4
Adrenals	109	2.7
Insulins	15	0.4
Eye, Ear, Nose, and Throat	122	3.1
Antibiotics (topical)	53	1.3
Enzymes	64	1.6
Local anesthetics	23	0.6
Serum, Toxoids, and Vaccines	22	0.6
Tetanus toxoid	21	0.5
Expectorants and Cough	22	0.6
Vitamins	20	0.5
Cardiovascular	8	0.2
Other	4	0.1
None dispensed	941	23.7
Total	3,974	100.0

TABLE 11.5
Number(N) and Percent(%) of Infirmary Visits
by Primary Diagnostic Test or Therapeutic
Procedure Administered

Test or Treatment	N	%
Psychotherapy	430	10.8
Asepsis	220	5.5
Physical medicine	217	5.5
Dressing and bandaging	143	3.6
Dental procedures	86	2.2
X-Rays	61	1.5
Suture insertion or removal	54	1.4
Blood tests	45	1.1
Urinalysis	36	0.9
Minor surgery	34	0.9
Other	164	4.1
None adminstered	2,484	62.5
Total	3,974	100.0

infective agents were the second most common medication (15.9%), and were principally comprised of systemic antibiotics (15.1%). More than 8% of the visits resulted in the use of skin and mucous membrane medications, and antihistamines were prescribed in 7.6% of the visits.

One or more diagnostic tests or therapeutic procedures were employed for 37.5% of all visits. Table 11.5 presents the number and percent of visits by primary diagnostic test or therapeutic procedures. These data differ from those of Table 11.2 regarding the Treatment and Diagnostic, Screening, and Preventive Modules because the latter dealt with diagnostic tests or therapeutic procedures as reasons for the visit, whereas the former pertain to tests and procedures performed during the visit regardless of reason. The single most common was psychotherapy. More than 10% of all visits included this procedure. Injury-related treatments were also frequent, e.g., asepsis and debridement (5.5%), physical medical (5.5%), and dressing and bandaging (3.6%). Dental procedures like extractions, fillings, and cleaning were also performed (2.2%).

Twenty-four hospitalizations occurred among 20 members of the cohort during their incarceration. More than 70% were for chronic and pre-existing disorders. The average length of stay was 22 days. The number and percent of hospitalizations by diagnosis is given in Table 11.6. Almost one half were for mental disorders, notably schizophrenia (16.7%) and personality disorders (16.7%). Injury and poisoning accounted for one-fifth of the hospitalizations, whereas smoke inhalation was the most frequent subdiagnosis (8.3%). Musculoskeletal and genitourinary diseases explained 12.5% and 8.3% of the hospitalizations, respectively. Reflecting the most common diag-

TABLE 11.6
Number(N) and Percent(%) of Hospitalizations
by Diagnosis

Diagnosis	N	%
Mental Disorders	10	41.7
Schizophrenia	4	16.7
Personality disorders	4	16.7
Injury and Poisoning	5	20.8
Smoke inhalation	2	8.3
Musculoskeletal Diseases	3	12.5
Genito-urinary Diseases	2	8.3
Digestive Diseases	1	4.2
Circulatory Diseases	1	4.2
Blood Diseases	1	4.2
Infectious Diseases		4.2
Total	24	100.0

nosis, the most frequently employed hospital procedure was psychiatric mental status determination (43.5%). Other procedures included splenectomy, arthroscopy, and respiratory therapy.

The distribution of number of infirmary visits per inmate per 100 days was plotted and indicated unimodality with substantial skewing to the right (Fig. 11.1). A small number of inmates was responsible for a disproportionately high number of visits. An attempt was made to determine the effect on inmate visits of socio-demographic background, health status at intake, previous medical contact, personality characteristics, and environment. In almost all cases, the assessment of these variables was made within the first few days of imprisonment and antedating all or nearly all infirmary visits by the inmates. Table 11.7 indicates these relationships. A multiple regression analysis of infirmary visits was completed to identify the significant predictors of utilization of the infirmary.

Among all socio-demographic variables, only age (Table 11.7) successfully predicted infirmary visits in a negative direction. Younger inmates went to the infirmary more often. It should be noted that the method of analysis we employed adjusts simultaneously for the influence of other variables in the prediction, including the influence of health conditions. For a given level of previous health problems, younger inmates have more visits. Older inmates, of course, have more health problems. The more medical conditions identified by the physician at intake and the greater the number of previous hospitalizations, the greater was the number of infirmary visits. Men who overreported health conditions, i.e., those who believed their health was poorer than the physician did have relatively more visits also. Significantly more visits were also observed among those who were in prison for a shorter time and among men who subsequently were transferred or escaped. The data suggest that younger men and those who escaped or transferred might have used the

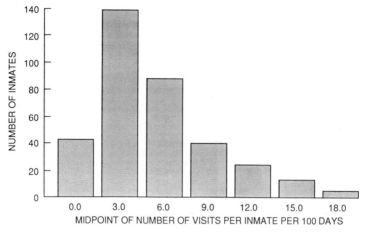

FIG. 11.1.   Distribution of number of infirmary visits per inmate for 100 days.

infirmary in part as a means of coping with the demands of their environment.

Medical utilization was also examined by month for the first 3 and last 3 months of imprisonment for men who were imprisoned for 6 or more months (Fig 11.2). The frequency of infirmary visits was highest during the first month and then declined significantly to a plateau that continued until discharge.

Only one other assessment had a time trend similar to that of infirmary visits. That is hours per week spent reading books or magazines. Anxiety scale scores, like infirmary visits, started high and then leveled off, but rose again at the release interview. Thus, for all but the last interview before release, anxiety, the solitary activity of reading and infirmary visits paralleled each other. All three, anxiety, reading, and infirmary visits may be considered as responses to the novel and threatening aspects of imprisonment. The levels are high initially and then decline as the prison became more predictable and understandable. The rise in anxiety at the release interview may not have been reflected in infirmary visits because the latter may have been perceived as delaying release. There is another plausible explanation. The release anxiety may have been clearly related in the inmates mind with the outside world and would not have required attempts to cope with the inside environment by such means as infirmary visits.

DISCUSSION

Comparisons with Other Prison Health Studies

These findings are generally in agreement with earlier descriptions of the health problems of inmates. However, differences in methodology render di-

TABLE 11.7
Multiple Regression of Total Number of Visits per Inmate per 100 Days
on all Independent Variables ($N = 325$)

	b	F	p	R²(%)
Sociodemographic				
Age	−0.0770	5.28	.022	1.24
Race		1.60	.207	0.38
Non-white–white	1.0035			
Nativity		0.59	.442	0.14
Foreign–native	0.7006			
Education	0.1709	0.67	.413	0.16
Religion		1.73	.179	0.82
Catholic–Protestant	0.9164			
Other–Protestant	−0.1030			
Marital status		0.26	.770	0.12
Previously–currently	−0.2026			
Never–currently	−0.4316			
Background				
Parental status		0.55	.652	0.38
One or both died–both alive	0.0966			
Divorced/separated–both alive	0.5603			
Other–both alive	−0.8061			
Childhood residence (urban/rural)	−0.0587	0.07	.734	0.02
Recidivism		0.12	.734	0.03
First-time offender–recidivist	−0.1426			
Health Status at Intake				
Physician assessment	16.2444	32.74	.001	7.71
Previous Medical Contact				
Number of previous hospitalizations	0.5345	16.77	.001	3.95
Personality				
"Over-reporting" of health conditions	3.8285	9.56	.002	2.25
Suppression of aggression	−0.5899	2.59	.109	0.61
Environmental				
Length of sentence	−0.0002	0.25	.615	0.06
Length of confinement	−0.0037	5.38	.021	1.27
Disposition		6.43	.002	3.03
Transferred	2.6105			
Escaped	0.3614			

Summary ANOVA

Source	df	Sum of Squares	Mean Square	F	p	R²(%)
Model	21	1494.48	17.17	5.76	.001	28.90
Error	303	3731.45	12.32			
Total	324	5225.93				

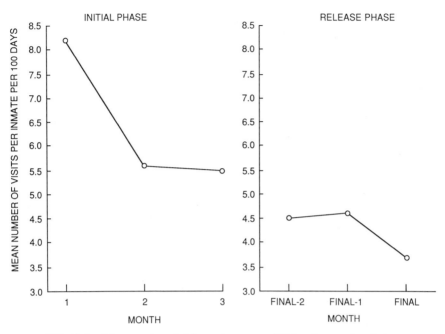

FIG. 11.2.   Mean number of visits per inmate per 100 days by month and phase.

rect comparisons among studies difficult, although the figure of 51.7% for inmates with at least one abnormality upon examination agrees closely with the 54% estimate by Novick and Al-Ibrahim (1977) for males. The rank ordering of the abnormalities according the frequency is also similar across studies. Disorders of the oral cavity were the most common problem in the Michigan (1975) and Derro (1978a) studies, and the second most frequent condition found by Novick and Al-Ibrahim (1977). The observed proportion of 31.7% may in fact be an underestimate because the examination was performed by physicians and not dentists. Dentists were employed in the Michigan research, and found that 96% of the men needed dental treatment excluding cleaning. The prevalences of some other abnormalities are very similar, e.g., 8.9% for musculoskeletal abnormalities compared to 8.6% for Derro's work (1978b), and 6.5% for skin abnormalities versus 5.8% for men in the Michigan study (1975).

Similarities are also apparent when health histories are compared. For instance, 91.2% of the inmates in this study reported at least one previous or current health condition, whereas the corresponding figure for the most recent AMA investigation was 90% (Modlin, 1979). Psychologic problems are ranked highly in other studies, but the observed frequency of 52.7% is exceeded only by the Michigan (1975) estimate of 83.8% for men. This difference may reflect the fact that in the current study, the health history asks about psychologic symptoms, whereas most other studies focus on psychiatric diagnoses. When comparable items are employed, comparable results are observed. For instance, 44.6% of inmates in the Derro (1978a) research scored high on the Zung Depression Index upon admission.

The figure of 52.4% for a history of trauma is higher than the estimates from other studies, but previous investigators have ascertained its prevalence differently. Derro (1978a) for example, has found that 25.2% of all medical care episodes in the year before imprisonment were for trauma. Novick and Al-Ibrahim (1977) have observed evidence of new trauma in 10% of the males examined and signs of old trauma in 14%. The frequencies of other disorders, however, are similar. For instance, the self-reported prevalence of epilepsy in Novick, Della Penna, Schwartz, Remmlinger, and Loewenstein's (1977) study (3.6% for males) approximates the 5.4% figure noted in the current study. The tuberulosis estimates were 1.8% and 2.8% respectively.

In general, the prevalences of health conditions or organ system abnormalities at intake were greater according to inmate self-report than physician assessment. This difference may be a simple function of the fact that the health history included more items and organ systems than the clinical assessment. The health history also measures lifetime prevalence, whereas the physician assessment deals with point prevalence. The former includes previous conditions which may have been resolved by the time of the examination, in addition to current problems; the former addresses only conditions presently evident. Self-report, of course, is subject to biases, but it serves as a useful adjunct to physician assessment and is the only way some types of information may be gathered.

The frequent history of alcohol and tobacco use corroborates the findings of other researchers. The 85% who reported that they currently smoke cigarettes is virtually identical to the 82% figure for males noted by the Michigan (1975) study. The findings that they have been smoking for an average of 10 years suggests that many started smoking when very young, because the mean age upon admission to prison was 25 years. The 36% who described themselves as alcoholics is greater than the 18% and 8.5% estimates of Novick, Della Penna, Schwartz, Remmlinger, and Loewenstein (1977) and the Michigan (1975) group, but is equal to Derro's (1978b) figure of 36.6% for "drinking problem," and is exceeded by the AMA's 50% "daily alcohol users" (Modlin, 1979).

No investigation, however, has reported drug-use prevalences as great as the 50% to 60% values observed in the current study. This difference may result from the fact that most other studies assess only drug addiction. Supporting this contention is the fact that Novick and Al-Ibrahim (1977) have found a drug abuse rate of 16% among male inmates, but when they asked for a history of illicit drug use (past or current), 41% responded affirmatively. The frequency of alcohol and drug use in this population of young

men may contribute to their relatively high prevalence of hepatitis and seizure disorders.

Similarities may also be discerned when comparing across studies the
health problems presented to prison medical staff by inmates after admission. The mean of 1.41 reasons per infirmary visit approximates the 1.23 estimate of Derro (1978b). When the data of Table 11.3 are reorganized by organ
system, the most frequent category is injury. Its value of 22.1% was obtained
by adding visits in the Injury and Adverse Effects Module to visits in other
modules that were for reasons that were injury-induced (e.g., dressing and
bandaging). Injury was also the most frequent complaint in Derro's study,
and this reason was the second most common condition in the work by
Young and Carr (1976). Their figures were 15.4% and 19.4%, respectively.

Respiratory symptoms and diseases were the second most frequent organ
system category in the current study, totalling 15.4%. They were the fourth
most common problem in the investigations by Derro (9.2%) and Young and
Carr (10.5%). Psychologic reasons ranked third in the present study. They
accounted for 15.3% of the visits when psychotherapy, psychologic symptoms, and psychologic diseases were combined. They were the most common
problem in Engebretsen and Olson's (1975) analysis, explaining more than
one third of the visits.

The hospitalization pattern paralleled that reported by Derro (1978b). In
his study, the two most common reasons for hospitalization were also psychiatric disorders and injury. The proportions were similar to those found in the
current study (respectively, 43% and 41.7% for psychiatric, and 29% vs.
20.8% for injury). Derro (1978b) has also reported family histories for diabetes, hypertension, and tuberculosis that approximate the estimates noted in
this investigation.

Other variables investigated in this chapter have not been examined previously by other studies. These include the results that most of the contacts
were initial visits for acute and newly diagnosed conditions. Only a small proportion of visits were associated with bed disability or restriction of activity,
indicating that most inmates were able to continue their daily routines without serious disruption.

Comparison with General Population Estimates

A comparison with data pertaining to the health status of the general population is also useful. The NCHS is an important source, although comparable
data do not exist for all the characteristics of interest. To improve the validity
of the comparison, estimates obtained during 1975 through 1978 (the years of
the current study) were used, unless otherwise noted. These figures are presented by age and sex when possible, because the prison population consisted
of young males.

Data from the National Health Interview Survey of NCHS (1977, 1979b) provide self-reported estimates of the prevalence of selected chronic diseases. For example, among men 17 to 44 years old, the prevalence of epilepsy was 3.6/1,000, diabetes 6.9/1,000, gastric or duodenal ulcer 23.0/1,000, and asthma 24.6/1,000 (235-237). These values are 2 to 20 times less than the estimates obtained in this study.

Levels of psychologic distress in the general population may be obtained from the National Health Examination Survey of NCHS (1970c). For men 18 to 24 years old, 43.4% stated they were anxious, and 20.4% had trouble falling asleep. The corresponding figures for men 25 to 34 years old were 47.5% and 16.7%. These values approximate the 39.4% and 28.5% estimates of the present investigation for the same two conditions (Table 11.2). The items from the former study, however, pertain to any experience of anxiety or insomnia in the respondent's lifetime, not recurrent or persistent problems. They would therefore produce greater prevalence estimates than questions assessing the occurrence of frequent anxiety and insomnia that was the procedure utilized in this study. A high level of depressive symptomatology was noted for 17.3% in the same survey (NCHS, 1980). Because this estimate was not presented by age and sex, however, comparisons with the 21.9% value for this study may not be valid.

The National Center for Health Statistics (1970b) has also conducted dental studies. Their results were presented not as the proportion with specific clinical diagnoses, but as the number of decayed, missing, or filled teeth per person, and in terms of a periodontal index. Direct comparisons with the findings of this study, therefore, are not possible. Dental treatment was nevertheless required for 76.9% of the males in the general population between 18 and 44 years of age. Nearly 25% of these persons needed cleaning only, in contrast to the Michigan (1975) estimate of 96% who required dental treatment excluding cleaning.

The prevalence of cigarette smoking among males 18 to 24 years old is 39.6% according to the National Center for Health Statistics (NCHS, 1970a). For men 25 to 34 years of age, 48.5% are current smokers. These values are one half the prevalence of 85% obtained in this study. Data concerning lifetime use of illicit drugs are available from the National Survey on Drug Abuse (Abelson, Fishburne, & Cisin, 1977). Their estimates for heroin, amphetamines, and barbituates were much lower than the 50% to 60% values for the current investigation, i.e., respectively 3.6%, 21.2%, and 18.4% for persons 18 to 25 years of age and 0.8%, 4.7% and 2.6% for those 26 years or older. A national survey of drinking practices and problems related to alcohol by Cahalan, Cisin, and Crossley (1969) has reported a rate of "heavy" drinking among men equal to 21%. "Heavy" drinkers included both problem drinkers and those suffering from the disease alcoholism. This value is one half the magnitude of the 44% estimate obtained in this study for prisoners who were self-admitted alcoholics or problem drinkers.

Methodologic differences limit the extent to which data from samples of the general population may be contrasted with the findings of this study. Prisoners are, on the average, of lower socioeconomic status than the national population. Differences may also exist in reporting tendencies between prisoners and non-incarcerated populations, resulting in biased comparisons. The magnitude of the discrepancies in prevalence, however, support the contention that these inmates use alcohol, tobacco, and illicit drugs more frequently than the general population, and that they suffer disproportionately from many health problems.

Information regarding characteristics of physician visits in the general population are available from the National Ambulatory Medical Care Survey of NCHS (1980). These data were transcribed by the physician or his staff onto specially prepared forms at the time of the visit. In contrast, the data for the present study were coded a posteriori from medical records. The comparison of results between the two studies is nevertheless a worthwhile endeavor, since both employ the same classification scheme (NCHS, 1980).

The Symptom Module was the most frequent reason for visit category in both studies. The estimate for men in the NCHS survey was 56.9%, versus 51.4% for the current investigation. The proportions for the Disease and Abnormal Test Results Modules were also similar (10.1% and 0.4%, respectively, for men in the general population, and 7.0% and 0.6%, respectively, for inmates). The Diagnostic, Screening, and Preventive Module, however, ranked second for men in the NCHS survey (12.6%), compared to fifth for the current study (4.3%). The reverse trend was noted for injuries and Adverse Effects, i.e., it was the second most common module for inmates (18.5%), whereas it ranked fifth for men in the general population (6.7%). Treatment-related visits were third in this study, accounting for 15.3% of all encounters, whereas they were fourth in the NCHS survey at 9.2%.

The most commonly presented health problems when reclassified by organ system among men in the general population were respiratory ailments. This was the second most frequent organ system category in the current study, and the respective proportions of 16.9% and 15.4% closely agree. Injuries were ranked third among males in the NCHS survey, with 10.9% of visits carrying that diagnosis. In contrast, they were the most common of all health problems among prisoners, at more than twice that of the national rate (22.1%). Other differences concerned the fact that visits for special conditions and examinations without sickness accounted for 12.7% of all visits for men in the NCHS survey, compared to almost no visits among the prison population. Only 4.3% of all visits for men in the general population were for psychologic problems, versus 15.3% for the current study. One should not interpret these data as indicating incidence (i.e., new conditions or problems), but they do illustrate some fundamental differences in reasons for ambulatory medical care between this prison population and the general community.

The prison medical staff apparently responded to this differential caseload by dispensing medication more frequently than other health-care providers (76.3% vs. 53.6% for the NCHS survey). This difference may reflect the fact that the former had proportionately fewer visits for preventive services. It may also be a result of the fact that the prison medical department controlled over-the-counter as well as prescription drugs. One may nevertheless speculate that the prison's medical staff depended on medication more heavily than community physicians because they lacked the resources for more extensive diagnostic and therapeutic procedures.

The prison study results also differ in other visit characteristics from the national study. For example, most physician visits among the general population were follow-up visits (59.8%), mostly for chronic conditions (50.6%). The reverse pattern was evident in this study of prison inmates. The fact that the population examined in this study was relatively young probably explains this discrepancy. More acute conditions are presented by younger persons, and visits for acute conditions are more likely to be initial visits.

12 Job-Related Stress Among Correctional Officers

It was not originally our intention to study the effects of the correctional environment on the prison staff. However, we changed our mind when some officers reported a good deal of interest in the study of inmates and indicated to us that the prison environment was difficult for the officers as well as for the inmates. As we became more familiar with prison personnel and their work and attitudes, we were able to identify with increasing clarity some problems of the officers. The purpose of this chapter is to describe the job-related problems expressed most often by prison personnel and the methods and results of a pilot study of the officers and staff in three corrections institutions.

GENERAL COMMENTS OF CORRECTIONAL OFFICERS AT BILLERICA

These comments are based on conversations between correctional officers and our chief interviewer, Eleanor Eliopoulos supplemented by our contacts with prison officials and officers.

Many, perhaps most, of the 59 correctional officers we surveyed at Billerica saw their jobs as entry level positions leading to careers in police, parole, and probation work. As the months and years went by and no such advancement occurred, there was increasing frustration and bitterness. Correctional staff was perceived by its members as divided into two groups, one owing its jobs and potential advancement to political patronage, the other having no such affiliation. Both groups came to believe, whether justified or not, that political support, rather than performance at work, determined career progress. Correctional officers without political support or inclination to establish such support felt isolated by those with such support, and there was rivalry, hostility, and jealousy.

Some officers reported that early in their employment they tended to be sympathetic toward inmates, only to be taken advantage of later. The daily jibes, curses, and taunts hurled by the prisoners remained a source of distress even among officers who thought of themselves as particularly tough.

The majority of correctional officers we encountered had profound conflicts about their jobs, their duties, and their proper behavior. They reported that much of their work is repressive and that they are required to enforce and perpetuate penal codes that offer only token rehabilitation services and a harsh prison environment. Society, they believe, does not want them to be lenient or humane officers but enforcers. However, society is quick to criticize them for enforcement. The prison administration is viewed as demanding strict enforcement but, for the sake of community relations, blames the harsher features of enforcement on its own staff and undercuts them by implying that the officers do not need to be so harsh with inmates.

Some correctional officers are torn between their role demands, which call for sternness and severity, and their need for acceptance as sensitive, humane individuals. They are sometimes embarrassed by their role but defiant and bitter about what they perceive as the public's ignorance and unwillingness to learn about that role. Correctional officers can usually accept the notion that their job of enforcement is not intended as an indignity to prisoners and that it is a job most of society believes is necessary, but they have difficulty understanding why society often mistrusts them and criticizes them when their job involves a risk to life for pay they regard as marginally adequate.

These comments made to us by prison personnel led us both to review the relevant literature on the social environment, the health, and mental health of correctional staff, and to carry out a pilot study in three institutions.

REVIEW OF LITERATURE ON PROBLEMS OF CORRECTIONAL STAFF

Most often reported among the problems of correctional staff are overcrowding and understaffing, role ambiguity and conflict, uncooperative inmates, lack of administrative support, physical threats, and the need for constant vigilance (Brodsky, 1977; Cheek & Miller, 1979; Hepburn & Albonetti, 1978, 1980; McCall, 1979; Poole & Regoli, 1980a; Thomas, 1974). The correctional officer carries out his duties in isolation and confinement, where his role is generally custodial, but still rather ambiguous. Other correctional staff, such as teachers, social workers, and health professionals may have better-defined roles, but their authority and status are unclear in the custody-oriented organizational hierarchy (Weber, 1957; Zald, 1962).

A national survey of state correctional institutions in 50 states and the District of Columbia revealed that in 1976, the average annual turnover rate for correctional officers was 27% (May, 1976). In New Mexico, the 1976 turnover rate was 65%, a statistic that may help explain the New Mexico prison riot of 1980. A study of New York State correctional staff found that their time off for disability was 300% higher than the state average (May, 1976) whereas in California, total disability payments for correctional officers would be sufficient to pay each active officer approximately $12,000 per year (Dahl & Thomas, 1979).

INTRODUCTION TO OUR STUDY OF PRISON STAFF

Because changes in blood pressure were serving successfully as non-self-report indicators of the effect of the prison environment on inmates, we undertook a pilot study to determine whether such changes served to illuminate interactions between the correctional staff and their environment. Basic demographic and work characteristics and before and after work blood pressures were recorded for prison staff in the same way as in earlier studies of inmates. We postulated that blood pressure measurements just before and near the end of the work day would allow for analysis of the impact of the work environment. It was hypothesized that two factors would be associated with larger increases in blood pressure during the work day; the degree of security in the institution and the job requirement of close contact with inmates. Maximum security institutions and close contact with inmates should be perceived by officers as threatening and uncertain, requiring great vigilance and maintenance of arousal and therefore leading to higher blood pressures on the job (Ostfeld & Shekelle, 1967).

METHOD

Study Settings

Data were collected from three institutions for men in Massachusetts. Concord is a maximum security state prison, Billerica is a medium security county facility, and New England Correctional Center (NECC) is a minimum security state farm. Most of the inmates at Concord were convicted of felonies or other serious crimes, and their behavior was closely monitored and controlled. They were allowed 2 hours per day outside of their cells for exercise and recreation. Men in Billerica were primarily convicted of misdemeanors and some were permitted to leave the facility for work release programs. Those participating in work release programs spent 10 to 11 hours per day outside of their cells. The inmates of NECC included men convicted of minor crimes, as well as those convicted of more serious offenses who had demonstrated "good behavior" in higher security level institutions where they had been previously incarcerated. Relatively little control was exerted over these inmates and they were allowed to go to and from their cells throughout the day.

Study Population

Every staff member from each of the three institutions was asked to volunteer for the study. The numbers who participated and participation rates were: Concord, 237 (90%); Billerica, 95 (91%); and NECC, 44 (92%). The study population was 89% male and 11% female, with a mean age of 35.5 years. The distribution by race was 93% whites, 7% non-white. The job category breakdown included 12% treatment staff, 32% service staff, and 56% custodial staff (i.e., guards or correctional officers).

PROCEDURE

Those who agreed to participate were interviewed in an administrative office immediately after arrival at work and punching in at the time clock, but before having contact with any inmates or attending to any work responsibilities. After the participant had been seated for a minimum of 5 minutes, blood pressure readings were taken in the same way as in the study of inmates. When hypertensive range blood pressures were found, the participant was notified and standard advice about consulting a physician was offered. Two blood pressure readings were taken at the beginning of the shift and repeated when the officer returned, 10 to 15 minutes before the shift ended some 8 hours later. The mean of the two pre- and the two post-blood pressure readings have been used in subsequent analyses.

Data collected at all three institutions included the participant's race, age, and job title, as well as measurements of height and weight. The staff of each institution were asked whether they had direct contact with inmates while on duty ("yes" or "no"), and shift assignment was also recorded ("Day – 8 a.m. to 4 p.m.," "evening – 4 p.m. to 12 a.m.," and "Midnight – 12 a.m. to 8 a.m.").

ANALYSIS

Two sets of multiple regression analyses were conducted, one for guards and one for correctional treatment, clerical, and service personnel. In the analysis for guards, change in blood pressure was the dependent variable, and inmate contact, institution, and shift were the independent variables. Age, race, and ponderal index were entered as covariates. Sex was not considered as all guards were men. The analysis for other correctional staff included change in blood pressure as the dependent variable, and institution, shift, sex, and job category as the independent variables. Again, age, race, and ponderal index were entered as covariates. The levels for job category were correctional treatment staff, and clerical, maintenance, and other non-professional and support staff. Correctional treatment staff had contact with inmates, the latter categories did not.

Parameters representing the main and interaction effects were estimated as if each were the last to enter the model, and they were assessed for statistical significance with partial F-tests (Draper & Smith, 1966). As a consequence, the main and interaction effects for one variable were adjusted simultaneously for the main and interaction effects of the others. Non-significant terms were deleted beginning with the three-way interaction to obtain a final model by using a backward elimination algorithm. Pairwise contrasts between groups were performed with two-tailed t-tests for independent samples after the partial F-tests to determine which mean blood pressure changes were different. Two-tailed t-tests for paired samples were used to determine if each mean change differed significantly from zero. The .05 significance level was employed, and SAS computer programs were used.

A parallel set of analyses were carried out in which an additional covariate was introduced into the multiple regression: the initial (pre-workday) value of systolic or diastolic blood pressure for each subject. This was done to adjust for possible systematic differences in initial blood pressure that could then influence blood pressure change. Because the results were substantially the same as those reported here, they are not presented in any detail.

RESULTS

Correctional Officers' Change in Blood Pressure by Institution, Inmate Contact, and Shift

Variables included in the final regression models of the guards' analysis are shown in Table 12.1A and 12.1B. The grand mean of 5.63 mmHg indicates that, on the average, systolic blood pressure increased during the work day among guards, and the increase was significantly greater than zero ($p <$ .001). The corresponding mean change for diastolic blood pressure was 3.02 mmHg ($p < $ .001).

The final regression models for systolic and diastolic blood pressure change each contained a significant main effect for institution ($p = $ .048 and $p = $ .026, respectively). The findings reveal that only the guards at Concord

TABLE 12.1A
Pre-Shift to Post-Shift Changes in Systolic Blood Pressure
Among Guards

			Mean Change		
		N	$\bar{x}$*	F	p
Ponderal Index				0.78	0.38
Age				0.02	0.89
Race				0.32	0.57
Contact with Inmates				0.29	0.59
No		11	7.66		
Yes		188	5.50		
Institution				4.27	0.02
Concord		124	6.36		
Billerica		59	5.82		
NECC		16	−0.75		
Shift				0.47	0.63
Day		90	7.54		
Evening		72	3.73		
Midnight		37	4.63		
Contact	Shift			2.53	0.08
No	Day	5	1.51		
No	Evening	5	13.07		
No	Midnight	1	12.09		
Yes	Day	85	7.89		
Yes	Evening	67	3.18		
Yes	Midnight	36	4.19		

*Subgroup means as predicted by the model. Observed
means are very similar.

and Billerica experienced a significant increase in blood pressure; those at
NECC showed a small, non-significant decrease. The ordering of the three
institutions from maximum to minimum security is reflected in the ordering
of the means in blood pressure changes. This would suggest that working in
higher security prison settings is more stressful for the guards and will be reflected in higher blood pressure increases at the end of the work day.

The main effects for Inmate Contact and Shift were not significant, but the
shift by contact interaction term was of borderline significance for systolic
blood pressure ($p = .066$). It is quite atypical for a guard to have no contact
with inmates and the small group of such guards could be an unrepresent-
ative, self-selected group (e.g., they applied for such jobs or were transferred
to them). Thus, the data on them are both unstable (small N) and difficult to
interpret. Aside from these reservations, however, Table 12.1A does suggest
that on a day shift, contact with inmates is associated with greater increase in
systolic blood pressure than no contact, whereas on the evening and night
shifts, the effect seems reversed.

TABLE 12.1B
Pre-Shift to Post-Shift Changes in Diastolic Blood Pressure
Among Guards

		Mean Change		
	N	$\bar{x}$*	F	p
Ponderal Index			1.05	0.31
Age			0.64	0.43
Race			0.01	0.93
Contact with Inmates			1.78	0.18
No	11	1.12		
Yes	188	3.11		
Institution			9.14	0.001
Concord	124	3.76		
Billerica	59	2.29		
NECC	16	−0.08		
Shift			0.40	0.67
Day	90	3.59		
Evening	72	2.72		
Midnight	37	2.12		
Contact Shift			0.37	0.69
No Day	5	0.71		
No Evening	5	2.47		
No Midnight	1	−0.52		
Yes Day	85	3.56		
Yes Evening	67	2.74		
Yes Midnight	36	2.28		

*Subgroup means, as predicted by the model. Observed
means are very similar.

Correctional Treatment, Service, and Clerical Staffs' Blood Pressure Changes by Sex, Institution, and Job Category

The models for systolic and diastolic blood pressure are shown in Table 12.2A and 12.2B, respectively. The grand mean for systolic blood pressure change was 5.13 mmHg ($p < .001$), and 2.19 mmHg for diastolic blood pressure ($p < .001$). Thus, this group of employees experienced a blood pressure increase during the work day that was of a similar magnitude as that for the guards.

The final regression models for systolic and diastolic blood pressure change each contained significant main effects for institution ($p = .044$ and $p = .024$, respectively) and job category ($p = .023$ and $p = .027$, respectively). The highest increase in blood pressure was again seen in the maximum security institution, Concord. The other two institutions showed small changes that were close to each other. With respect to job category, Tables

TABLE 12.2A

Pre-Shift to Post-Shift Changes in Systolic Blood Pressure
Among Correctional Treatment, Service, and Clerical Staff by
Demographic, Institution, and Job Characteristics

			Mean Change		
		N	$\bar{x}$*	F	p
Ponderal Index				0.22	0.64
Age				3.19	0.08
Race				0.26	0.61
Sex				0.48	0.49
Female		40	3.14		
Male		116	5.53		
Institution				4.78	0.01
Concord		105	6.75		
Billerica		33	1.92		
NECC		18	1.62		
Job Category				6.17	0.01
Rx†		41	6.48		
Clerical		115	4.36		
Sex	Job Category			9.08	0.001
Female	Rx	13	12.10		
Female	Service/Clerical	27	−0.05		
Male	Rx	28	4.54		
Male	Service/Clerical	88	5.89		

*Subgroup means, as predicted by the model. Observed
means are very similar.

†In this and subsequent tables the designation Rx means
treatment.

12.2A and 12.2B indicate that treatment personnel had a greater increase in
blood pressure than did the clerical and service personnel.

A significant interaction between sex and job category can also be seen in
Tables 12.2A and 12.2B. That is, the differential blood pressure increase
due to job category is seen only among females, whereas the males do not
seem to respond differentially in the two job categories.

An additional analysis was also undertaken to explore the possibility that
inmate contact was operating as an intervening variable and was responsible
for the association between job category and blood pressure change on the
job. The job category classification was strongly related to inmate contact,
because 93% of staff employed as treatment personnel had inmate contact,
compared to 60% for service workers. A multiple regression (Tables 12.3A
and 12.3B) that substituted inmate contact for job category among treatment
and service staff indicated that inmate contact was also a significant predictor of change in systolic blood pressure change ($p = .0037$) and marginally related to change in diastolic blood pressure change ($p = 0.557$). The sex

TABLE 12.2B
Pre-Shift to Post-Shift Changes in Diastolic Blood Pressure
Among Correctional Treatment, Service, and Clerical Staff by
Demographic, Institution, and Job Characteristics

			Mean Change		
		N	$\overline{x}$*	F	p
Ponderal Index				1.48	0.22
Age				1.55	0.22
Race				0.00	0.99
Sex				0.06	0.80
Female		40	1.41		
Male		116	2.33		
Institution				5.22	0.01
Concord		105	3.24		
Billerica		33	−0.27		
NECC		18	0.61		
Job Category				6.35	0.01
Rx		41	3.30		
Clerical		115	1.66		
Sex	Job Category			5.76	0.02
Female	Rx	13	6.01		
Female	Service/Clerical	27	−0.23		
Male	Rx	28	2.37		
Male	Service/Clerical	88	2.81		

*Subgroup means, as predicted by the model. Observed
means are very similar.

by contact interactions, however, became somewhat attenuated, compared
to the sex by job category interactions seen in Tables 12.2A and 12.2B.

The results in Tables 12.2 and 12.3 can be collapsed by creating three job
groupings: treatment, clerical/service with inmate contact, and clerical/
service without contact. Now, the nature of the interaction with sex becomes
clearer. Among women employees, inmate contact is associated with a size-
able increase in systolic and diastolic blood pressure when it is the context of
a treatment job; inmate contact in the clerical/service categories is associated
only with a modest increase, not much higher than for females with no inmate contact. Among male employees, the distinction between contact and
no contact makes less of a difference for differential increase in blood pressure, as does the distinction (within the group of male employees with contact) between treatment and clerical/service.

The re-analyses of Table 12.1–12.3, using initial (pre-work day) blood
pressure values as an additional covariate (together with age, race, and ponderal index) produced no major changes and can be summarized as follows:
(a) For Tables 12.1A and 12.1B, the effect of institution becomes more sig-

TABLE 12.3A

Pre-Shift to Post-Shift Changes in Systolic Blood
Pressure Among Correctional Treatment, Service,
and Clerical Staff by Demographic Characteristics,
Institution, and Contact with Inmates

		Mean Change		
	N	$\bar{x}*$	F	p
Ponderal Index			0.02	0.90
Age			2.93	0.09
Race			0.21	0.65
Sex			2.36	0.13
Female	40	5.76		
Male	116	5.35		
Contact with Inmates			7.89	0.01
No	49	2.19		
Yes	107	6.95		
Institution			3.83	0.02
Concord	105	6.49		
Billerica	33	3.08		
NECC	18	0.99		
Sex Contact			2.82	0.10
Female No	20	− 0.94		
Female Yes	20	8.83		
Male No	29	3.27		
Male Yes	87	6.30		

*Subgroup means, as predicted by the model.
Observed means are very similar.

nificant, but the other effects remain about the same. (b) For Tables 12.2A
and 12.2B, all three effects (institution, job category, and sex by job category
interaction) became more significant with no change in the direction of effects. (c) For Tables 12.3A and 12.3B, the effects of contact and institution
again became stronger, but the interaction term remained of borderline
significance.

In summary, there are three sets of findings that stand out, in the sense that
they reveal statistically reliable results that are replicated on both systolic and
diastolic blood pressure measurements: (a) Working in the prison setting is
associated with blood pressure increases from before the start of the work
day to the end of it. (b) This effect is stronger in high security institutions,
and holds true both for guards and treatment/service/clerical personnel. (c)
Actual contact with inmates is associated with a greater increase in blood
pressure with the effect strongest for a specific subset of employees: females
in the treatment job category. It is less striking for male treatment/service/
clerical employees, and does not hold at all for (male) guards.

TABLE 12.3B
Pre-Shift to Post-Shift Changes in Diastolic Blood
Pressure Among Correctional Treatment, Service,
and Clerical Staff by Demographic Characteristics,
Institution, and Contact with Inmates

		Mean Change			
		N	x*	F	p
Ponderal Index				0.66	0.42
Age				1.82	0.18
Race				0.01	0.93
Sex				1.23	0.27
Female		40	2.63		
Male		116	2.33		
Contact with Inmates				4.15	0.04
No		49	1.43		
Yes		107	2.85		
Institution				4.48	0.01
Concord		105	3.16		
Billerica		33	−0.04		
NECC		18	0.66		
Sex	Contact			3.42	0.07
Female	No	20	−0.61		
Female	Yes	20	4.12		
Male	No	29	2.13		
Male	Yes	87	2.41		

*Subgroup means, as predicted by the model.
Observed means are very similar.

DISCUSSION

These findings confirm a priori hypotheses, which suggest the notion that
differential environmental stress is reflected in differential blood pressure response. Specific differences in environments include mode of housing and
different inmate populations. NECC inmates are housed in single, carpeted
rooms physically resembling a college dormitory. The other two institutions
contain cells, as well as "dormitories" consisting of a large room with multiple beds. Criminal histories, length of sentence, and availability of space are
among the determining factors in assignment to a particular correctional institution; however, excessive generalization about the inmate population is
precluded by inevitable overlap between institutions. The presence of certain
inmates, known to have violent tendencies, may elicit fear and greater vigilance among some staff members. The institutions studied differ somewhat
with respect to their inmate populations, and one may have more violent inmates than another, as determined by the type of crime for which inmates are

incarcerated. The need for greater vigilance, real or imagined, may play a role in the association of elevated blood pressure among staff with inmate contact, and in the significant institutional differences in mean blood pressure change.

The shift contact interaction in the guards' regression model suggests that inmate contact may have different implications for staff on the day shift than for those on other shifts. Inmates undoubtedly spend more time away from their cells or dormitories involved in work or recreational activities at this time. The relatively greater amount of inmate movement in the prison may require considerably more vigilance during this shift.

Inmate contact, as a dichotomous variable, is only a crude measure of that contact. Knowledge of the type and frequency of contact would allow a more meaningful assessment of its impact. Other types of activity during the day place extra demands on guards who work the day shift. Sick call generally takes place early in the day, and may require intervention on the part of the guard to screen inmates, or accompany them to the medical area. Visits by family, friends, or lawyers may also disrupt the routine for the day shift guards, whereas guards working other shifts would encounter fewer disruptions.

There is no shift variance for treatment or service staff; for the most part they work during the day. However, the significant increase in blood pressure among guards who work the day shift leads us to question whether the presence of other staff members (e.g., administrative, treatment, and service staff) is a factor that causes stress, because guards working the evening or midnight shift would have extremely limited contact with non-custodial staff. Conflict between administrators and guards has frequently been cited as a source of stress for guards, because of contradictions in expectations. "Guards who enforce the rules are seen as rigid and punitive; contradictorily overlooking infractions leads to accusations of incompetence or corruption" (Poole & Regoli, 1980b, p. 26). Guards may also find that the directives of custodial responsibility are incompatible with the goals of treatment staff, resulting in frequent conflicts over threats to security (Cressey, 1965, 1968; Hepburn & Albonetti, 1980).

Ninety-three percent of the women categorized as treatment staff report that they have inmate contact. It is possible that women who have inmate contact may feel threatened by inmates, and thus maintain a state of greater vigilance than men, or than women with no inmate contact. Perhaps this accounts for the blood pressure increases they exhibit on the job. Men with inmate contact may feel less vulnerable, or simply better equipped to protect themselves.

Differences in blood pressure change between treatment and service staff may also be reflecting characteristics other than inmate contact. The organizational structure of the prisons may cause conflict for staff members carrying out the divergent responsibilities of custody-related and treatment activities. If guards perceive the treatment staff as interfering with their custodial objectives, they may view them with resentment, or even antagonism. The data lead us to consider whether this is particularly the case for women, as guards, all of whom were men, may view them as more of a threat to security than they would view male treatment staff. General understaffing may have been a problem at the time of the study, in light of the relatively high staff turnover. Of the guards studied, nearly one third had been hired within the last 2 years. This would suggest that, if staffing is a problem, the burden of custodial responsibility may be indirectly placed on all staff members, including those whose functions are largely therapeutic or educational.

Outside of correctional institutions, similar occupations with therapeutic or educational functions have many stressful features, such as excessive caseloads, barriers to goal attainment, role ambiguity or conflict, and uncomfortable working conditions (Daley, 1979). These features are frequently common to the prison environment. Treatment-oriented programming, including medical care, counseling, and education, have generally had low philosophical and financial priority in the view of most correctional administrators. Security is the primary goal of those drawing up correctional budgets; thus, treatment staff may be left with a low level of input in program planning and implementation. As to whether women are more negatively affected by this problem than men, cannot be adequately answered here. However, it is highly probable that these institutions, as an alien subculture comprised of men, presents more difficulties for women in integration into the organization, and in the achievement of professional goals.

Some qualification is needed with respect to the blood pressure data. The change score analysis we employed assumes that all participants start at their own "baseline" blood pressures before work begins and that the increment during the shift is a reflection of job stress. This may not be the case. Some employees may have higher pressures at the beginning of the work day because of anticipation of difficulties or the stress of commuting to the job. In such cases it need not be expected that pressures would rise further during the working day. Our use of change scores may underestimate the impact of the occupational stress of working in prison.

When blood pressure is measured repeatedly at brief intervals over hours or days, the social situation has far more effect on its level than any diurnal variation (Harshfield, Pickering, Kleinert, Blank, & Laragh, 1982; Littler, West, Honour, & Sleigth, 1978; Perloff & Sokolow, 1978). Therefore, any change during the work day may properly be attributed to the work itself.

We have attributed the differing blood pressure effects of the time of the shifts worked, to inmate contact, noting that pressures increase most during the day when inmates are most active and more likely to be out of their cells. We cannot exclude the possibility, however, that employees select their work shifts and that some of the effect we noted may be attributed to differential apprehension about the job.

SUMMARY

In summary, a pilot study of correctional staff examined occupational stress among correctional officers, treatment staff, and service staff, using blood pressure change during the work day as an indicator of stress in the prison environment. Among prison guards, a significant positive association was found between systolic and diastolic blood pressure increase, and higher levels of institutional security. A marginally significant association in the same direction was found for systolic blood pressure change and the inmate contact × shift interaction. Among non-custodial staff, institutional differences in blood pressure change were similar to those for guards. Also, an interaction term examining sex × job category demonstrated that women in treatment occupations had significantly greater mean increases in blood pressure than women in other occupations, and greater than men in similar or different occupations.

IMPLICATIONS OF THE DATA

The results of this pilot study have implicated several aspects of the prison work setting as possible sources of stress. Institutional differences in blood pressure among staff are highly suggestive of an environmental impact, as are differences in inmate contact. Variation in blood pressure change by sex and job category is suggestive of stressful features within certain occupational groups (Cobb & Rose, 1973) and although the presence or absence of inmate contact appears to be a contributing factor, it does not entirely explain the variance.

The recent literature on stress among correctional staff (Kalimo, 1980) may provide further clues as to the nature of this stress, and means for alleviation. Role conflict and ambiguity have received much attention, as has the topic of conflict between staff with custodial versus treatment objectives. Johnson (1977) notes that conflict between custodial and treatment staff is unavoidable, as the persons who fill these roles often have substantially differing personal values and orientations, and may even view each other as obstacles to effective role performance. Given the inevitability of these coexisting directives, any solution must take the objectives of each view into account.

Job training has been a stated need for correctional officers (Grenfell, 1976) and recommended by administrators and others involved in the criminal justice system. In 1976, 40 states required only a high school diploma for correctional officer positions. Several of these required an unspecified type of additional work experience, and only the District of Columbia required that correctional officers have either a college degree or 3.5 years of experience in counseling or supervising. Former Chief Justice Warren E. Burger (1981), speaking at commencement ceremonies at the George Washington University Law School, recommended the establishment of a national academy for the training of prison personnel. Similar training offered to police officers, at the FBI's national police academy, has helped police work in terms of efficiency and law enforcement.

Correctional officers are often called on to settle disputes, calm nerves, and respond to the fear or anger of inmates. A certain amount of responsibility for intervention and referral of inmate problems ultimately rests with the guard who controls access to administrative and treatment personnel. Some guards see this as an integral part of their role, whereas others view it as alien to the custodial role. As staff who represent the first line of contact for inmates, they are forced to assess the problems and needs of inmates, and decide whether to intervene or refer. Janus, Bess, Cadden, and Greenwald (1979) have stated that there is a strong need for training police officers in crisis intervention, and such training seems equally appropriate to the role of the correctional officers.

Janus, Bess, Cadden, and Greenwald compared a control group of policemen receiving the usual training, to an experimental group who had received instruction on various aspects of psychopathology and symptom identification in stressed persons. The training enabled officers in the experimental group to differentiate much of the time between psychopathology and normal stress reactions, and to take appropriate action. An additional benefit was that police officers felt more comfortable communicating with mental health professionals, and gained increased respect for these individuals. This approach has obvious relevance to prison guards, given the wide gap in orientation between custodial and treatment personnel, and the desirability of training correctional officers in crisis intervention. Grenfell (1976) reports that the guards' highest priority for additional training is in human relations (e.g., to be able to assess and predict inmate behavior, increasing their awareness of potentially violent situations).

A team approach among correctional staff has been cited as a means of alleviating conflicts between personnel with diverse responsibilities. Hepburn and Albonetti (1978) examined a program that brings various levels of correctional staff together, with the inmates, to discuss and resolve issues relating to work and cell assignment, disciplinary action, furlough requests, and merit time consideration. The team approach has been significantly associated with more favorable imate attitudes toward living and work assignments, and staff. It is significantly related to more favorable staff attitudes toward inmates and other staff, a positive view of work assignment, and a lower level of orientation to punishment and role conflict.

Participation in decision making will help staff feel they are part of an integrative team, and they may perceive interpersonal differences as less threatening (Hazelrigg, 1968). There is a logical reason for guards to contribute to this process: they deal with inmates on day-to-day basis, and become intimately aware of inmates' reactions to this environment and other inmates.

Our analysis of a relationship between working in the prison environment and elevations in blood pressure is suggestive of substantial occupational stress. The literature also supports this finding. Much has been written about sources of work stress for correctional staff, and the focus of this research has been the conflict between staff and inmates, administrative obstacles, and tension between staff with custodial roles and those with treatment functions. The data obtained in this pilot study demonstrate that type of institution and inmate contact are related to blood pressure increases, and support a priori hypotheses that inmate contact and degree of institutional security would be positively associated with blood pressure increases due to a perceived need for greater vigilance. That higher blood pressure is associated with staff with a treatment role rather than clerical or service occupations may be a reflection of inmate contact, since those in clerical positions are unlikely to have inmate contact. It may also suggest that there are inherently stressful features of positions with treatment functions. The finding that women who are in treatment occupations demonstrate highly significant increases in blood pressure as compared with other women, and compared with men in similar positions, deserves further study.

Much of the theoretical discussion of such problems has been confined to the topic of guards; however, the present study has implicated the prison environment as a stressful one for other staff members, as well. The results of this pilot study serve to strongly recommend that a full scale study be undertaken. More background information is required of all staff, including demographic variables, medical history, length of employment and job training. An extensive analysis of psychologic factors, e.g., perceptions of the work environment, inmates, and other staff members, in conjunction with an objective assessment of the work environment and job responsibilities, is required to differentiate between the impact of the work environment, and differential susceptibility to elevations in blood pressure.

13 Summary, Synthesis, and Recommendations

SUMMARY OF RESULTS

The results are summarized in terms of five categories of variables and their relation to blood pressure. The categories are sociodemographic factors, background characteristics, current situational variables, social support indicators, and psychological scale scores concerned with mood, perception, and symptoms. In some cases, these categories correlate contemporaneously with blood pressure levels or changes; in other cases they predict subsequent blood pressure level or change. After summarization of these relationships, the implications of these data for further research, for prison policy, for inmates, for inmate's family and friends, and for prison medical care are presented.

Sociodemographic Variables and Blood Pressure

Before proceeding with the details of these relationships, it is necessary to repeat that we did observe a significant positive correlation between blood pressure and body bulk and between blood pressure and age. This relationship was noted for both systolic and diastolic pressure. Such correlations are to be expected (see chapter 3) and need not concern us further.

[Aside from its correlation with blood pressure, age was an important vari- mm3p177 -g able in another way. In moving from cell to dormitory, younger men tended to show larger increases in systolic blood pressure than older men; the largest increase occurred in the 20–22 age grouping. This effect of age is not easy to interpret, but it may indicate that—given their broader and more extensive

177

life experience — older inmates are better able to adapt to the change in housing mode.

At the first interview, but not subsequently, black inmates had higher pressures than white inmates. The fact that this relationship was present only very early in imprisonment suggests that the difference was not a consequence of the usually higher pressures in blacks. If that were the case, the difference would have persisted. We interpret the finding to mean that blacks, because they were such a small proportion of inmates (and of prison staff), were more apprehensive and vigilant because they expected difficulties with whites early in the sentence, but later were less concerned.

Religiosity was significantly and positively related to systolic pressures at the 2-week interview for the entire group. Men who reported themselves as deeply religious had higher systolic pressures than men who described themselves as "against religion." Perhaps religious men find more guilt and shame attached to imprisonment. They may repress feelings of anger and hostility. Perhaps their past manner of living and relations with others make them unusual compared to other inmates. They may not fit in and may feel isolated, vulnerable, and defenseless. Such characteristics, if present, may help explain the relationship between self-reported strength of religious beliefs and systolic blood pressure.

We expected that men with more education would have higher pressures because they also did not fit in well with most of the other inmates who were less well educated. Although not systematically recorded, differences in manner of communication, subject matter of conversations, and other behavior were observed in men with different educational attainment. At several time periods both systolic and diastolic pressures were positively correlated with amount of education. As expected, the contrast was largest between those with eighth grade education and those with some college. In a wide variety of noninstitutionalized U.S. population, education, and other measures of social class have been inversely correlated with blood pressure (Dawber et al., 1967; Harburg, Erfurt, Chape, Hauenstein, Schull, & Schork, 1973; McDonough, Garrison, & Hames, 1966; NCHS, 1981; Ostfeld & D'Atri, 1977; Skinner, Benson, McDonough & Hames, 1966). The prison results are thus unique to the prison setting.

At the initial interview, the relatively small proportion of men born outside the United States had significantly higher systolic pressures than natives. The former group also showed an increase in diastolic pressure between the first and second interview, whereas natives showed a drop in pressure. In subsequent interviews, natives and non-natives exhibited no differential blood pressure trends. Non-native status thus was associated with blood pressure in the same way as being black, and the same interpretation may be offered. The foreign born, small in number, and less familiar with American society and its institutions were more vigilant and apprehensive early in their sentences, but later became less concerned.

Men who were married and men with children had higher pressures than single, childless men, controlling for the fact that married fathers were older as a rule. Prisoners with families may have more shame and guilt about their imprisonment. Their families may be deprived of fathers' income or socially ostracized because of fathers' crime. Awareness of these problems may contribute to higher pressures in married fathers.

Thus, we observed that blacks, the foreign born, and older married fathers who had more education and more religious feelings were a numerical minority in prison and had higher pressures at some times in the prison stay than men not so characterized. The majority of inmates in this study are white U.S. natives, young, with less than 4 years of high school, unmarried, childless, and without strong religious feelings.

Background Characteristics and Blood Pressure

The hypothesis that first time offenders would experience greater difficulty in coping with imprisonment than recidivists, and as a result would exhibit higher blood pressures, was supported at the initial, 2-week, and 2-month interviews. Confirmatory evidence for the same hypothesis emerged from the 4-month and 6-month interviews, when blood pressures were significantly negatively correlated with number of previous times in jail or prison.

Transiency of residence before imprisonment was assessed through recording the number of residential changes the inmate experienced since age 10. That age cutoff was selected because moves before age 10 might not have been accurately recalled. The length of stay at last residence before imprisonment was also recorded. At T1 length of stay at last residence was positively associated with systolic and diastolic pressures. At 1 month, 2 months, and 3 months, blood pressure was either positively correlated with length of stay at last residence or negatively correlated with number of residential moves since age 10, or both. The proposed explanation for the relationship is the expectation that frequent moves promote the ability to cope with additional moves and related changes in the social and physical environment. Residential mobility may be related to other sociodemographic characteristics that correlate with blood pressure. Married men, for example, stayed longer at last residence before prison than single men.

On moving from cell to dormitory, men whose pre-imprisonment residence was more urban had virtually no change in systolic blood pressure, whereas a small increase was recorded among men from more rural places of residence. At 2 weeks, men of large city, small city, or town background, had lower pressures than rural men. These results suggest that more urban experience facilitates early adaptation to imprisonment and to the dormitory setting. Before we become too comfortable with these associations, we must point out that at 1 month, 3 months, and release, the pressures of rural men were several millimeters of mercury lower than of men of more urban background. Although several explanations for these seemingly disparate results come to mind none of them is sufficiently plausible to warrant presentation here.

At 3 months, 6 months, and release, men whose mothers had died when they were children had higher pressures than men with both parents in the home. The relationship between pressures and either father's death or both parents' absence from the home was less consistent in direction (father's death) or less frequently observed (both parents absent). The early presence of mother in the home may have contributed to a view of the world as a more stable, more predictable, and less threatening place. The opposite orientation among those with mother gone would favor the development of apprehension, fear of uncertainty, and adverse life expectation that, in prison, could lead to higher blood pressures.

Current Situational Variables and Blood Pressure

As expected, men in cells had significantly lower blood pressures than those in any other form of housing, whether dormitory, work release dormitory, infirmary, or protective custody. Dormitory and work release dormitory and their relationship to blood pressure level and change have been discussed in detail (chapter 8). The higher pressures in the infirmary and in protective custody require additional comment. The infirmary resembles a dormitory in that the men share the same housing and therefore, presumably, they also share the loss of privacy and risk of conflict with others. Illness and the anxiety connected with it may also have had some effect in raising blood pressure. Men are usually placed in protective custody because of the prison staff's belief that other inmates may harm the man if he were to remain in the usual housing. Men suspected by other inmates of being informants of the guards, men whose crimes cause contempt of other inmates such as molesting children, and men who have been attacked, beaten, or sexually assaulted are the kind of inmates who reside in protective custody. The higher pressure in these men may reflect the self-evident higher threat and arousal experienced by these men.

At 1 month and 6 months, relationships between family financial problems and blood pressure were noted. Men who described the financial problems as "desperate" had higher pressures than those inmates who reported "some" financial problems. And men with "some" financial problems had higher pressures than those denying family financial problems. These relationships may help explain why married fathers had higher pressures than single childless men, controlling for the older age of the former. Men with wives and children are more likely to report family financial problems than men without such relationships.

Men who had jobs while in prison and those who had monthly furloughs had lower pressures than those men without jobs or furloughs. These relationships were noted at the 2-week and 2-month periods. A number of activities were also related to blood pressure levels. On five occasions, either systolic or diastolic pressures were negatively associated with amount of time spent exercising. Listening to the radio and reading books were also negatively correlated with pressures at one or more times. Amount of time spent "taking it easy" was positively associated with blood pressures. Time spent "sitting and thinking" and "going for walks" were once negatively and once positively correlated with pressures. While these correlations are reliable, the underlying pattern of causality is unclear to us. Jobs, furloughs, exercising, and listening to the radio are, in this institution, activities carried out with other people. Perhaps these activities involving others may lead to feelings of support and security and to the orientation that the prison is not so ambiguous and threatening. Thus, apprehension is less and pressures are lower. Time spent "taking it easy" was anything but "easy." It meant time spent alone, ruminating about problems. The withdrawal and social isolation may reinforce the perception that prison is an uncertain place, threatening and harmful. Increased social contact may mean less vigilance and arousal; isolation may mean more.

Men who moved from a cell to a dormitory, or from a cell to a work release dormitory reported improved perception of housing mode. This was not true for men moving from a cell to a work release cell. Men moving from a cell to a dormitory or to a work release cell reported a less favorable view of guards. Going from a cell to a dormitory resulted in reports of loss of privacy accompanied by the perception of greater safety and more open spacious quarters. Inmates transferred from cells to a work release dormitory reported no change in privacy but did note feelings that the housing was safer, more open, and permitting greater freedom to do what they liked. Men moving from cell to work release cell reported no change in any of these perceptions of housing mode.

The same changes in housing mode also evoked changes in other mental health indicators. Men in all three groups showed decreases in anxiety, hostility, depression, and psychophysiologic symptoms. The size of the changes is not significantly different across the three groups, but the changes tended to be larger in the cell-to-work-release-dormitory group and least in the cell-to-work-release-cell men.

On moving from cell to dormitory, the largest increases in blood pressure occurred in younger men of rural background and in those who responded to the move by withdrawal and "sitting around thinking." Blood pressure change after the cell-to-dormitory move was also higher in those who reported a large loss or privacy, an increase in danger, and an increase in psychophysiologic symptoms.

The 40 men with the highest systolic blood pressure increases between any two examinations had many more adverse prison experiences between these examinations than a random sample of the remaining men. The adverse experiences included solitary confinement, being locked into cells, being caught with illicit drugs or alcohol, and movement from cell to dormitory. Our data suggest that, had the data collection been timed differently, even larger blood pressure changes would have been noted. For example, if one interview had occurred weeks before the adverse event during a period of relative tranquility and the second immediately after the detection of alcohol or solitary confinement, the increase could have been greater than we noted on our fixed schedule of data collection.

Social Support Indicators and Blood Pressure

We had anticipated that frequency of social contact by visit or telephone would be negatively associated with blood pressure. Reflection convinced us that this notion is too simple. A visitor may cheer or upset. A phone call may bring good news or bad. Frequent visits or calls are, perhaps, as likely to soothe as to upset. Frequency of telephone use was positively related to diastolic pressure at the fifth month. At 2 weeks and at 1 month, men who reported visits by friends had lower pressures than men not visited by friends. However, men who reported visits from outsiders (neither family nor friends) had higher pressures at 4 months than men with no outside visitors. Outside visitors are usually legal counsel, clergy, former employers, and representatives of social agencies. It is tempting to speculate that visits of friends lessen anxiety and vigilance and visits by outsiders have the opposite effect. We did not collect enough information about precisely who visited nor did we record the reasons for visits, so our speculation remains only that, speculation.

Psychological Self-Report Indicators and Blood Pressure

Inmates serially rated the institution, their residence, and the prison guards, but not other prison employees. Self reports of anxiety, hostility, depression, and symptoms related to anxiety were obtained at the same times. Unfavorable rating of inmate residence was significantly correlated with blood pressure at the initial, 2-week, and first, second, third, fifth and sixth-month interviews. Such unfavorable ratings mirrored perceptions of the residence as crowded, uncomfortable, dangerous, lacking in privacy, and feeling not at home. Negative perceptions of the institution were correlated with blood pressure at the third month. The negative perception reflected a view of the prison as more dangerous, unpleasant, unfriendly, isolated, and produced a desire to leave the institution. Changes in perception of guards in the more negative direction were associated with a higher blood pressure increase, but only among inmates who at the same time had a more negative change in their views of privacy.

Our expectation that background characteristics, current situational variables, perceptions of the environment, and social support indicators would be more frequently and strongly related to blood pressure at the beginning and at the end of imprisonment was partly borne out. Omitting the expected associations of blood pressure with age and ponderal index, we noted seven categories of data significantly correlated with systolic pressure, and seven with diastolic pressure at the first interview. At the release interview, seven categories were significantly associated with systolic pressure and five with diastolic pressure. For systolic pressure, with the exception of the first-month data, there was a U-shaped relationship over time with the highest number of correlations at the first and release interviews. No clear trend was evident for diastolic pressures.

There was a characteristic pattern of inmates' activities, behaviors, and perceptions over the course of imprisonment. Early in prison, there were higher scores on measures of anxiety, reports of smaller number of inmates known well enough to talk to, and more solitary use of leisure. Nearer the midpoint of imprisonment, there were self-reports of less anxiety, more frequent visits, increase in the number of inmates known, more use of leisure and an increase in group leisure activities coupled with decreases in solitary leisure pursuits. Toward the end of the sentence, self-reports of anxiety, hostility, and depression increased, and leisure activity and number of inmates known decreased.

Inmate Health

In several important respects, inmates were much more unhealthy than a national sample of young men, and exhibited behavior that threatened their future health to a great degree. Inmates reported from 2 to 20 times as much epilepsy, diabetes, stomach and duodenal ulcer, and asthma as the national sample. Inmates were 3 to 16 times as likely to report use of heroin, amphetamines, and barbituates, twice as likely to be cigarette smokers, and twice as likely to be problem drinkers or alcoholics.

Change in Inmates after Release

Changes associated with release from prison (i.e., difference between the last interview in prison and the first interview after release) included the following: a substantial improvement in rating "the area you are living in now" compared to the evaluation of the prison, a significant decline in anxiety, hostility, depression, and symptoms of discomfort, and a significant drop in systolic blood pressure.

EVALUATION OF THE RESEARCH

The research described here has several important strengths. Defined populations of inmates and prison employees constitute the participants. The participation rates among all groups studied exceeded 90%. The possibility of bias that occurs when studying volunteers or when participation rates are low has been avoided. The longitudinal method employed in the study of inmates also provides benefits to the study. The serial collection of data over time reduces errors caused by faulty recollection, provides more precise information about the chronological relationships of changes in mood, perception, and response to stress over time, and makes causal inferences more feasible than in the more usual cross-sectional or case-control studies. Such serial data collection also provides us the opportunity to understand how the inmates' mood, behavior, and stress responses changed during the sentence. The repeated determination of blood pressure provides us a non self-report measure of response to the prison environment and its change over time in association with alteration in mood, perception, and behavior.

The research also has limitations and problems. We have studied thoroughly only one institution, and generalizations of our experience there to other institutions, differing in size, security, types of offenders, correctional orientation, prison staff, and degree of crowding, may be unwise or misleading. The institution we studied changed in at least one important respect while we were studying it; that is the construction of new cells for work release prisoners. The presence of our personnel in the prison may have altered the behavior of inmates and staff, although we have no evidence that this was so. The degree of crowding at Billerica while we were there was certainly small as compared to many other institutions.

As with most other sources of medical data, the prison medical records presented some problems. The data were collected for purposes other than research. Standard medical nomenclature was not always used, notes were telegraphic in style, and some entries were very hard to read.

Our understanding of the prison setting was further handicapped by the requirement of measuring blood pressure and collecting data on a fixed schedule. We could not measure pressures and collect data immediately before, during, and immediately after fights, thefts, disciplinary actions, struggles for dominance, and important phone calls and visits. This protocol requirement made it likely that we underestimated the amount of blood pressure and psychological change in inmates occurring because of such prison events.

The research provides partial answers to a number of important questions.

To what kinds of inmates is the prison particularly stressful? The majority of the inmates we studied were young, white, unmarried, childless, and without much education or religious inclination. Men who were not like that provided evidence of greater stress than we identified in the majority. It was the older, married fathers with more education and more religious inclination who exhibited greater responses to stress in prison. Men with one or more parents gone from the home when they were children found prison more stressful than men whose parents were in the home during the inmates' childhood. Men who had changed residence more frequently exhibited less response to stress than men whose address was more stable. On the initial interview but not subsequently, black and foreign-born inmates had higher pressures than white inmates.

What in the prison was particularly stressful? First is minority status. Men belonging to the numerical minority in terms of age, race, marital and family status, education, religious inclination, and stability of home address exhibited evidence of more responses to stress than did men who belonged to the majority in terms of these characteristics. This sociodemographic heterogeneity in men housed in dormitories probably led to the development of majority and minority status or to the development and competition of groups of inmates homogeneous in themselves, who warred with each other and thereby contributed to the greater evidence of stress in the dormitories. The effect of such warring factions could operate around the clock for dormitory men but only during much more limited times for men housed in cells.

First time offenders exhibited greater response to stress than recidivists. Men who believed their families were having financial problems showed greater response to stress and the more severe the financial problems were, the greater was the response.

The relatively small groups of men in the infirmary and in protective custody had the highest pressures of all. The correlation suggests that these men found the prison particularly stressful either because of the psychological effects of illness or the need to be isolated and protected from other inmates. There is no reason to believe that the kinds of illnesses necessitating infirmary residence were themselves responsible for raising blood pressure. Men in the infirmary because of injury during a fight or knifing may have exhibited higher pressures because of the psychological effects of the assault and the injury, not because of tissue damage or blood loss. Men with major injury or illness are not kept in the infirmary; they are hospitalized.

Those inmates who perceived and reported the prison in negative terms showed more response to threat than those who reported a more positive view, particularly early in the sentence. Scores on measures of anxiety and hostility also were higher both early in the sentence and just before release, and exhibit lower levels around the midpoint of the stay in prison. Our data confirm the chronology of inmates' perception and behavior defined by Miller (1973) in his definitions of the initial, middle, and terminal phase of the inmates' life in prison. There is evidence in our data of the "short time syndrome" described by Miller (p. 17).

The major stressful events of prison life, such as lockups, solitary confinement, and being caught with illicit drugs or alcohol have pronounced effects on blood pressure.

What factors appear to reduce stress in prison? Inmates who have a job detail, who are on work release programs, who spend more time socializing with other inmates, who spend more time outside their prison residence, who report more visits from family and friends, and who have more monthly furloughs are stressed less than those without these characteristics. The relationships between these prison activities and levels of stress indicators are stronger early and late in the prison sentence and less so during the intermediate months of imprisonment.

The protective effect of social networks appears to operate in the house of correction as in so many other settings. Inmates who have friends among other inmates and whose family and friends visit them in prison more often are spared some of the feelings of uncertainty, threat, and loneliness that affect other inmates with less of these supports or none of them.

Finally, we need to remind the reader that in our work, blood pressure is used as an index of the effect of the prison environment on the people who live and work there. We have not used blood pressure as a precursor of cardiovascular disease. The size of the blood pressure levels and changes in the inmates and staff we studied is not enough in most cases to suggest increased risk of high blood pressure and its cardiovascular consequences in these people. About one inmate in five going from cell to dormitory had an increase in systolic pressure of 20 mmHg or more or a diastolic pressure increase of 10 mmHg or more. Changes of this magnitude not only are statistically significant but may have long term health implications if they persist. Whether living or working in prison increases the risk of cardiovascular disease is a question to which our research provides no clear answer.

RECOMMENDATIONS

Before we begin listing our recommendations, some additional comments need to be made. To aid the reader in evaluating our recommendations, it is, of course, essential to understand the data we have collected. But it is also important to understand our non-systematic, possibly biased, but strong impressions of prison officials, guards, inmates, and the prison itself. The upper echelon prison officials were impressive. They all appeared concerned about the welfare of inmates and their prospects for rehabilitation. They supported our studies even though we inconvenienced their staff. They made no attempt to cover up problems or to limit our inquiries. Some of the favorable impression they made on us could be attributable to their skill in public relations. But their words and their behavior showed no change during the months and years of our study. We believe that they were honest with us and troubled about the limitations on money, staff, and resources that made their efforts less than successful.

There was a total polarization between correctional officers (guards) and inmates. One belonged either to one faction or to the other. An example may be illuminating: After our study on inmates had been going on for a year, the guards showed interest in what we were doing and asked many questions of our staff about the purpose and methods of the study. They then asked us, through our staff, to begin a similar study on themselves. We agreed to carry out a pilot study of the correctional officers and instructed our staff to start. When the time came to begin the guard pilot study, none of the guards scheduled showed up. The problem was that our staff had worked with inmates and were identified as being on the side of the inmates. The guards would participate only if new staff who had never worked with inmates would carry out the studies on them.

Individual guards had widely divergent views about the inmates. Some felt that they were ordinary people who had had bad breaks in life, while others regarded them as "scum." The prevailing view was that the inmates were "psychopaths," congenitally inferior people for whom nothing could be done.

When we began the study, we were generally favorably inclined toward the inmates and treated them with respect, even with empathy. But their behavior made it difficult to maintain this attitude. An example will clarify our difficulty: When we examined the inmates after they had been released, we always agreed to meet them at a motel for data collection. We did not ask the inmates for their addresses or phone numbers on the outside. When inmates came into the motel lobby, some would look around to see if anyone was at the registration desk. If no one was, they would take the nickels, dimes and quarters out of the displays inviting donations to multiple sclerosis, leukemia, or crippled children's funds. Such actions made it difficult to remain favorably disposed toward inmates. Perhaps we were particularly distressed because of our medical orientation.

Communication between inmates and guards was stylized and sometimes made us feel as if we were watching a play. The inmates shouted their lines before their audience. The guards shouted their lines before their audience. Nobody really talked to anybody. The "posturing and dissembling" that Hans Toch (1975, 1977) described were clearly seen.

One experience, more than any other, typifies for us life in prison. A prisoner and a guard were shouting jaw to jaw like a baseball manager and an umpire. The inmate suddenly broke off the confrontation and walked away, weeping, with his head down. The guard said — perhaps intended for us to hear, although he didn't look our way — "that poor dumb son of a bitch, he's sick and his old lady walked out and all he can do is act tough."

Do we believe that if some of our suggestions are implemented things will get better? Better for whom? For the guards, sharply divided into those with and without political support, ambivalent about their work in a dangerous, underpaid, and often demeaned profession? For the inmates, often frightened and depressed but admitting nothing, feeling better on the outside, but unable in so many cases to avoid return to prison? For the prison so sharply polarized into inmates and staff?

Many people unconnected with the prison system are also polarized in their views about crime and criminals, and that polarization may result inevitably from a single basic belief about the human being identified as a criminal. A person accepting the premise that an inmate is not directly responsible for his crime may view the guards as brutes and the prison as hell. A person believing the inmate is directly responsible for his misdeed may believe that the guards are wardens of public safety and that the prison is a barricade protecting the innocent.

The system is the way it is for powerful reasons, not as a result of haphazard events. The behaviors of guards and inmates continue to meet each other's expectations and are cemented into self-fulfilling prophecies, while the public isn't sure how it wants prisons to run.

The point of the discussion is this: Efforts to improve the prison will fail if we begin as advocates either for inmates or for prison personnel. We cannot start change by advocating a better deal for inmates or begin by pressing for higher salaries and better working conditions for guards. We shall have to start by acknowledging that all who live and work in prison have a tough time and all need improved conditions without taking sides or saying who is right and who is wrong.

Our recommendations must follow logically from our findings, but they must make sense in terms of what is known. They must also be feasible and have some promise for success. A very literal and rigid view of some of the associations in our data would lead to some absurd recommendations. For instance, although anxiety increases just before release, we do not recommend that men remain in prison. Even though married inmates have higher pressures than single men, we do not fatuously conclude that divorce is advisable.

For Further Research

There may be other studies involving prison health that are longitudinal, but we have been unable to find any. The longitudinal method, the advantages of which are described earlier in this chapter, needs to be applied to this kind of research. An additional benefit of this method needs to be mentioned: Incidence rates for specific illnesses, infirmary visits, certain kinds of behavior, suicide attempts, and other prison occurrences are readily calculable for data collected longitudinally.

Studies of prison health should be designed to provide for careful examination of health at intake and reasons for visiting the prison infirmary after admission, while simultaneously testing hypotheses derived from a strong theoretical base. A great need exists for research that follows inmates from admission to discharge and links health status and change in health status over time to antecedent events. Studies of the health of prison personnel and of the effect of their occupation on their health are almost non-existent.

Most of our data come from a medium security institution, not extremely crowded, and with white males constituting nearly 90% of the inmates. To learn more with our methods, additional studies need to be carried out on maximum security institutions and on inmate populations of women, blacks and Hispanics.

The data indicate that personnel employed in the prisons show blood pressure responses to psychosocial stress on the job. Contact with inmates and degree of prison security are positively correlated with blood pressure. Longitudinal studies of these relationships are needed to understand and deal with the occupational stresses of prison employment.

Devices for monitoring blood pressure and pulse at times no more than a few minutes apart and worn by inmates and guards throughout the day could provide much more information about interactions between people and the social environment in prison.

One may take the position that imprisonment should be as stressful and difficult as possible on the grounds that that kind of experience is both punishment and deterrent. Our data do indicate that prison is stressful for inmates, but they also reveal that the environment of the prison is difficult for employees as well. Will attempts to improve the working conditions of employees and the prison lives of inmates reduce the effectiveness of imprisonment as a deterrent to crime? We do not know.

The authors of this book are a part of the helping and healing tradition that underlies public health and much of the social, behavioral, and biomedical sciences. In the absence of evidence to the contrary, we assume that attempts to make prison a little more bearable for the people who live and work there will not increase new criminal acts and recidivism, will benefit prison employees, and will leave some inmates less angry and embittered, less likely to kill or injure themselves, and less likely to have chronic psychiatric problems because of the effects of imprisonment. Our subsequent recommendations are based on these views.

For Prison Policy

The fact that men in the work release dormitory had higher pressures than men in cells is a very instructive point. Men housed in work release dormitories lived in settings resembling family residences. There was plenty of space for each man and many of the features of home, including kitchen facilities for their own cooking, comfortable chairs, curtains on the windows, provision for a variety of leisure activities, and a more comfortable, less crowded setting in which to see visitors.

The relative comfort and freedom of the work release dormitories did not counteract the stress of group living. This finding suggests that making dormitories more attractive and livable may have little effect on the stressful aspects of dormitory living. The opportunity for threatening interactions in dormitories may not be mitigated by improvements in the physical environment.

The stressful effects of the dormitory (not housing work release inmates) were limited to younger men of rural origin who reported more psychological distress, reduced privacy, and more solitary activities in the dormitory. It is clear that crowding by itself is not a useful construct for interpreting our findings and drawing implications for prison policy. The conclusion is that some men, identifiable by relatively simple means, may find dormitory living difficult and that correctional staff can use this information in developing a more humane policy of prison housing. An improved policy of housing new inmates in cells could have some benefit by allowing the inmate to begin to understand the prison routine, the staff and other inmates without some of the apprehension that dormitories may induce. Cells will continue to be needed for new inmates, to protect some inmates from others, and to reduce the alarm some men show in dormitories.

Work release programs were associated with lower pressures and family financial problems with higher readings. Work release programs may therefore be particularly beneficial to those men with family financial problems.

Dormitory residents should be as homogeneous as possible in terms of age, race, education, and occupational background. Several smaller dormitories instead of one or two large ones may give staff more flexibility in keeping dormitory populations more homogeneous.

If the aim of prison disciplinary actions is to induce experiences that are quite stressful to inmates, non-self-report measures indicate that they are achieving that aim. This knowledge may help prison officials employ such disciplinary actions appropriately.

Work release programs, leisure activities, and furloughs do reduce the stress of prison living and should be encouraged.

Visits from family and friends are helpful to inmates. Liberal visiting hours and more privacy in visiting areas may be advisable.

For Inmates and Their Family and Friends

It is advisable for inmates to pursue recreation with groups rather than alone. Talking to family and friends on the telephone and encouraging them to visit will be helpful. Inmates with no visits from family or friends and those with weekly visitors experienced greater stress than those with visitors coming once a month. The data suggest that some intermediate frequency of visitors is better than none or more frequent visits. When there is time for leisure, the inmates who take it easy or just sit and think should try to enter group activities. If an inmate is frightened by dormitory residence, he should ask to go to a cell. Prison staff should not view such a request as disgraceful or cowardly but as an opportunity to reduce stress and the risk of being terrorized by other inmates.

Exercise as a leisure activity was rather consistently associated with blood pressure levels indicative of less stress. Exercise should therefore be encouraged by prison authorities and engaged in by inmates.

For Prison Medical Care

Our data indicate that guards would benefit from training in psychopathology and symptom identification in stressed persons. Guards themselves recognize the need for training in human relations. After such training, they could more accurately predict inmate behavior and identify potentially violent situations before they erupt. Such training should be provided not only by persons skilled in human behavior but also by those who know prisons and inmates. Knowledge provided by training might reduce the gap in orientation between custodial and treatment personnel and enable both groups to work together more effectively and less stressfully.

The system of prison medical care should be prepared to treat a wide variety of illness, both bodily and psychological, and these illnesses will tend to be concentrated in a relatively small part of the inmate population. Among the four most common prison health problems are alcoholism, drug addiction, traumatic injury, and dental diseases. Only for injury was there a systematic program; handling minor trauma in prison and promptly hospitalizing those with more serious injury. Thus, very little is now being done for 3 of the 4 most common prison health problems. If the prison is responsible for minimum adequate care, it will need the resources to do the job.

The relatively poor health of inmates poses another burden for prison medical care; that of attempting to reduce future morbidity through screening, disease detection, and utilization of preventive measures. In the institutions we observed such programs were virtually non-existent. Even in a time of scarce resources, preventive measures can be justified on the grounds of reducing future illness and its related expense.

Health providers in prison should expect many visits to the infirmary, most of them for minor illnesses and trauma, but more serious illness will not be rare. Inmates who visit the infirmary often should not necessarily be penalized for doing so. The more frequent visits may help them cope with the environment.

Finally, a two-tiered system of medical care (Howe, Froom, Culpepper, & Mangone, 1977) may promote more efficient operation of the infirmary without jeopardizing care of inmates. Because so many inmate visits are for routine, non life-threatening problems and are usually treated by medications not requiring a prescription, most of these visits can be handled by physicians' assistants, nurses, or nurse practitioners. This would allow physicians to treat the relatively infrequent serious injuries and illnesses, and thus reduce expenses for medical care.

APPENDIX A:
Correctional Institutions Environmental Scale

Form C

Institution: _____ Name: _____

Unit: House — Single cell (which tier?)   _____

             Dormitory (which section?)   _____

      Work release —   _____

Age: _____ Sex: Male __ Female __

Date: _____

Are you: Inmate _____Staff member _____

How long have you been (or worked) on this unit? __ yrs __ mths __ wks

In your lifetime, how much time have you spent __ yrs __ mths __ wks
(or worked) in correctional institutions?

If you are a staff member, what is your title? (no abbreviations please)

_____

Instructions

There are 86 statements in this form. They are statements about correctional
units. You are to decide which statements are true of your unit, and which are
not.

True: — Circle the T when you think the statement is True or mostly True of your unit.

False: — Circle the F when you think the statement is False or mostly False of your unit.

Please be sure to answer every statement.

T   F   1. Inmates say anything they want to the counselors.
T   F   2. Staff have very little time to encourage inmates.
T   F   3. This unit emphasizes training for new kinds of jobs.
T   F   4. The staff make sure the unit is always neat.
T   F   5. Inmates are rarely asked personal questions by staff.
T   F   6. Inmates put a lot of energy into what they do around here.
T   F   7. Things are sometimes very disorganized around here.
T   F   8. Once a schedule is arranged for an inmate, he must follow it.
T   F   9. The staff discourage criticism.
T   F   10. Inmates are careful about what they say when staff are around.
T   F   11. Staff go out of their way to help inmates.
T   F   12. Staff care more about how inmates feel than about their practical problems.
T   F   13. The day room is often messy.
T   F   14. Inmates are expected to share their personal problems with each other.
T   F   15. Staff tell inmates when they're doing well.
T   F   16. The staff very rarely punish inmates by restricting them.
T   F   17. The staff act on inmates' suggestions.
T   F   18. Inmates rarely help each other.
T   F   19. Inmates here are expected to work toward their goals.
T   F   20. Inmates rarely talk about their personal problems with other inmates.
T   F   21. Staff are involved in inmate activities.
T   F   22. Inmates are always changing their minds here.
T   F   23. Inmates will be transferred from this unit if they don't obey the rules.
T   F   24. When inmates disagree with each other, they keep it to themselves.
T   F   25. Staff are interested in following up inmates once they leave.
T   F   26. There is very little emphasis on making plans for getting out of this institution.
T   F   27. The staff help new inmates get acquainted on the unit.
T   F   28. Many inmates look messy.
T   F   29. Staff are mainly interested in learning about inmates' feelings.
T   F   30. Staff sometimes argue with one another.

T   F   31. If an inmate's program is changed, someone on the staff always tells him why.

T   F   32. Staff don't order the inmates around.

T   F   33. Inmates are expected to take leadership on the unit.

T   F   34. Inmates are encouraged to show their feelings.

T   F   35. Counselors have very little time to encourage inmates.

T   F   36. Inmates are encouraged to plan for the future.

T   F   37. The unit has very few social activities.

T   F   38. Inmates' activities are carefully planned.

T   F   39. The inmates are proud of this unit.

T   F   40. If one inmate argues with another, he will get into trouble with the staff.

T   F   41. New treatment approaches are often tried on this unit.

T   F   42. Inmates never know when a counselor will ask to see them.

T   F   43. All decisions about the unit are made by the staff, and not by the residents.

T   F   44. It is hard to tell how inmates are feeling on this unit.

T   F   45. The more mature inmates on this unit help take care of the less mature ones.

T   F   46. Staff encourage group activities among inmates.

T   F   47. The unit usually looks a little messy.

T   F   48. Personal problems are openly talked about.

T   F   49. Very few things around here ever get people excited.

T   F   50. If an inmate breaks a rule, he knows what will happen to him.

T   F   51. Inmates may criticize staff members to their faces.

T   F   52. Inmates here are encouraged to be independent.

T   F   53. Staff and inmates say how they feel about each other.

T   F   54. Counselors sometimes don't show up for their appointments with residents.

T   F   55. Inmates must make plans before leaving this unit.

T   F   56. The staff set an example for neatness and orderliness.

T   F   57. The staff discourage talking about sex.

T   F   58. Discussions are pretty interesting on this unit.

T   F   59. Inmates never know when they will be transferred from this unit.

T   F   60. The staff give inmates very little responsibility.

T   F   61. Staff rarely give in to inmate pressure.

T   F   62. There is very little emphasis on what inmates will be doing after they leave the unit.

T   F   63. This is a friendly unit.

T   F   64. Staff try to help inmates understand themselves.

T   F   65. Inmates don't do anything around here unless the staff ask them to.

T F   66. On this unit, staff think it is a healthy thing to argue.

T F   67. The residents know when counselors will be on the unit.

T F   68. Inmates can call staff by their first names.

T F   69. Staff encourage inmates to start their own activities.

T F   70. People say what they really think around here.

T F   71. Inmates are encouraged to learn new ways of doing things.

T F   72. This is a very well organized unit.

T F   73. Inmates hardly ever discuss their sexual lives.

T F   74. Inmates here really try to improve and get better.

T F   75. Staff are always changing their minds here.

T F   76. The unit staff regularly check up on the inmates.

T F   77. There is no inmate government on this unit.

T F   78. Inmates tend to hide their feelings from the staff.

T F   79. The staff know what the inmates want.

T F   80. There is very little emphasis on making inmates more practical.

T F   81. Inmates on this unit care about each other.

T F   82. Discussions on the unit emphasize understanding personal problems.

T F   83. There is very little group spirit on this unit.

T F   84. When inmates first arrive on the unit, someone shows them around and explains how the unit operates.

T F   85. Inmates are rarely kept waiting when they have appointments with the staff.

T F   86. Inmates have a say about what goes on here.

Appendix B: Zuckerman and Lukin Adjective Check List

NOW SOME WORDS THAT MAY OR MAY NOT DESCRIBE HOW YOU HAVE FELT RECENTLY. AS YOU READ EACH WORD PLEASE INDICATE WHETHER IT IS TRUE OR FALSE FOR YOUR RECENT FEELINGS. (MARK T TRUE OR F FOR FALSE NEXT TO EACH WORD). (To be self-administered).

_____ good natured	_____ active	_____ frightened
_____ hostile	_____ angry	_____ strong (physically)
_____ agitated	_____ calm	_____ unhappy
_____ contented	_____ merry	_____ alive
_____ powerful	_____ rejected	_____ cheerful
_____ easy going	_____ nervous	_____ happy
_____ alone	_____ afraid	_____ blue
_____ bored	_____ aggressive	_____ offended
_____ lonely	_____ bitter	_____ irritated
_____ upset	_____ glad	_____ gloomy
_____ sullen	_____ hopeless	_____ awful
_____ panicky	_____ cautious	_____ cooperative
_____ mad	_____ low (in spirits)	_____ annoyed
_____ complaining	_____ critical	_____ peaceful
_____ secure	_____ desperate	_____ cross
_____ suspicious	_____ clean	_____ lost
_____ miserable	_____ lively	_____ tired
_____ cruel	_____ trusting	_____ left out
_____ discouraged	_____ confused	_____ sad

_____ wide awake   _____ loved by others   _____ lonesome
_____ kind   _____ worried   _____ daring
_____ furious   _____ impatient   _____ resentful
_____ destroyed   _____ dirty   _____ tormented
_____ fit   _____ stubborn   _____ mean
_____ tense   _____ terrified   _____ energetic
    _____ shaky   _____ disgusted

Appendix C:
Symptom Scale, National Center for Health Statistics

Interviewer: Please circle one category for each item.

Have you ever had a nervous breakdown?	Yes	No
Have you ever felt you were going to have a nervous breakdown?	Nearly all the time Pretty often Sometimes	 Rarely Never
Have you ever been bothered by nervousness feeling fidgety and tense?	Nearly all the time Pretty often Sometimes	 Rarely Never
Have there ever been times when you couldn't take care of things because you couldn't get going?	Nearly all the time Pretty often Sometimes	 Rarely Never
Do you ever have any trouble getting to sleep, or staying asleep?	Nearly all the time Pretty often Sometimes	 Rarely Never
Are you bothered by nightmares?	Nearly all the time Pretty often Sometimes	 Rarely Never
Are you bothered by your hands sweating so that you feel damp and clammy?	Nearly all the time Pretty often Sometimes	 Rarely Never

How often have you fainted or blacked out?	Nearly all the time Pretty often Rarely Sometimes Never
In the past few years, how often have you had headaches?	Nearly all the time Pretty often Rarely Sometimes Never
How often have you had spells of dizziness?	Nearly all the time Pretty often Rarely Sometimes Never
How often have you been bothered by your heart beating hard?	Nearly all the time Pretty often Rarely Sometimes Never

Appendix D:
Anger–Aggression Scale

CIRCLE ONE:

How often do you have a feeling of being irritable?

Nearly all the time
Pretty often
Sometimes
Rarely
Never

How often do you feel a little irritated or annoyed?

Nearly all the time
Pretty often
Sometimes
Rarely
Never

In general, are you?

Quick to get irritated
Somewhat quick to get irritated
Somewhat slow to get irritated
Slow to get irritated

When was the last time you were really angry?

Today or yesterday
A few days ago
Last week

(Continued)

Last month
A few months ago
A year ago or more

How easy are you to annoy?

Very easy
Quite easy
Hard
Very hard

How often do you *feel* like swearing?

Nearly all the time (few times a day)
Pretty often (once a day)
Sometimes (few times a week)
Rarely (once or twice a month)
Never

When you're around people you don't like, how often do you *feel* like being rude to them?

Nearly all the time
Pretty often
Sometimes
Rarely
Never

How often do you *feel* like losing your temper at someone you *like?*

Nearly all the time
Pretty often
Sometimes
Rarely
Never

How often do you *feel* like picking a fight or arguing with someone?

Nearly all the time
Pretty often
Sometimes
Rarely
Never

How often do you *feel* like smashing things?

Nearly all the time
Pretty often
Sometimes
Rarely
Never

How often *do* you swear?

Nearly all the time
Pretty often
Sometimes
Rarely
Never

How often *are* you rude to people?

Nearly all the time
Pretty often
Sometimes
Rarely
Never

How often *do* you lose your temper at someone you like?

Nearly all the time
Pretty often
Sometimes
Rarely
Never

How often *do* you pick a fight or argue with someone?

Nearly all the time
Pretty often
Sometimes
Rarely
Never

How often *do* you smash things?

Nearly all the time
Pretty often
Sometimes
Rarely
Never

When you are angry, how long does your anger last?

A week or more
Several days
A day
A few hours
A few minutes

When something happens to get you very angry *at someone you like,* how long do you think about it?

A week or more
Several days

(Continued)

A day
A few hours
A few minutes

I feel that it is alright for me to swear (out loud), is this?

Very true of you
Fairly true
Not very true
Not true at all

I feel it is wrong to be rude, is this?

Very true of you
Fairly true
Not very true
Not true at all

I feel it is wrong to pick a fight or argue, is this?

Very true of you
Fairly true
Not very true
Not true at all

I feel it is alright to lost my temper, is this?

Very true of you
Fairly true
Not very true
Not true at all

I would feel guilty if I yelled, is this?

Very true of you
Fairly true
Not very true
Not true at all

Appendix E:
Analytic Methods and Details
of Results

The methods of statistical analysis employed in chapters 7 and 9 are described here in greater detail than would have been desirable in those chapters.

For each time period the first and second blood pressure measurements of both systolic and diastolic pressures were averaged. The two means were considered the dependent variables in a multiple regression analysis. The sociodemographic, background, situational variables, and social support and psychological scale scores were entered as independent variables. Categorical factors such as race, marital status, and housing mode were represented by dummy variables (Kleinbaum & Kupper, 1978).

The analysis included the computation of univariate statistics; that is, frequencies and percentiles of the discrete variables and frequencies, percentiles, and means of the continuous variables. Based on these results, error checks and transformations were carried out. Bivariate statistics were computed next resulting in histograms, bar graphs, and correlations for the continuous variables.

A stepwise algorithm (i.e., forward selection with backward elimination) was utilized to determine the final regression models. Partial F values were then calculated for every variable if the entrance significance level ($p = .5$ for the forward selection of variables) was met and variables were systematically deleted if the elimination significance level was not met until equations with only significant terms remained. Variables were first deleted if they did not maintain a p value of at least .25 in the elimination step of the stepwise algorithm. The next step was to enter into the model only those significant variables from the previous step, again using a significance level of .25 as the criterion for eliminating variables. The third step involved using the remaining subset of variables but reducing the criterion for elimination to $p = .10$. The final model was obtained by then introducing into the model only those variables found to be significantly ($p \leq .10$) related to blood pressure in the previous step. As a cross check, all possible regressions were then calculated among the variables obtained in the final model; that is, choosing a model that minimized Cp — a measure of bias, maximized R^2, and selected variables significant at the .10 level. To facilitate the analysis, the Stepwise Procedure and the General Linear Models (GLM) Procedure, both in the SAS Computer package (Helwig & Council, 1979) and the "all possible regressions" program (BMDP9R) of the BMDP Computer package (Dixon & Brown, 1979) were employed.

The GLM procedure was employed in the final step. In this way, additional comparisons between various levels of the nominal variables could be made. As a consequence of this procedure, all variables in the model were simultaneously adjusted for the effects of all other variables with the calculation of Type IV sums of squares. Residual analyses and normal probability plots were then made to insure that the models that were fit adequately described the data at each time point of data collection.

It should be noted that in all analyses, the GLM procedure constructs dummy variables within its program and uses the level with the highest numeric value as the comparision group. However, in the stepwise procedure, one can construct dummy tables and enter specific levels into the regression models as independent variables. In this way, one can pre-select comparison groups independently of the computer package. Comparison groups were chosen to represent the levels of "non-activity" according to the a priori hypotheses tested. For example, men never married, non-smokers, and those not receiving any visitors were compared to men currently or previously married, smokers, and men with visitors respectively. The parameter estimates given in the tables in chapter 7 represent those calculated by subtracting various coefficients from the GLM output to correspond to the methodology used for constructing the dummy variables in the stepwise procedure.

TABLE E. 1
Summary Table of All Significant Independent Variables Based on Entire Group Models Mean Systolic Blood Pressure

Variable	2-Week	1-Month	2-Month	3-Month	4-Month	5-Month	6-Month	Release
Sociodemographic factors								
Age	0.3821	0.4140	0.4278	0.4364	0.2214			0.3251
Ponderal Index	−2.6676	−2.1146						
Education								
Grade 8	−5.7116							
(Some College)*								
Religiosity								
Deeply religious	5.8496							
(Neutral)*								
Children								
Yes					6.0344			
(No)*								
Race								
White								
Black								
(Other)*								
Background characteristics								
Recidivism								
First-time offender	4.1805		3.2965					
(Recidivist)*								
Length of stay at last residence								
<3 years		−0.4114						
3–5 years		−5.6681						
(5+ years)*								
No. of residential changes since age 10		−0.0873						
Parents alive and present as a child								
No, mother died								8.5016
No, father died								6.1844
No, both absent								2.9715
(Yes, both present)*								
Number of times previously in jail					−1.0763			

(Continued)

TABLE E. 1 (Continued)

Variable	2-Week	1-Month	2-Month	3-Month	4-Month	5-Month	6-Month	Release
Current situation variables								
Housing mode								
Protective custody and infirmary				9.5715		3.9762		
Dormitory				6.6864		5.3801		
Work release				6.6680		8.4151		
(Single cell)*								
Smoking history								
1/2 pack cig/day					-5.6777			8.2875
1/2-1 1/2 packs cig/day					-5.3131			-1.8044
2 Packs Cig/Day					-3.2487			-1.3348
(Currently non-smoker)*								
Financial problems								
Some		2.9181					0.0899	
Desperate		6.0563					6.9505	
(None)*								
Hours per week:								
Exercising	0.0716							
Sitting and thinking			-0.3251					
Listening to radio				-0.0658		-0.1075		
Going for walks								-0.1327
Social support indices								
CIES social support scale			-0.6151					
Frequency of visits by friends								
Monthly		-3.5841						
(Never)*								
Psychological assessment								
Anxiety		0.6066						
Hostility		0.8569						
Perception of residence				-0.4095		-0.2392	-0.2520	
Perception of prison guards								
NCHS—physical anxiety scale								

*A comparison group to which particular levels of *discrete* variables were compared is given in parentheses.

TABLE E. 2
Summary Table of All Significant Independent Variables Based on Entire Group Models Mean Diastolic Blood Pressure

Variable	2-Week	1-Month	2-Month	3-Month	4-Month	5-Month	6-Month	Release
Sociodemographic factors								
Age	0.3617	0.3606	0.4129	0.2734	0.2991	0.2248	0.3114	0.3222
Ponderal index	-2.3098	-1.4440		-2.6062	-0.0281	-2.6537	-2.9708	-1.7913
Education								
Grade 8	-1.6471	-1.9874			-3.2281			
Grades 9-11	-2.2432	-3.2692						
(Some college)*								
Children								
Yes					1.8732			
(No)								
Background characteristics								
Recidivism								
First time offender			1.8520					
(Recidivist)*								
Parents alive and present as a child								
No, mother died				2.0609			2.0249	
No, father died				-3.9470			-2.0024	
(Yes, both present)*								
Number of times previously in jail							-1.1109	
Childhood residence								
Large city				6.3917				5.3789
Small city				4.8877				4.2134
Town				5.4144				3.9501
(Rural)*								

(Continued)

TABLE E. 2 (Continued)

Variable	2-Week	1-Month	2-Month	3-Month	4-Month	5-Month	6-Month	Release
Current situation variables								
Housing mode								
Protective custody and infirmary				3.6306				
Dormitory				2.2053				
Work release				3.7386				
(Single cell)*								
Job detail								
Yes	-1.9383							
(No)*								
Smoking history								
<1/2 pack cig/day					-2.4262			
1/2-1 1/2 packs cig/day					-3.6282			
≥2 packs cig/day					-1.8954			
(Currently non-smoker)*								
Frequency of telephone use								
Daily						-2.5084		
(No use)*								
Financial problems								
Some		1.6926						
Desperate		3.9160						
(None)*								
Hours per week:								
Exercising			-0.1258					
Going for walks							-0.2420	
Taking it easy							0.0534	-0.0473

Social support indices			
Frequency of social contact among inmates	−0.1494	−0.2160	
Frequency of outside visitors			
Weekly			4.2374
Monthly			2.6530
(Never)*			
Frequency of visits by friends			
Monthly	−3.3721		
(Never)*			
Psychological assessment scales			
Anxiety	0.2951	0.4094	
Depression			−0.3714
Perception of institution		−0.1347	
Perception of residence	−0.0992		−0.1704
NCHS—physical anxiety scale			−0.2984

*A comparison group to which particular levels of *discrete* variables were compared is given in parentheses.

Summary Table of All Significant Independent Variables Based on the
Core Group Models Mean Systolic Blood Pressure

Variable	2-Week	1-Month	2-Month	3-Month
Initial mean systolic blood pressure	0.5469	0.5246	0.5496	0.3373
Sociodemographic factors				
Age	0.2231			
Education				
Grade 8				
(Some college)*				
Children				
Yes		2.7676	2.7169	3.7727
(No)*				
Background characteristics				
Recidivism				
First-time offender	2.1060			
(Recidivist)*				
Length of stay at last residence				
<3 years				−3.1117
3–5 years				−0.5193
(5+ years)*				
Childhood residence				
Large city				7.2006
Small city				4.7754
Town				2.8913
(Rural)*				
Current situation variables				
Housing mode				
Protective custody and infirmary		16.5316	15.7081	
Dormitory		3.8506	0.9357	
Work release dormitory		10.2477	9.9493	
(Cell)*				
Job detail				
Yes				
(No)*				
Smoking history				
<1/2 pack cig/day			−5.7328	
1/2-1 1/2 packs cig/day			−1.6182	
>2 packs cig/day			−5.4967	
(Currently non-smoker)*				
Frequency of telephone use				
Daily or weekly		1.4496		
(No use)*				
Hours per week:				
Exercising			−0.2359	−0.3495
Listening to radio				
Taking it easy			0.0386	
Reading books				−0.1403

TABLE E. 3 *(Continued)*

Variable	2-Week	1-Month	2-Month	3-Month
Social support indices				
CIES social support scale				
Frequency of visits by friends				
Weekly		0.4105		
Monthly		− 3.2424		
(Never)*				
Psychological assessment scales				
Depression				
Perception of residence	− 0.2009			− 0.3590

*A comparison group to which particular levels of *discrete* variables were compared is given in parentheses.

Summary Table of All Significant Independent Variables Based on the
Core Group Models Mean Diastolic Blood Pressure

Variable	2-Week	1-Month	2-Month	3-Month
Initial mean diastolic blood pressure	0.5499	0.3865	0.2961	0.4562
Sociodemographic factors				
Age	0.1554	0.1474	0.4110	
Ponderal index	−1.5626	−1.0928		
Education				
Grades 9–11		−2.3144		
(Some college)*				
Background characteristics				
Length of stay at last residence				
<3 years		−1.0717		
3–5 years		−1.5176		
(5 + years)*				
Number of residential changes since age 10			−0.0693	
Childhood residence				
Large city	−1.9485	5.6455		10.2941
Small city	−3.7194	4.9877		6.3514
Town	−0.9208	4.9958		8.8575
(Rural)*				
Current situation variables				
Frequency of furloughs				
Monthly			−3.4780	
(Never)*				
Smoking History				
<1/2 pack cig/day			−3.9043	
1/2-1 1/2 packs cig/day			−1.6066	
>2 packs cig/day			−3.9651	
(Currently non-smoker)*				
Hours per day outside residence	−0.2544	−0.2434	−0.2339	
Frequency of telephone use				
Daily or weekly	−2.8031			
(No use)*				
Hours per week:				
Exercising	−0.1802			−0.2151
Listening to radio				
Reading books			−0.1011	
Going for walks		0.1932		
Social support indices				
Frequency of social contacts among inmates	−0.2069			
CIES social support scale				
Psychological assessment scales				
Anxiety		0.9873	0.4880	
Hostility		0.5914		
Perception of residence	−0.1506		−0.1427	
Perception of prison guards				
Perception of institution				
NCHS − physical anxiety scale				

*A comparison group to which particular levels of *discrete* variables were compared is given in parentheses.

TABLE E. 5
Descriptive Statistics of All Variables Employed in the Data Analysis

Variable	Statistic*	Initial+	2-Week	1-Month	2-Month	3-Month	4-Month	5-Month	6-Month	Release
Hours per day outside residence	N		398	377	329	295	232	164	141	280
	$\bar{x}$		9.430	9.175	8.350	8.339	7.849	8.451	8.064	7.989
	S		4.000	4.117	4.034	4.001	4.288	4.164	4.224	4.210
Number of inmates know well	N		402	379	321	299	232	164	143	281
enough to stop and talk to	$\bar{x}$		20.893	30.309	33.825	37.498	39.138	41.982	37.545	36.409
	S		24.222	28.286	30.231	30.985	32.437	34.056	30.524	29.775
Frequency of social contact	N		402	380	332	298	232	164	143	281
among inmates	$\bar{x}$		2.811	2.097	2.232	2.228	2.371	2.061	2.245	2.149
	S		5.353	3.741	4.370	4.205	4.919	3.878	3.820	4.003
Anxiety scale	N		400	379	330	294	228	162	142	278
	$\bar{x}$		2.360	2.137	2.030	2.014	2.079	1.870	1.754	3.122
	S		2.385	2.251	2.204	2.297	2.230	2.213	2.101	1.596
Hostility scale	N		402	380	332	299	232	164	143	281
	$\bar{x}$		16.898	16.911	16.837	16.699	16.797	16.866	17.147	17.352
	S		2.420	2.297	2.582	2.752	2.536	2.639	2.426	2.494
Depression scale	N		402	380	332	299	232	164	143	281
	$\bar{x}$		18.886	19.563	19.645	19.615	19.543	19.854	20.084	20.847
	S		4.034	3.828	3.876	4.044	3.882	4.016	3.887	3.814
NCHS anxiety symptom scale	N		402	380	332	299	232	164	143	281
	$\bar{x}$		45.306	46.105	46.389	46.773	47.168	47.762	48.343	47.623
	S		6.904	6.372	6.482	6.683	6.832	6.106	5.632	6.404
Perception of institution	N		402	380	332	299	232	164	143	281
	$\bar{x}$		27.159	28.921	28.684	29.090	27.819	27.921	28.210	28.270
	S		7.758	9.237	9.036	9.332	8.708	8.796	9.053	8.862
Perception of residence	N		402	380	332	299	232	164	142	281
	$\bar{x}$		16.766	18.826	18.635	19.224	18.047	18.732	19.211	19.352
	S		7.018	7.584	7.014	7.333	7.221	7.227	8.035	7.433

(Continued)

215

TABLE E. 5 (Continued)

Variable	Statistic*	Initial +	2-Week	1-Month	2-Month	3-Month	4-Month	5-Month	6-Month	Release
Perception of prison guards	N		401	379	330	298	231	164	143	279
	$\bar{x}$		45.045	43.512	42.139	41.607	41.147	44.494	40.587	41.283
	S		10.501	12.207	12.362	12.584	12.755	12.581	12.857	11.860
Hrs per week watching television	N		401	380	332	299	230	164	143	281
	$\bar{x}$		25.287	25.813	25.036	24.348	25.678	24.622	24.448	22.473
	S		21.853	21.381	20.558	20.172	20.619	18.647	18.259	18.560
Hrs per week listening to radio	N		399	380	331	298	230	163	143	281
	$\bar{x}$		18.409	21.132	21.275	20.621	21.913	22.890	19.979	20.434
	S		22.362	23.756	24.169	23.567	23.347	23.910	21.708	22.021
Hrs per week working on hobbies	N		401	379	329	299	231	163	143	279
	$\bar{x}$		2.362	3.158	3.292	3.020	1.667	2.761	2.161	2.330
	S		8.548	9.531	9.512	10.172	5.664	8.293	7.996	8.781
Hrs per week reading books and magazines	N		401	377	332	297	231	164	143	281
	$\bar{x}$		12.067	9.247	8.410	8.084	8.173	8.079	6.895	7.420
	S		13.456	11.519	10.030	10.581	12.843	12.070	9.843	10.936
Hrs per week sittig and thinking	N		399	378	331	295	230	164	142	280
	$\bar{x}$		8.739	9.556	8.858	9.661	12.148	10.061	9.739	9.532
	S		13.838	15.899	14.663	16.534	19.119	15.544	16.056	15.301
Hrs per week taking it easy	N		398	377	332	298	230	163	141	279
	$\bar{x}$		43.053	41.326	41.675	43.369	44.283	42.098	43.411	41.785
	S		28.392	27.721	27.871	27.353	28.528	27.810	28.147	27.880
Hrs per week going for walks	N		401	376	331	299	231	163	61	280
	$\bar{x}$		3.085	3.168	3.423	3.100	3.411	2.350	7.410	3.664
	S		5.691	7.788	7.788	6.774	6.262	3.679	12.876	10.937
Hrs per week spent exercising	N		397	378	329	297	231	161	142	278
	$\bar{x}$		6.189	6.352	6.286	5.428	5.537	5.273	4.254	4.906
	S		7.678	8.889	7.264	6.262	6.763	5.804	5.496	6.931

216

Housing Mode									
Cell	N	402	380	331	299	232	164	143	281
	n	396	297	236	172	140	85	66	126
	%	98.50	78.16	71.30	57.53	60.34	51.83	46.15	44.84
Dormitory	n	4	51	53	54	44	31	28	47
	%	1.00	13.42	16.01	18.06	18.97	18.90	19.58	16.73
Work Release	n	0	22	32	60	38	30	38	79
	%	0.00	5.79	9.67	20.07	16.38	18.29	26.57	28.11
Other (prot. cust. and infirmary)	n	2	10	10	13	10	18	11	29
	%	0.50	2.63	3.02	4.35	4.31	10.98	7.69	10.32
Job Detail									
Yes	N	402	380	330	298	232	164	142	281
	n	277	292	220	207	148	122	115	203
	%	68.91	76.84	66.67	69.46	63.79	74.39	80.99	72.24
No	n	125	88	110	91	84	42	27	78
	%	31.09	23.16	33.33	30.54	36.21	25.61	19.01	27.76
Frequency of visits by family member	N	366	354	309	258	217	163	140	278
Weekly	n	48	91	93	95	73	51	36	71
	%	13.11	25.71	30.10	36.82	33.64	31.29	25.71	25.54
Monthly	n	223	175	134	108	89	62	47	102
	%	60.93	49.44	43.37	41.86	41.01	38.04	33.57	36.69
Never	n	95	88	82	55	50	50	57	105
	%	25.96	24.86	26.54	21.32	25.35	30.67	40.71	37.63
Frequency of visits by friends	N	370	349	307	249	220	158	140	274
Weekly	n	48	85	92	80	62	46	43	62
	%	12.97	24.36	29.97	32.13	28.18	29.11	30.71	22.63
Monthly	n	197	160	120	95	77	49	41	92
	%	53.24	45.84	39.09	38.15	35.00	31.01	29.29	33.58
Never	n	125	104	95	74	81	63	56	120
	%	33.78	29.80	30.94	29.72	36.82	39.87	40.00	43.79

(Continued)

TABLE E. 5 (Continued)

Variable	Statistic*	Initial+	2-Week	1-Month	2-Month	3-Month	4-Month	5-Month	6-Month	Release
Frequency of outside visitors	N		390	379	327	292	230	161	141	279
Weekly	n		69	110	114	114	84	62	50	87
	%		17.69	29.02	34.86	39.04	36.52	37.80	35.46	31.18
Monthly	n		277	231	173	137	115	76	63	134
	%		71.03	60.95	52.91	46.92	50.00	46.34	44.68	48.03
Never	n		44	38	40	41	31	26	28	58
	%		11.82	10.02	12.23	14.04	13.48	15.85	19.86	20.79
Frequency of phone use	N		395	379	331	298	230	164	143	280
Daily	n		322	292	246	205	171	125	110	213
	%		81.52	77.04	74.32	68.79	74.35	76.22	76.92	76.01
Weekly	n		4	12	15	20	10	8	5	7
	%		1.01	3.17	4.53	6.71	4.35	4.88	3.50	2.50
None	n		69	75	70	73	49	31	28	60
	%		17.47	19.79	21.15	24.50	21.30	18.90	19.58	21.43
Financial problems	N		400	377	331	297	230	162	141	362
Yes	n		125	122	109	109	86	66	58	140
	%		31.25	32.36	32.93	36.70	37.39	40.74	41.13	38.67
No	n		275	255	228	188	144	96	83	222
	%		68.75	67.64	69.18	63.30	62.61	59.26	58.87	61.33
Amount of financial problems	N		400	379	325	292	231	158	138	356
Some	n		103	97	87	69	58	33	29	88
	%		25.75	25.59	26.77	23.63	25.11	20.89	21.01	24.72
Desperate	n		194	193	167	162	127	84	78	190
	%		48.50	50.92	51.38	55.48	54.98	53.16	56.52	53.37
None	n		103	89	71	61	46	41	31	78
	%		25.75	23.48	21.85	20.89	19.91	25.95	22.46	21.91

*N = sample size $\bar{x}$ = mean value S = standard deviation.

References

Aaby, P., Bukh, J., Lisse, I. M., & Smits, A. J. (1984). Overcrowding and intensive exposure as determinants of measles mortality. *American Journal of Epidemiology, 120,* 49–63.

Abeles, H., Feibes, H., Mandel, E., & Girard, J. A. (1970). The large city prison — a reservoir of tuberculosis. *American Review of Respiratory Diseases, 101,* 706–709.

Abelson, H. I., Fishburne, P. M., & Cisin, I. (1977). *National survey on drug abuse, 1977: A nationwide study — Youth, young adults, and older people.* Rockville, MD: National Institute on Drug Abuse.

Aiello, J. R., Baum, A., & Gormley, F. P. (1981). Social determinants of residential crowding stress. *Personality and Social Psychology Bulletin, 7,* 643–649.

Aiello, J. R., & Thompson, D. (1980). Personal space, crowding, and spatial behavior in a cultural context. In I. Altman, A. Rappoport, & J. Wohlwill (Eds.), *Human behavior and environment* (Vol. IV). New York: Plenum.

Alexander, F. (1939). Emotional factors in essential hypertension. *Psychosomatic Medicine, 1,* 173–179.

Altman, I. (1975a). *The environment and personal behavior.* Monterey, CA: Brooks/Cole.

Altman, I. (1975b). *The environment and social behavior.* Monterey, CA: Brooks/Cole.

American Medical Association. (1973). *Report on the 1972 AMA medical survey of U.S. jail systems.* Chicago: Author.

American Medical Association. (1979). *American Medical Association standards for health services in jails.* Chicago: American Medical Association, Program to Improve Medical Care & Health Services in Correctional Institutions.

Archea, J. (1977). The place of architectural factors in behavioral theories of privacy. *Journal of Social Issues, 33*(3), 116–137.

Ayman, D. (1933). The personality type of patients with arteriolar essential hypertension. *American Journal of Medical Sciences, 186,* 213–223.

Ayman, D., & Goldshine, A. D. (1940). Blood pressure determinations by patients with essential hypertension. I. Difference between clinic and home readings before treatment. *American Journal of Medical Sciences, 200,* 465–474.

Baker, D. B. (1985). The study of stress at work. *Annual Review of Public Health, 6,* 367–381.

Baldassare, M. (1978). Human spatial behavior. *Annual Review of Sociology, 4,* 29–56.

Baron, R. M., Mandel, D. R., Adams, C. A., & Griffen, L. M. (1976). Effects of social density in university residential environments. *Journal of Personality and Social Psychology, 34,* 434–446.

Bauer, G. E., & Clark, J. A. (1976). Personality deviancy and prison incarceration. *Journal of Clinical Psychology, 32,* 279–283.

Baum, A., Aiello, J. R., & Calesnick, L. E. (1978). Crowding and personal control: Social density and the development of learned helplessness. *Journal of Personality and Social Psychology, 36,* 1000–1011.

Baum, A., Calesnick, L. E., Davis, G. E., & Gatchel, R. J. (1982). Individual differences in coping with crowding: Stimulus screening and social overload. *Journal of Personality and Social Psychology, 43,* 821–830.

Baum, A., Davis, G. E. (1980). Reducing the stress of high-density living: An architectural intervention. *Journal of Personality and Social Psychology, 38,* 471–481.

Baum, A., Shapiro, A., Murray, D., & Wideman, M. V. (1979). Interpersonal mediation of perceived crowding and control in residential dyads and triads. *Journal of Applied Social Psychology, 9,* 491–507.

Baum, A., & Valins, S. (1977). *Architecture and social behavior: Psychological studies of social density.* Hillsdale, NJ: Lawrence Erlbaum Associates.

Beebe, G. W. (1975). Follow-up studies of World War II and Korean prisoners. II. Morbidity, disability, and maladjustments. *American Journal of Epidemiology, 101,* 400–422.

Beigel, A., & Russell, H. E. (1972). Suicide attempts in jails: Prognostic considerations. *Hospital and Community Psychiatry, 23,* 361–363.

Berkowitz, L. (1962). *Aggression: A social psychological analysis.* New York: McGraw-Hill.

Booth, A. (1976). *Urban crowding and its consequences.* New York: Praeger.

Booth, A., & Cowell, J. (1976). Crowding and health. *Journal of Health and Social Behavior, 17,* 204–220.

Booth, A., Johnson, D. R., & Edwards, J. N. (1979). Urban crowding and the family. *Journal of Population, 2,* 74–86.

Booth, A., Johnson, D. R., & Edwards, J. N. (1980a). Reply to Gove and Hughes. *American Sociological Review, 45,* 870–873.

Booth, A., Johnson, D. R., & Edwards, J. N. (1980b). In pursuit of pathology: The effects of human crowding (Comment on Gove, Hughes, and Galle). *American Sociological Review, 45,* 873–878.

Botterell, E. H. (1972). *Enquiry into the health care system.* Toronto: Ministry of Correctional Services.

Brett, G. Z., & Benjamin, B. (1957). Housing and tuberculosis in a mass radiography survey. *British Journal of Preventive and Social Medicine, 11,* 7–9.

Brod, J., Fencl, V., Hejl, Z., & Jirka, J. (1959). Circulatory changes underlying blood pressure elevations during acute emotional stress (Mental Arithmetic) in normotensive and hypertensive subjects. *Clinical Science, 18,* 269–279.

Brodsky, C. M. (1977). Long-term work stress in teachers and prison guards. *Journal of Occupational Medicine, 19*(2), 133–138.

Burch, M. A., & Walker, J. L. (1978). Effects of population density and information overload on state of anxiety and crowding perception. *Psychological Record, 28,* 207–214.

Burger, J. M., Oakman, J. A., & Bullard, N. G. (1983). Desire for control and the perception of crowding. *Personality and Social Psychology Bulletin, 9,* 475–479.

Burger, W. E. (1981). Commencement address. George Washington University School of Law.

Cahalan, D., Cisin, I. H., & Crossley, H. M. (1969). *American drinking practices.* New Brunswick, NJ: Publications Division, Rutgers Center of Alcohol Studies.

Calhoun, J. B. (1962). Population density and social pathology. *Scientific American, 206,* 139–148.

Cappon, D. (1971). Mental health in high-rise. *Canadian Journal of Public Health, 62,* 426–431.

Centerwall, B. S. (1984). Race, socioeconomic status, and domestic homicide, Atlanta, 1971-1972. *American Journal of Public Health, 74,* 813–815.

Cheek, F. E., & Miller, M. D. (1979, November). *Managerial styles and correction officer stress.* Paper presented at the Annual Meeting of the American Society of Criminology, Philadelphia, PA.

Choldin, H. M. (1978). Urban density and pathology. *Annual Review of Sociology, 4,* 91–113.

Christian, J. J. (1961). Phenomena associated with population density. *Proceedings of the National Academy of Sciences, 47,* 428–449.

Climent, C. E., Rollins, A., Ervin, F. R., & Plutchik, R. (1973). Epidemiological studies of women prisoners, I: Medical and psychiatric variables related to violent behavior. *American Journal of Psychiatry, 130*(II), 985–990.

Cobb, S., & Rose, R. M. (1973). Hypertension, peptic ulcer, and diabetes in air traffic controllers. *Journal of the American Medical Association, 224,* 489–492.

Cohen, S., & Sherrod, D. R. (1978). When density matters: environmental control as a determinant of crowding effects in laboratory and residential settings. *Journal of Population, 1,* 189–202.

Commission on Accreditation for Corrections. (1977). *Manual of standards for adult correctional institutions.* Rockville, MD: Commission for Corrections.

Cox, V. C., Paulus, P. B., & McCain, G. (1984). Prison crowding research: The relevance for prison housing standards and a general approach regarding crowding phenomena. *American Psychologist, 39,* 1148–1160.

Cox, V. C., Paulus, P. B., McCain, G., & Karlovac, M. (1982). The relationship between crowding and health. In A. Baum & J. E. Singer (Eds.), *Advances in environmental psychology, Vol. 4, Environment and health.* Hillsdale, NJ: Lawrence Erlbaum Associates.

Cox, V. C., Paulus, P. B., McCain, G., & Schkade, J. K. (1979). Field research on the effects of crowding in prisons and on offshore drilling platforms. In J. R. Aiello & A. Baum (Eds.), *Residential crowding and design.* New York: Plenum.

Cressey, D. R. (1965). Prison organizations. In J. G. March (Ed.), *Handbook of organizations.* Chicago: Rand-McNally.

Cressey, D. R. (1968). Contradictory directives in complex organizations: The case of the prison. In L. E. Hazelrigg (Ed.), *Prison within society.* Garden City, NY: Doubleday.

Dahl, J. J., & Thomas, J. (1979). *Management of stress in corrrections. Participant's handbook.* Washington, DC: University Research Corporation for the National Institute of Justice.

D'Atri, D. A., & Ostfeld, A. M. (1975). Crowding: Its effects on the evaluation of blood pressure in a prison setting. *Preventive Medicine, 4,* 550–566.

Daley, M. R. (1979). 'Burnout': Smoldering problem in protective services. *Social Work, 24,* 375–379.

Davies, M. H. (1971). Is high blood pressure a psychosomatic disorder? A critical review of the evidence. *Journal of Chronic Diseases, 24,* 239–258.

Dawber, T. R., Kannel, W. B., Kagan, A., Donabedian, R. K., McNamara, P. M., & Pearson, G. (1967). Environmental factors in hypertension. In J. Stamler, R. Stamler, & T. N. Pullman (Eds.), *The epidemiology of hypertension.* New York: Grune & Stratton.

Dean, L. M., Pugh, W. M., & Gunderson, E. K. E. (1978). The behavioral effects of crowding: Definitions and methods. *Environment and Behavior, 10,* 419–431.

Derro, R. A. (1978a). Admission health evaluation of inmates of a city-county workhouse. *Minnesota Medicine, 61,* 333–337.

Derro, R. A. (1978b). Health problems in a city-county workhouse. *Public Health Reports, 93*(4), 379–385.

Dixon, W. J., & Brown, M. B., (Eds.). (1979). *BMDP-79 Biomedical Computer Program P-Series.* Berkeley: University of California Press.

Dohrenwend, B. S., & Dohrenwend, B. P. (1970). Class and race as status-related sources of stress. In S. Levine & N. A. Scotch (Eds.), *Social stress.* Chicago: Aldine.

Draper, N. R., & Smith, H. (1966). *Applied regression analysis.* New York: Wiley.

Duvall, D., & Booth, A. (1978). The housing environment and women's health. *Journal of Health and Social Behavior, 19,* 410–417.

Ehrstrom, M. CH. (1945). Psychogene Blutdruckssteigerung. Kriegshypertonien. *Acta Medica Scandinavica, 122,* 546–570.

Ekland-Olson, S., Barrich, D. M., & Cohen, L. E. (1983). Prison overcrowding and disciplinary problems: An analysis of the Texas prison system. *Journal of Applied Behavioral Science, 19,* 163–176.

Engebretsen, B., & Olson, J. W. (1975). Primary care in a penal institution: A study of health care problems encountered. *Medical Care, 13,* 775–781.

Epstein, Y. M. (1981). Crowding stress and human behavior. *Journal of Social Issues, 37*(1), 126–144.

Farrington, D. P., & Nuttall, C. P. (1980). Prison size, overcrowding, prison violence, and recidivism. *Journal of Criminal Justice, 8,* 221–231.

Fischer, J. D., & Byrne, D. (1975). Too close for comfort: sex differences in response to invasions of personal space. *Journal of Personality and Social Psychology, 32,* 15–21.

Fraser, J., & Cowell, E. M. (1919). A Clinical Study of the Blood Pressure in Wound Conditions. In *Medical research committee reports of the special investigation committee on surgical shock and allied conditions* (No. II). London: His Majesty's Stationery Office at the University Press, Oxford.

Freedman, J. (1975). *Crowding and behavior.* San Francisco: Freeman.

Freedman, J. L. (1979). Reconciling apparent differences between the responses of humans and other animals to crowding. *Psychological Review, 86,* 80–85.

Freedman, J. L., Levy, A. S., Buchanan, R. W., & Price, J. (1972). Crowding and human aggressiveness. *Journal of Experimental and Social Psychology, 8,* 528–548.

Galle, O., Gove, W., & McPherson, J. M. (1972). Population density and pathology: What are the relations for man? *Science, 176,* 23–30.

Geddes, R., & Gutman, R. (1977). The assessment of the built environment for safety: Research and practice. In L. E. Hinkle, Jr., & W. C. Loring (Eds.), *The effect of the man-made environment on health and behavior.* Atlanta: Center for Disease Control, DHEW Publication No. (CDC) 77-8318.

Gillis, A. R. (1977). High-rise housing and psychological strain. *Journal of Health and Social Behavior, 18,* 418–431.

Gillis, A. R. (1979). Household density and human crowding: Unravelling a non-linear relationship. *Journal of Population, 2,* 104–117.

Goldfarb, R. L. (1975). *Jails: The ultimate ghetto.* Garden City, NY: Anchor Press.

Goldsmith, S. B. (1975). *Prison health — Travesty of justice.* New York: Prodist.

Goodman, L. A., & Kruskal, W. H. (1953). Measures of association for cross-classification. *Journal of the American Statistical Association, 49,* 732–764.

Gordon, R. A. (1967). Issues in the ecological study of delinquency. *American Sociological Review, 32,* 927–944.

Gormley, F. P., & Aiello, J. R. (1982). Social density interpersonal relationships, and residential crowding stress. *Journal of Applied Social Psychology, 12,* 222–236.

Gove, W. R., & Hughes, M. (1980a). The effects of crowding found in the Toronto study: some methodological and empirical questions (A comment on Booth and Edwards). *American Sociological Review, 45,* 864–870.

Gove, W. R., & Hughes, M. (1980b). In pursuit of preconceptions: a reply to the claim of Booth and his colleagues that household crowding is not an important variable. *American Sociological Review, 45,* 878–886.

Gove, W. R., Hughes, M., & Galle, O. R. (1979). Overcrowding in the house: An empirical investigation of its possible pathological consequences. *American Sociological Review, 44,* 59–80.

Graham, J. D. P. (1945). High blood-pressure after battle. *Lancet, I,* 239–240.

Gruchow, H. W. (1977). Socialization and the human physiologic response to crowding. *American Journal of Public Health, 67,* 455–459.

Gunn, J. (1974). Social factors and epileptics in prison. *British Journal of Psychiatry, 124,* 509–517.

Gunn, J. C. (1977). *Epileptics in prison.* London: Academic Press.

Gunn, J., & Fenton, G. (1969). Epilepsy in prisons: A diagnostic study. *British Medical Journal, 4,* 326–328.

Guyton, A. C. (1977). *Basic human physiology: Normal function and mechanisms of disease.* Philadelphia: Saunders.

Guze, S. B. (1976). *Criminality and psychiatric disorders.* New York: Oxford University Press.

Guze, S. B., Goodwin, D. W., & Crane, J. B. (1969). Criminality and Psychiatric Disorders. *Archives of General Psychiatry, 20,* 583–591.

Guze, S. B., Woodruff, R. A., & Clayton, P. J. (1974). Psychiatric disorders and criminality. *Journal of the American Medical Association, 227,* 641–642.

Hall, E. T. (1966). *The hidden dimension.* New York: Doubleday.

Harburg, E., Erfurt, J. C., Chape, C., Hauenstein, L. S. Schull, W. J., & Schork, M. A. (1973). Socioecological stressor areas and black–white blood pressure: Detroit. *Journal of Chronic Diseases, 26,* 595–611.

Harburg, E., Erfurt, J. C., Hauenstein, L. S., Chape, C., Schull, W. J., & Schork, M. A. (1973). Socio-ecological stress, suppressed hostility, skin color and black–white male blood pressure: Detroit. *Psychosomatic Medicine, 35*(4), 276–296.

Hare, E. H. (1956). Mental Illness and social conditions in Bristol. *Journal of Mental Science, 102,* 349–357.

Harris, M. H. (1982). *Social class and mean blood pressure in the State of Connecticut: Findings from the Connecticut High Blood Pressure Survey 1978–79.* Unpublished master's thesis, Yale University School of Medicine.

Harshfield, G. A., Pickering, T. G., Kleinert, H. D., Blank, S., & Laragh, J. H. (1982). Situational variations of blood pressure in ambulatory hypertensive patients. *Psychosomatic Medicine, 44*(3), 237–245.

Hazelrigg, L. E. (Ed.). (1986). *Prison within society.* Garden City, NY: Doubleday.

Hejl, Z. (1957). Changes in cardiac output and peripheral resistance during simple stimuli influencing blood pressure. *Cardiologia, 31,* 375–381.

Helwig, J. T., & Council, K. A. (Eds.). (1979). *SAS user's guide* (1979 Ed.). Raleigh, NC: SAS Institute, Statistical Analysis System.

Henry, J. P., Meehan, J. P., & Stephens, P. M. (1967). The use of psychosocial stimuli to induce prolonged systolic hypertension in mice. *Psychosomatic Medicine, 29,* 408–432.

Henry, J. P., & Stephens, P. M. (1977). *Stress, health and the social environment. A sociobiological approach to medicine.* New York: Springer-Verlag.

Henry, J. P., Stephens, P. M., Axelrod, J., & Mueller, R. A. (1971). Effect of psychosocial stimulation on the enzymes involved in the biosynthesis and metabolism of noradrenaline and adrenaline. *Psychosomatic Medicine, 33,* 227–237.

Henry, J. P., Stephens, P. M., & Santisteban, G. A. (1975). A model of psychosocial hypertension showing reversibility and progression of cardiovascular complications. *Circulation Research, 36,* 156–164.

Hepburn, J. R., & Albonetti, C. A. (1978). Team classification in state correctional institutions: Its association with inmate and staff attitudes. *Criminal Justice and Behavior, 5,* 63–73.

Hepburn, J. R., & Albonetti, C. A. (1980). Role conflict in correctional institutions. An Empirical Examination of the Treatment-Custody Dilemma Among Correctional Staff. *Criminol-*

ogy, 17(4), 445–459.

Hickam, J. B., Cargill, W. H., & Golden, A. (1948). Cardiovascular reactions to emotional stimuli. Effect on the cardiac output, arteriovenous oxygen difference, arterial pressure and peripheral resistance. *Journal of Clinical Investigation, 27,* 290–298.

Holmes, T. H., & Rahe, R. H. (1976). The social readjustment rating scale. *Journal of Psychosomatic Research, 11,* 213–218.

Howe, B., Froom, J., Culpepper, L., & Mangone, D. (1977). Adoption of the sick role by prisoners. *Social Science and Medicine, 11,* 507–510.

Hughey, D. W. (1983). Effects of living accommodations of high proximity on the self-perceptions of college students residing in university housing facilities. *Psychological Reports, 53,* 1013–1014.

Hypertension Detection and Followup Program Cooperative Group. (1979). Five-year findings of the hypertension detection and followup program. I. Reduction in mortality of persons with high blood pressure, including mild hypertension. *Journal of the American Medical Association, 242,* 2562–2577.

The Jails and Prisons Task Force of the Program Development Board of the American Public Health Association. (1976). *Standards for health services in correctional institutions.* Washington, DC: American Public Health Association.

James, S. A., & Kleinbaum, D. G. (1976). Socioecological stress and hypertension related mortality rates in North Carolina. *American Journal of Public Health, 66*(I), 354–358.

Janus, S. S., Bess, B. E., Cadden, J., & Greenwald, H. (1979). The police officer as street psychiatrist. *Police Studies, 2*(3), 27–31.

Johnson, R. (1977). Ameliorating prison stress—Some helping roles for custodial personnel. *International Journal of Criminology and Penology, 5*(3), 263–273.

Jones, D. A. (1976). *The health risks of imprisonment.* Lexington, MA: Lexington Books.

Kagan, A., Gordon, T., Kannel, W. B., & Dawber, T. R. (1958). Blood pressure and its relation to coronary heart disease in the Framingham study. In F. F. Skelton, (Ed.), *Hypertension, Vol. 7, Drug action, epidemiology and hemodynamics: Proceedings of the council for high blood pressure research.* New York: American Heart Association 43.

Kalimo, R. (1980). Stress in work: conceptual analysis and a study on prison personnel. *Scandinavian Journal of Work Environment and Health, 6*(3), 9–124.

Kalis, B. L., Harris, R. E., Sokolow, M. D., & Carpenter, L. G. (1957). Response to psychological stress in patients with essential hypertension. *American Heart Journal, 53,* 572–578.

Karlin, R. A., Epstein, Y. M., & Aiello, J. R. (1978). Strategies for the investigation of crowding. In A. Esser & B. Greenbie (Eds.), *Design for community and privacy.* New York: Plenum.

Kasl, S. V. (1976). Effects of housing on mental and physical health. In *Housing in the seventies, working papers 1.* Washington, DC: U.S. Department of Housing and Urban Development.

Kasl, S. V. (1984a). Chronic life stress and health. In A. Steptoe & A. Mathews (Eds.), *Health care and human behaviour.* London: Academic Press.

Kasl, S. V. (1984b). Stress and health. *Annual Review of Public Health, 5,* 318–341.

Kasl, S. V. (1985). Environmental exposure and disease: an epidemiological perspective on some methodological issues in health psychology and behavioral medicine. In J. E. Singer & A. Baum (Eds.), *Advances in environmental psychology, Vol. 5, Methods and environmental psychology.* Hillsdale, NJ: Lawrence Erlbaum Associates.

Kasl, S. V., & Cobb, S. (1970). Blood pressure changes in men undergoing job loss: A preliminary report. *Psychosomatic Medicine, 32,* 19–38.

Kasl, S. V., & Cobb, S. (1980). The experience of losing a job: some effects on cardiovascular functioning. *Psychotherapy and Psychosomatics, 34,* 88–109.

Kasl, S. V., & Harburg, E. (1975). Mental health and the urban environment: Some doubts and second thoughts. *Journal of Health and Social Behavior, 16,* 268–282.

Kasl, S. V., & Rosenfield, S. (1980). The residential environment and its impact on the mental health of the aged. In J. E. Birren & R. B. Sloane (Eds.), *Handbook of mental health and aging.* Englewood Cliffs, NJ: Prentice-Hall.

King, L., & Geis, G. (1977). Tuberculosis transmission in a large urban jail. *Journal of the American Medical Association, 237,* 791–792.

King, L. N., & Whitman, S. (1981). Morbidity and mortality among prisoners: An epidemiologic review. *Journal of Prison Health, 1*(1), 7–29.

King, L. N., & Young, Q. D. (1978). Increased prevalence of seizure disorders among prisoners. *Journal of the American Medical Association, 239,* 2674–2675.

Kirmeyer, S. L. (1978). Urban density and pathology: A review of research. *Environment and Behavior, 10,* 247–269.

Kleinbaum, D. G., & Kupper, L. L. (1978). *Applied regression analysis and other multivariable methods.* North Scituate, MA: Duxbury Press.

Kliman, A. (1971). Australia antigen in volunteer and paid blood donors. *New England Journal of Medicine, 284,* 109.

Koplan, J. P., Walker, J. A., Bryan, J. A., & Berquist, K. R. (1978). Prevalence of hepatitis B surface antigen and antibody at a state prison in Kansas. *Journal of Infectious Diseases, 137,* 505–506.

Kosa, J., Antonovsky, A., & Zola, I. K. (Eds.). (1969). *Poverty and health. A sociological analysis.* Cambridge, MA: Harvard University Press.

Kriesberg, L. (1968). Neighborhood setting and the isolation of public housing tenants. *Journal of the American Institute of Planners, 34,* 43–49.

Krotoski, W. A. (1972). Hepatitis in prisoner blood donors. *New England Journal of Medicine, 286,* 159.

Langner, T. S. (1962). A twenty-two item screening score of psychiatric symptoms indicating impairment. *Journal of Health and Human Behavior, 3,* 269–276.

Lee, R. E., & Schneider, R. F. (1958). Hypertension and arteriosclerosis in excutive and nonexecutive personnel. *Journal of the American Medical Association, 167,* 1447–1450.

Levy, L., & Herzog, A. N. (1974). Effects of population density and crowding on health and social adaptation in the Netherlands. *Journal of Health and Social Behavior, 15,* 118–240.

Lipowski, Z. J. (1974). Sensory overloads, information overloads and behavior, *Psychotherapy and Psychosomatics, 23,* 264–271.

Litt, I. F., & Cohen, M. I. (1974). Prisons, adolescents, and the right to quality medical care. *American Journal of Public Health, 64,* 894–897.

Littler, W. A., West, M. J., Honour, A. J., & Sleigth, P. (1978). The variability of arterial pressure. *American Heart Journal, 95*(1), 180–186.

Lundberg, U. (1976). Urban commuting: Crowdedness and catecholamine excretion. *Journal of Human Stress, 2*(3), 26–32.

Manton, K. G., & Myers, G. C. (1977). The structure of urban mortality. A methodological study of Hannover, Germany, Part II. *International Journal of Epidemiology, 6,* 213–223.

Marshall, J. E., & Heston, R. (1975). Boys and girls together: sexual composition and the effect of density and group size on cohesiveness. *Journal of Personality and Social Psychology, 31,* 952–961.

Mathews, R. W., Paulus, P. B., & Baron, R. A. (1979). Physical aggression after being crowded. *Journal of Nonverbal Behavior, 4,* 5–17.

May, E. (1976). Prison guards in America: The inside story. *Corrections Magazine,* Dec.

McCain, G., Cox, V. C., & Paulus, P. B. (1976). The relationship between illness complaints and degree of crowding in a prison environment. *Environment and Behavior, 8,* 283–290.

McCallum, R., Rusbult, C. E., Hong, G. K., Walden, T. A., & Schopler, J. (1979). Effects of resource availability and importance of behavior on the experience of crowding. *Journal of Personality and Social Psychology, 37,* 1304–1313.

McCarthy, D., & Saegert, S. (1978). Residential density, social overload, and social withdrawal. *Human Ecology, 6,* 253–272.

McDonough, J. R., Garrison, G. E., & Hames, C. G. (1964). Blood pressure and hypertensive disease among Negroes and Whites: a study in Evans County, Georgia. *Annals of Internal Medicine, 61,* 208–228.

McEvoy, G. K., McQuarrie, G. M., & Douglas, P. M. (Eds.). (1979). *American hospital formulary service.* Bethesda, MD: American Society of Hospital Pharmacists.

Megargee, E. I. (1977). The association of population density, reduced space and uncomfortable temperatures with misconduct in a prison community. *American Journal of Community Psychology, 5*(3), 289–298.

Metropolitan Life Insurance Company. (1967). Cardiac mortality and socioeconomic status. *Statistical Bulletin, 48,* 9–11.

Meyer, R.G. (1968). *Chronic high blood pressure, essential hypertension, and the inhibition of aggression.* Proceedings of the 76th Annual Convention of the American Psychological Association.

Michelson, W. (1970). *Man and his urban environment: A sociological approach.* Reading, MA: Addison-Wesley.

Michigan State Office of Health and Medical Affairs. (1975). *Key to health for a padlocked society.* Lansing, MI: State of Michigan.

Milgram, S. (1970). The experience of living in cities. *Science, 167,* 1461–1468.

Miller, W. B. (1973). Adaptation of young men to prison. *Corrective and Social Psychiatry and Journal of Applied Behavior Therapy, 19*(4), 15–26.

Mitchell, E. D. (1971). Some social implications of high sensity housing. *American Sociological Review, 36,* 18–29.

Mitford, (1973). *Kind and usual punishment: The prison business.* New York: Knopf.

Modlin, H. C. (1979). Medical care in correctional institutions: The AMA Project. *American Academy of Psychiatry and the Law Bulletin, 7,* 118–124.

Moos, R. H. (Ed.). (1976). *Human adaptation, coping with life crises.* Lexington, MA: Lexington Books.

Moos, R. H. (1979). Social-ecological perspectives on health. In G. C. Stone, F. Cohen, & N. E. Adler (Eds.), *Health psychology — A handbook.* San Francisco: Jossey-Bass.

Morrison, D. F. (1976). *Multivariate statistical methods.* New York: McGraw-Hill.

Muniz, F. J., Malyska, H., & Levin, W. C. (1971). Au antigen in blood from prisoners. *New England Journal of Medicine, 284,* 501–502.

National Center for Health Statistics. (1970a). *Changes in cigarette smoking habits between 1955 and 1966.* Vital and Health Statistics, Data from the National Health Survey, Series 10, No. 59, DHEW Publication No. (PHS) 1000, Rockville, MD.

National Center for Health Statistics. (1970b). *Need for dental care among adults, United States 1960-1962.* Vital and Health Statistics, Data from the National Health Survey, Series 11, No. 36, DHEW Publication No. (PHS) 1000, Washington, DC.

National Cancer for Health Statistics. (1970c). *Selected symptoms of psychological distress.* Vital Health Statistics, Data from the National Health Survey, Series 11, No. 37, Public Health Service Publication No. 1000. Rockville, MD.

National Center for Health Statistics. (1977). *Prevalence of chronic conditions of the genitourinary, nervous, endocrine, metabbolic and blood and blood-forming systems and of other selected chronic conditions, United States, 1973.* Vital and Health Statistics, Data from the National Health Survey, Series 10, No. 109, DHEW Publication No. (HRA) 77-1536, Rockville, MD.

National Center for Health Statistics. (1979a). *A reason for visit classification for ambulatory care.* Vital and Health Statistics, Data from the National Health Survey, Series 2, No. 78, DHEW Publication No. (PHS) 79-1352, Hyattsville, MD.

National Center for Health Statistics. (1979b). *Prevalence of selected chronic digestive conditions, United States 1975.* Vital and Health Statistics, Data from the National Health Survey, Series 100, No. 123, DHEW Publication No. (PHS) 70-1558, Hyattsville, MD.

National Center for Health Statistics. (1980). *The national ambulatory medical care survey: 1977 summary, United States, January–December, 1977.* Vital and Health Statistics, Data from the National Health Survey, Series 13, No. 44, DHEW Publication No. (PHS) 80-1795, Hyattsville, MD.

National Center for Health Statistics. (1981). *Hypertension in adults 25–74 years of age. United States 1971–1975.* Vital and Health Statistics, Data from the National Health Survey, Series, 11, No. 221, DHHS Publication (PHS) 81-1671, Washington, DC.

Nefzger, M. D. (1970). Follow-up studies of World War II and Korean War prisoners. I. Study plan and mortality findings. *American Journal of Epidemiology 91*(2), 123–138.

Nicosia, G. J., Hyman, D., Karlin, R. A., Epstein, Y. M., & Aiello, J. R. (1979). Effects of bodily contact on reactions to crowding. *Journal of Applied Social Psychology, 9,* 508–523.

Novick, L. F., & Al-Ibrahim, M. S. (1977). *Health problems in the prison setting: A clinical and administrative approach.* Springfield, IL: Thomas.

Novick, L. F., Della Penna, R., Schwartz, M. S., Remmlinger, E., & Loewenstein, R. (1977). Health status of the New York City prison population. *Medical Care, 15,* 205–216.

Novick, L. F., & Remmlinger, E. (1978). A study of 128 deaths in New York City correctional facilities (1971–1976): Implications for prisoner health care. *Medical Care, 16,* 749–756.

Nunnally, J. C. (1978). *Psychometric theory.* New York: McGraw-Hill.

O'Brien, G. E., & Pembroke, M. (1982). Crowding, density, and the job satisfaction of clerical employees. *Australian Journal of Psychology, 34,* 151–164.

Obrist, P. A., Langer, A. W., Grignolo, A., Sutterer, J. R., Light, K. C., & McCubbin, J. A. (1979). Blood pressure control mechanisms and stress: Implications for the etiology of hypertension. In G. Onesti & C. R. Klimt (Eds.), *Hypertension determinants, complications, and interventions.* New York: Grune & Stratton.

Ostfeld, A., & D'Atri, D. (1977). Rapid sociocultural change and high blood pressure. In S. V. Kasl & F. Reichsman (Eds.), *Advances in psychosomatic medicine. Epidemiologic studies in psychosomatic medicine.* (Vol. 9). Basel: Karger.

Ostfeld, A. M., & Shekelle, R. B. (1967). Psychological Variables and Blood Pressure. In J. Stamler, R. Stamler, & T. Pullman (Eds.), *The epidemiology of hypertension. Proceedings of an international symposium.* American Heart Association. New York: Grune & Stratton.

Paul, O., Lepper, M. H., Phelan, W. H., Dupertuis, G. W., MacMillan, A., McKean, H., & Park, H. (1963). A longitudinal study of coronary heart disease. *Circulation, 28,* 20–31.

Paulus, P., Annis, A. B., Seta, J. J., Schkode, J. K., & Mathews, R. W. (1976). Density does affect task performance. *Journal of Personality and Social Psychology, 34,* 248–253.

Paulus, P., Cox, V., McCain, G., & Chandler, J. (1975). Some effects of crowding in a prison environment. *Journal of Applied Social Psychology, 5*(1), 86–91.

Paulus, P. B., & McCain, G. (1983). Crowding in jail. *Basic and Applied Social Psychology, 4,* 89–107.

Paulus, P., McCain, G., & Cox, V. (1978). Death rates, psychiatric commitments, blood pressure and perceived crowding as a function of institutional crowding. *Environmental Psychology and Nonverbal Behavior, 3,* 107–116.

Paulus, P. B., McCain, G., & Cox, V. C. (1985). The effects of crowding in prisons and jails. In D. P. Farrington & J. Gunn (Eds.), *Reactions to crime: The public, the police, courts, and prisons.* Chichester: Wiley.

Perloff, D., & Sokolow, M. (1978). The representative blood pressure: usefulness of office, basal, home, and ambulatory readings. *Cardiovascular Medicine, 3*(6), 655–668.

Petrich, J. (1976). Rate of psychiatric morbidity in a metropolitan county jail population. *American Journal of Psychiatry, 133*(II), 1439–1444.

Pickering, G. W. (1974). *Hypertension: Causes, consequences and management.* New York: Churchill Livingstone.

Poole, E. D., & Regoli, R. M. (1980a). Role stress, custody orientation, and disciplinary actions. *Criminology, 18*(2), 215–226.

Poole, E. D., & Regoli, R. M. (1980b). Work relations and cynicism among prison guards. *Criminal Justice and Behavior, 7*(3), 303–314.

Power, J. G. P. (1970). Health aspects of vertical living in Hong Kong. *Community Health, 1,* 316–320.

Proshansky, H. M., Ittelson, W. H., & Rivlin, L. G. (1970). Freedom of choice and behavior in a physical setting. In H. M. Proshansky, W. H. Ittelson, & L. G. Rivlin (Eds.), *Environmental psychology, man and his physical setting.* New York: Holt, Rinehart & Winston.

Rainwater, L. (1970). *Behind ghetto walls.* Chicago: Aldine.

Rector, F. L. (1929). *Health and medical service in American prisons and reformatories.* New York: The National Society of Penal Information.

Reddy, D. M., Baum, A., Fleming, R., & Aiello, J. R. (1981). Mediation of social density by coalition formation. *Journal of Applied Social Psychology, 11,* 529–537.

Richardson, D. W., Honour, A. J., Scott, F. H., & Pickering, G. W. (1964). Diurnal variation in blood pressure. *Clinical Research, 12,* 57.

Rieger, W. (1971). Suicide attempts in a federal prison. *Archives of General Psychiatry, 24,* 532–535.

Robinson, W. S. (1950). Ecological correlations and the behavior of individuals. *American Sociological Review, 15,* 351–357.

Rohe, W. M. (1982). The response to density in residential settings. *Journal of Applied Social Psychology, 12,* 292–303.

Ronchi, D., & Sparacino, J. (1982). Density of dormitory living and stress: mediating effects of sex, self-monitoring, and environmental affective qualities. *Perceptual and Motor Skills, 55,* 759–770.

Rose, R. M. (1980). Endocrine responses to stressful psychological events. *Psychiatric Clinics of North American, 3*(2), 251–276.

Ross, M., Layton, B., Erickson, B., & Schopler, J. (1973). Affect, facial regards, and reaction to crowding. *Journal of Personality and Social Psychology, 28,* 69–76.

Roth, L. H., & Ervin, F. R. (1971). Psychiatric care of federal prisoners. *American Journal of Psychiatry, 128,* 424–430.

Ruback, R. B., & Carr, T. S. (1984). Crowding in a woman's prison: Attitudinal and behavioral effects. *Journal of Applied Social Psychology, 14,* 57–68.

Ruskin, A., Beard, O. W., & Schaffer, R. L. (1948). "Blast hypertension." Elevated arterial pressures in the victims of the Texas City disaster. *American Journal of Medicine, 4,* 228–236.

Schaeffer, G. H., & Patterson, M. L. (1980). Intimacy, arousal, and small group crowding. *Journal of Personality and Social Psychology, 38,* 283–290.

Schmidt, D. E., Goldman, R. D., & Feimer, N. R. (1979). Perceptions of crowding: Predicting at the residence, neighborhood, and city levels. *Environment and Behavior, 11,* 105–130.

Schmidt, D. E., & Keating, J. R. (1979). Human crowding and personal control: An integration of the research. *Psychological Bulletin, 86,* 680–700.

Schmitt, R. C. (1955). Housing and health on Oahu. *American Journal of Public Health, 45,* 1538–1540.

Schmitt, R. C. (1966). Density, health, and social disorganization. *Journal of the American Institute of Planners, 32,* 38–40.

Schwab, J. J., Nadeau, S. E., & Warheit, G. J. (1979). Crowding and mental health. *Pavlovian Journal of Biological Science, 14,* 226–233.

Sengel, R. A. (1978). A graph analysis of the relationship between population density and social pathology. *Behavioral Science, 23,* 213–224.

Seta, J. J., Paulus, P. B., & Schkode, J. K. (1976). Effects of group size and proximity under cooperative and competitive condition. *Journal of Personality and Social Psychology, 34,* 47-53.

Skinner, J. S., Benson, H., McDonough, J. R., & Hames, C. G. (1966). Social status, physical activity, and coronary proneness. *Journal of Chronic Diseases, 19,* 773-783.

Sommer, R. (1967). Small group ecology. *Psychological Bulletin, 67,* 145-152.

Sommer, R. (1969). *Personal space: The behavioral basis of design.* Englewood Cliffs, NJ: Prentice-Hall.

Stamler, J., Stamler, R., & Pullman, T. N. (Eds.). (1967). *The epidemiology of hypertension.* New York: Grune & Stratton.

Stamler, R., & Stamler, J. (1976). The challenge to conquer hypertension in the 20th century. *Urban Health* June, 24-33.

Stead, W. W. (1978). Undetected tuberculosis in prison. Source of infection for community at large. *Journal of the American Medical Association, 240,* 2544-2547.

Stein, L. (1950). A study of respiratory tuberculosis in relation to housing conditions in Edinburgh. *British Journal of Preventive and Social Medicine, 4,* 143-169.

Stevenson, A., Martin, E., & O'Neill, J. (1967). *High living: A study of family life in flats.* London: Melbourne University Press.

Stokols, D. (1972). On the distinction between density and crowding: some implications for future research. *Psychological Reviews, 79,* 275-277.

Stokols, D. (1976). The experience of crowding in primary and secondary environments. *Environment and Behavior, 8,* 49-86.

Stokols, D. (1979). A congruence analysis of human stress. In I. G. Sarason & C. D. Spielberger (Eds.), *Stress and anxiety* (Vol. 6). Washington, DC: Hemisphere Press.

Stokols, D., Ohlig, W., & Resnick, S. M. (1978). Perception of residential crowding, classroom experience, and student health. *Human Ecology, 6,* 233-252.

Stokols, D., Rall, M., Pinner, B., & Schopler, J. (1973). Physical, social, and personal determinants of the perception of crowding. *Environment and Behavior, 5,* 87-115.

Swank, G. E., & Winer, D. (1976). Occurrence of psychiatric disorder in a county jail population. *American Journal of Psychiatry, 133*(II), 1331-1333.

Syme, S. L., Oakes, T. W., Friedman, G. D., Feldman, R., Siegelaub, A. B., & Collen, M. (1974). Social class and racial difference in blood pressure. *American Journal of Public Health, 64*(1), 619-620.

Szilagyi, A. D., & Holland, W. E. (1980). Changes in social density: Relationships with functional interaction and perceptions of job characteristics, role stress, and work satisfaction. *Journal of Applied Psychology, 65,* 28-33.

Taylor, R. B. (1980). Conceptual dimensions of crowding reconsidered. *Population and Environment, 3,* 298-308.

Taylor, R. B. (1981). Perception of density: Individual differences? *Environment and Behavior, 13,* 3-21.

Thomas, J. E. (1974). The prison officer: A conflict in roles. *Journal of Psychosomatic Research, 18,* 259-262.

Thompson, D. H., Trachtman, L., & Greenberg, H. B. (1978). Our tuberculous prisoners. *Journal of the Louisiana State Medical Society, 130,* 203-204.

Toch, H. (1975). *Men in crisis: Human breakdowns in prison.* Chicago: Aldine.

Toch, H. (1977). *Living in prison.* New York: MacMillan.

Tolubeeva, N. A., & Flegontova, E. P. (1940). Disturbance of blood pressure regulation in hypertension. *Voprasy Kardiologic in Gematologi Leningrad, 121.*

Twaddle, A. C. (1976). Utilization of medical services by a captive population: An analysis of sick call in a state prison. *Journal of Health and Social Behavior, 17,* 236-248.

U.S. Department of Commerce, Bureau of Census. (1975). *Annual housing survey: 1973, Part*

B, indicators of housing and neighborhood quality for the U.S. and regions. Washington, DC: U.S. Government Printing Office, Current Housing Reports, Series H-150-73-B.

United States National Center for Health Statistics. (1978). *The international classification of diseases, ninth revision, clinical modification, ICD.9.CM.* Ann Arbor, MI: Commission on Professional and Hospital Activities.

Veale, A. M. O., Hamilton, M., Irvine, R. O. H., & Smirk, F. H. (1962). Population survey of casual and near-basal blood pressures: with comments on survey techniques. *New Zealand Medical Journal, 61,* 65–76.

Walden, T., & Forsyth, D. R. (1981). Close encounters of the stressful kind: affective, physiological, and behavioral reactions to the experience of crowding. *Journal of Nonverval Behavior, 6,* 46–64.

Walden, T. A., Nelson, P. A., & Smith, D. E. (1981). Crowding, privacy, and coping. *Environment and Behavior, 13,* 205–224.

Ward, S. K. (1975). Methodological considerations in the study of population density and social pathology. *Human Ecology, 3,* 275–286.

Weber, G. H. (1957). Conflicts between professional and non-professional personnel in institutional delinquency treatment. *Journal of Criminal Law, Criminology and Police Science, 48*(1), 26–43.

Williamson, R. C. (1981). Adjustment to the high rise: Variables in a German sample. *Environment and Behavior, 13,* 289–310.

Wilner, D. M., Walkley, R. P., Pinkerton, T. C., & Tayback, M. (1962). *The housing environment and family life.* Baltimore, MD: The Johns Hopkins Press.

Wolf, S. (1958). Cardiovascular reactions to symbolic stimuli. *Circulation, 18,* 287–292.

Wolf, S., Cardon, P., Shepard, E., & Wolff, H. (1955). *Life stress and essential hypertension. A study of circulatory adjustments in man.* Baltimore, MD: Williams & Wilkins.

Wolf, S., Pfeiffer, J. B., Ripley, H. S., Winter, O. S., & Wolff, H. G. (1948). Hypertension as a reaction pattern to stress; Summary of experimental data on variations in blood pressure and renal blood flow. *Annals of Internal Medicine, 29,* 1056–1076.

Worchel, S., & Teddlie, W. (1976). The experience of crowding: a two-factor theory. *Journal of Personality and Social Psychology, 34,* 30–40.

Worchel, S., & Yohai, S. M. L. (1979). The role of attribution in the experience of crowding. *Journal of Experimental Social Psychology, 15,* 91–104.

Wurtz, K. R. (1960). Some theory and data concerning attenuation of aggression. *Journal of Abnormal and Social Psychology, 60,* 134–136.

Yancey, W. L. (1971). Architecture, interaction, and social control: The case of a large-scale public housing project. *Environment and Behavior, 3,* 3–21.

Young, T. K. H., & Carr, P. (1976). Utilization of physician services in a prison population. *Canadian Journal of Public Health, 67,* 295–299.

Zald, M. N. (1962). Power balance and staff conflict in correctional institutions. *Administrative Science Quarterly, VII,* 22–49.

Zuckerman, M., & Lubin, B. (1965). *Multiple adjective checklist.* San Diego: Educational Testing Service.

Author Index

Subject Index